Introduction to

# The
# Criminal
# Justice 14
# Process

**Bryan Gibson** is a barrister and former clerk to the justices whose career has also included spells as legal adviser to the Magistrates' Association Sentencing of Offenders Committee and as co-editor of the weekly journal *Justice of the Peace*. His writings include *Introduction to the Magistrates' Court* (fourth edition 2001), *Domestic Violence and Occupation of the Family Home* (1999) (with Chris Bazell), *The Sentence of the Court* (as editor) (third edition 2002), *Human Rights and the Courts: Bringing Justice Home* (as editor) (1999) and *The Waterside A to Z of Criminal Justice* (forthcoming).

**Paul Cavadino** is chief executive of the crime reduction charity Nacro, for which he has worked since 1972. He was chair of the Penal Affairs Consortium from 1989 to 2000 and clerk to the Parliamentary All-party Penal Affairs Group from 1980 to 2001. He has written, spoken and broadcast widely on criminal justice issues. His publications include *Bail: The Law, Best Practice and the Debate* (with Bryan Gibson) (1993) and *Children Who Kill* (as editor) (1996).

**David Faulkner** is a senior research associate at the University of Oxford Centre for Criminological Research, where he writes about and teaches criminal justice, penology and government and public administration. He also works with charities concerned with penal reform, community safety and opportunities for young people. He was formerly Deputy Secretary of State at the Home Office including eight years in charge of the Criminal, Research and Statistical Departments and was Private Secretary to one Home Secretary (James Callaghan) and senior adviser to six others. He is the author of *Crime, State and Citizen: A Field Full of Folk* (2001).

Introduction to
# The Criminal Justice Process

## SECOND EDITION

**Published** 2002 by
WATERSIDE PRESS
Domum Road
Winchester SO23 9NN
**Telephone** 01962 855567
**Fax** 01962 855567
**E-mail** enquiries@watersidepress.co.uk
**Web-site** www.watersidepress.co.uk

**ISBN** Paperback 1 872870 27 9

**Cover design** John Good Holbrook Ltd, Coventry/Waterside Press

**Printing and binding** Antony Rowe Ltd, Chippenham

**First edition** 1995 ISBN 1 872 870 09 0

Introduction to

# The Criminal Justice Process

## SECOND EDITION

**Bryan Gibson** and **Paul Cavadino**

With the assistance of David Faulkner

WATERSIDE PRESS
WINCHESTER

Introduction to
# The Criminal Justice Process

## CONTENTS

## Part III: Key Actors

# Part IV: Aspects of Criminal Justice

# Foreword and Acknowledgements

The criminal justice process encompasses all the procedures and practices which flow from the detection and apprehension of offenders. It embraces police dealings with suspects; the charging, cautioning and prosecution of individuals; bail and remand decisions affecting the liberty of people not yet convicted of or sentenced for any offence; pleas, trials and sentencing; the arrangements for carrying out custodial and community sentences; and—for all but a handful of prisoners who stay behind bars for the rest of their lives—rehabilitation and reintegration into the community. An understanding of the process as a whole requires some knowledge of how systems work and how decisions are made at each of these stages.

We have sought to describe the different aspects in a way that will leave the reader with a clear picture of the overall structure. As with the first edition of this book our aim has been to avoid undue complexity but at the same time to provide a full enough description to enable the reader to grasp the central features. We hope the result will assist not only the beginner seeking a general overview—whether as a student or interested lay person—but also the practitioner who wants to strengthen his or her understanding of the wider context in which his or her day-to-day role is discharged.

## A time of change

This second edition comes at a vital time for the criminal justice process of England and Wales. A White Paper, *Justice for All*, published in 2002 contains wide-ranging proposals which if implemented in full (for certain aspects are not going unchallenged), could wholly transform the criminal justice landscape. Most of these proposals stem from (but do not wholly reproduce) earlier recommendations in Lord Justice Auld's report, *Review of the Criminal Courts* (2001), and John Halliday's report, *Making Punishments Work* (2001). Both of these were major exercises in themselves, involving an examination of the structure of the criminal courts and their sentencing powers respectively. We have noted ways in which *Justice for All* could alter the current arrangements at appropriate points in the text and have dealt with the White Paper more fully in *Chapter 15*.

## Other landmarks and updating

The first edition of this book was written not long after the Criminal Justice Act 1991—with its discernible philosophy and coherent sentencing framework (see *Chapter 9*)—was still fresh in people's minds. The 1991 Act seemed to offer some degree of permanence, despite the fact that Parliament made an early change of direction at key points. That framework is now to be overhauled, just one of many recurring motifs from the text—and which distinguish this edition from the last one—such as:

- developments in the way criminal justice services generally are provided, managed and co-ordinated, including moves towards 'joining up' criminal justice and greater central direction or involvement
- a renewed emphasis on crime prevention and crime reduction, key aims which now pervade the criminal process

- the incorporation of the European Convention On Human Rights into UK law, notably Article 6 (the right to a fair trial) and Article 14 (whereby such rights are guaranteed without discrimination)
- a fresh emphasis on victims, witnesses, reparation and restorative justice
- the creation of a National Probation Service (NPS), the re-naming of some community sentences, and stricter enforcement strategies
- the creation of a Criminal Defence Service and changes to 'legal aid'
- the Police Reform Act 2002 and changes in police work generally, including advances in technology which are altering methods of investigation and detection of crime and the prosecution of offenders
- the introduction of drug-testing at key points in the criminal process
- increased reliance on electronic monitoring of people under court orders and following release from prison on home detention curfew
- the changed ethos generated by the Macpherson report following the murder of the black teenager Stephen Lawrence, together with the introduction of racially-based offences and sentencing criteria
- an emphasis on confronting persistent offenders and conduct such as harassment, anti-social behaviour and domestic violence
- the creation of a Youth Justice Board and wholly revised arrangements for youth justice, including youth offending teams (YOTs), youth offending panels (who will soon deal with virtually all 'first time' juvenile offenders), and a statutory scheme of police reprimands and warnings
- an increase in the prison population to over 71,000 with its consequent impact on the capacity of HM Prison Service to maintain humane and safe regimes and effective strategies in terms of resettlement and programmes to reduce re-offending
- the creation of an Assets Recovery Agency to trace and recover proceeds of crime; and
- an emphasis on 'working together' and partnership across the agencies, and an enhanced role for both the private sector and the voluntary sector working with statutory criminal justice services.

These and many other developments that are changing the criminal justice process in England and Wales have been incorporated into the text.

### Acknowledgements

Very many people have contributed to this handbook with information, materials and suggestions including a number of other Waterside Press authors to whom we are most grateful. We would particularly like to thank David Faulkner of the Oxford Centre for Criminological Research, and also Gordon Barclay of the Home Office Research, Development and Statistics Department for commenting on *Chapter 16*. David Faulkner began by casting his eyes over the draft and making valuable suggestions, but a certain momentum took over. A better description of his involvement in this project now appears on the title page.

**Bryan Gibson** and **Paul Cavadino**
September 2002

# CHAPTER 1

# Overview

Looking back no-one ever paused to devise an overall blueprint for criminal justice in England and Wales. This is one reason why, in 1995, when this book first appeared, the title *Introduction to the Criminal Justice Process* was chosen. We explained then that what exists in England and Wales is a *process* of justice, typified by a network of closely linked organizations, each with its own role, aims, targets, culture and history. Put another way, the criminal justice process involves the completion of a sequence of discrete tasks by an assortment of individual services (or 'agencies') acting at arms length from one another. It is a description of these tasks, how they inter-relate and of the personnel involved that forms the subject matter of this book.

### The emerging criminal justice *system*

In recent times the organizations have come to more resemble a true *system*.[1] They still do not have a unified structure of management and political direction is divided between three government departments but over the past 20 years the dependence of individual services on one another for their effective operation has been increasingly recognised. Indeed, the once highly disparate nature of criminal justice began to diminish from the 1980s onwards, as a result of cross-agency working groups and inter-agency liaison, culminating from 1992 in a national Criminal Justice Consultative Council (and area committees) comprising leaders of the different services (*Chapter 17*).

In 2002 the White Paper, *Justice for All* (*Chapter 15*) set out a vision of a criminal justice system which builds on these and other developments and many of its proposals (noted at appropriate points in the text which follows) centre on linking component parts of the process in a more effective way. The White Paper acknowledges that each service 'has developed largely independently' but sets out a 'blueprint' for the future that is intended to send

> the clearest possible signal to those committing offences that the criminal justice system is united in ensuring their detection, conviction and punishment.

The proposals by which this will be achieved, it claims, provide 'a coherent strategy, from the detection of offences to the rehabilitation of offenders designed to focus the system on its purpose—fighting and reducing crime and delivering justice on behalf of victims, defendants and the community'.

## NATURE OF THE PROCESS

Some aspects of the criminal process are of quite ancient origin, such as the magistrates' court,[2] High Court and appellate jurisdiction of the House of

---

[1]   The term Criminal Justice System (CJS) is used extensively by the Home Office in its publications and at that department's web-site (www: homeoffice.gov.org).
[2]   See *History of the Justices of the Peace* (1994), Skyrme, T, Chichester: Barry Rose.

Lords—whilst others stem from Victorian or Edwardian times, or are of more recent origin such as the Crown Court (1971), Crown Prosecution Service (CPS) (1985) (but reorganized several times since), the youth court (1991) and the Youth Justice Board (1998). The National Probation Service (NPS)[3] and Criminal Defence Service (CDS) were created in their present form as recently as 2001 and the Assets Recovery Agency in 2002. The process is continually evolving.

One reason for a division of functions is the constitutional doctrine of the separation of powers—the principle that the Legislature (Parliament), Executive (Government) and Judiciary (Courts) should be independent of one another. In the criminal justice context this means that the government (or in practice the Home Secretary) can, with Parliament's independent and democratic agreement, legislate on law and order, but neither Parliament nor ministers of the Crown can dictate what a given law means or how it should be applied or enforced—when determination of the facts, interpretation of the law and the application of the law to the facts are ultimately matters for the courts.

In the case of judges and magistrates (known collectively as the judiciary) this relationship is known as 'judicial independence'. The courts have a long tradition of independent decision-making—of freedom from improper influence or 'back door' information. They act only on the basis of evidence or other admissible information and can be called to account only by other courts in the judicial hierarchy on appeal (and, since 2000, by the European Court of Human Rights).[4] Similarly, all other participants in the criminal justice process such as the police, Crown prosecutors, probation officers and prison governors have roles and working cultures where independent decision-making is the norm—and, for the most part, essential.

This fragmentation of responsibilities acts as a considerable restraint on the abuse of power or coercion. In a liberal democracy there may be strengths in a process in which the constituent parts—some of which operate more closely to the interests of the state (or are more susceptible to influence from the centre or from political interests) than others—function independently. But, as noted in the first edition of this book and now confirmed by *Justice for All*, it can also be a weakness.

Throughout this book there are examples of a general shift towards a nationwide agenda for participants in the criminal justice process including in relation to key aims such as crime reduction and crime prevention. Virtually all the criminal justice agencies now experience some degree of strategic direction at national level,[5] whilst decisions about day-to-day implementation are generally taken at area or local level. Services have been progressively reorganized, and new organizations have been created to operate at one remove from government. HM Prison Service and the Forensic Science Service became executive agencies under the 'Next Steps' reforms of 1992, and the probation service was centralised under a national directorate in 2001.

---

[3]   The Probation Service has existed in a localised form since the early 1900s.
[4]   See under *The European Convention* later in the chapter and *Chapter 10*.
[5]   Judicial decision-making is not in itself amenable to 'management' in the normal sense, national or otherwise—but there have been moves to monitor the performance of judges and magistrates. Since 2001, all criminal courts (including magistrates' courts, where many strategic decisions are also still made locally) are linked via the nationwide Court Service (*Chapter 2*).

Even when services are centralised, there has been a preference for some resources to be provided on a nationwide basis (such as the National Criminal Intelligence Service and National Crime Squad operated by the police: *Chapter 11*) or higher levels of co-ordination such that provided by the Court Service (*Chapters 2* and *3*). Further there is a cross-cutting Strategic Board of high ranking officials which *Justice for All* proposes replacing with a National Criminal Justice Board (*Chapter 15*).

## Separation of funding from decision-making

Similarly, justice cannot be allowed to be driven by financial priorities, profit motive or similar vested interest. The ethical problems of money or resources following criminal justice activities, e.g. the number of arrests or convictions or amount of fines imposed by courts seem obvious given the multi-billion pound a nature of the undertaking. Ultimately, if not immediately, priorities become distorted.

Generally speaking, criminal justice decision-making operates quite independently of funding considerations (or at the very least at arm's length). Similarly, one agency is not constrained by the knock-on effect elsewhere in the process of arriving at a correct and proper conclusion. A decision by the police to arrest someone or of a court to impose a particular sentence takes no direct account of the existence (or lack) of available resources.[6] The diversion of an offender away from the formal criminal justice process by means of a police caution (or in the case of a juvenile a warning or reprimand), or from imprisonment into a community-based sentence, does not mean that the comparatively high cost of bringing a case to court or the saving made by not using a prison cell can be transferred to some fresh purpose. Nor do resources follow offenders, such as those dealt with in the community instead of in prisons or young offender institutions (YOIs),[7] or a mental patient[8] who is treated in hospital rather than prosecuted and kept in prison.[9]

Since 1992 the Home Secretary has been under a statutory duty to publish information about the costs of criminal justice for the attention of people concerned with the administration of justice, so that whilst cost is not strictly a factor in decision-making it is something which—in the modern day and age—it is felt by Parliament that courts should be appraised of on a regular basis.

## An 'interdependent' process

The autonomous nature of criminal justice agencies sometimes allowed practices to develop which were insupportable—often geared to the aims and objectives of individual organizations (or even employees) and determined unilaterally. Acceptance of the idea that the agencies, whilst independent of one another, are

---

[6] But some connections are emerging. Thus prison overcrowding may be a reason to prefer a community sentence: see *Chapters 9* and *14* and an increasing number of functions are being linked in officialese and even statute, such as 'prisons and probation', 'courts and legal services'.

[7] There may be a greater rationale under the Youth Justice Board arrangements.

[8] Many offenders suffer from some form of mental disorder or personality disorder.

[9] Fines, e.g. are paid over to the Exchequer and do not for instance count towards court running costs or the outlay on a courthouse. A questionable trend, perhaps, is that whereby police forces in experimental areas have been allowed to retain speeding fines, a practice which it has been proposed should be extended nationwide.

'interdependent' surfaced from the mid-1980s onwards and this has gone hand-in-hand with the idea that the relevant services—*as an entity*—are responsible for the delivery of a key public service.

The underlying rationale of interdependence is that each of the component parts of the process is to some degree reliant on the rest in discharging its own role. The Crown Prosecution Service (CPS) relies on the police for information from which to make a decision about prosecution; the police often require legal advice from the CPS concerning the scope of an offence. Courts cannot sentence in serious cases without the benefits of a pre-sentence report (PSR) from the National Probation Service (NPS), which, in turn, needs to understand sentencing guidelines and the kind of factors courts regularly take into account in arriving at sentence decisions. A chain of communications may be involved in ensuring that HM Prison Service knows that a particular prisoner is a suicide risk.[10]

Thus, all criminal justice services bear joint responsibility for making the overall network of arrangements work. The trend is for the agencies to work towards better information, sound communications, improved performance, compatible working systems, agreed targets, protocols, understandings and common geographical boundaries—with Best Practice or National Standards a high priority within an agency and increasingly between and across agencies. Common mechanisms are codes of practice, liaison meetings, local or national task forces and user groups (such as court user groups at both Crown Court and magistrates' court level: the court representing a focal point for the participating organizations and for individuals caught up in the process of justice).

## CRIMINAL JUSTICE

As noted in the *Foreword* criminal justice is a broad topic touching on everything from the investigation of an offence through prosecution, trial and sentence to the discharging of punishments (or 'sanctions'). Within its outer reaches it takes in aspects of criminology,[11] penology (both subjects with their own flexible boundaries, perceptions and debates), criminal law and the rules of evidence. Criminal justice also has a more pragmatic dimension in terms of its links to crime prevention and crime reduction and the urgent and ever present demands of the law and order lobby—the general public, the media and politicians—for 'something to be done' about the latest threat (or perceived threat) to public safety. In this last sense in particular it is a constantly changing topic in terms both of its priorities and content.

It would be impossible now to describe criminal justice without reference to the Human Rights Act 1998 and European Convention On Human Rights and Fundamental Freedoms, not least the fair trials provisions of Article 6 and the various fundamental rights (such as the right not 'to be punished without law') and freedoms (such as those of assembly, association, expression, thought, conscience and religion) all of which are protected under the Convention. One particularly important impact has been the growth of a duty to give reasons and explanations for decisions (see later).

---

[10]  Similar examples appear throughout this book and emphasise the need for reliable data and co-ordinated information systems.

[11]  For a basic outline, see *Introduction to Criminology* (1999), Pond R, Winchester: Waterside Press.

**Anti-social behaviour: a note**

A modern dimension to 'criminal justice' which is worthy of note is that where certain kinds of anti-social behaviour are criminalised or singled out for formal action. Anti-social behaviour orders (ASBOs) were introduced under the Crime and Disorder Act 1998 to deal with what can broadly speaking be termed 'nuisance' behaviour (and not necessarily criminal activity). An application to a court for an ASBO is a *civil* matter and results from liaison and discussion between the police and local authority. But, once an ASBO is granted, then if it is later breached this has to be treated as a criminal matter due to the potential penalties involved. Human rights issues then arise, such as Article 6 ('fair trial') and Article 10 ('freedom of expression'): see later in the chapter. Civil remedies linked to criminal sanctions can also be seen in relation to harassment and football banning orders (*Chapter 9*) whilst the Police Reform Act 2002 allows so-called 'on the spot fines' for a range of (admittedly in this case criminal) offences which have been loosely categorised as 'anti-social behaviour' (*Chapter 11*). The theme of tackling anti-social behaviour continues in *Justice for All*.

**Criminal justice and the scheme of the book**

The approach has been to describe the framework of criminal justice organizations and participants by reference to the chain of events which begins once a criminal offence is committed. The book describes the criminal courts, their jurisdiction and powers (*Part I*); the chronological progress of a criminal case (*Part II*); and the key actors, their roles and responsibilities (*Part III*). Finally, *Part IV* looks at several free-standing topics: reform, discrimination, 'working together' and partnership, and victims, witnesses and restorative justice.

## STRATEGIC MANAGEMENT

There is no Ministry of Justice for England and Wales, nor any overall director of the various strands which make up the criminal justice process. At the highest level there is a balance of functions and responsibilities as between the Lord Chancellor and Home Secretary—broadly speaking resulting in a division between that for the judiciary and that for criminal justice policy respectively, and with each being ultimately accountable for criminal justice services which appropriately attach to their Parliamentary role (as outlined below). There is a cross-cutting Strategic Board of high ranking officials—which *Justice for All* proposes replacing with a National Criminal Justice Board—and there is also a Cabinet Committee chaired by the Home Secretary and including the Lord Chancellor and Attorney General 'to ensure a coherent approach to . . . reform'. There is also a Minister for Justice Systems Information Technology.[12]

**The Lord Chancellor**

The Lord Chancellor is appointed by the Queen on the recommendation of the Prime Minister. The office is of ancient origin and has lasted for about 1,000 years. Somewhat uniquely, under the British constitution, the role requires the

---

[12] And moves to create a Virtual Unified Case File to provide users across the criminal process with 'seamless access' to information about an individual case.

occupant to play a part in all three arms of state (see the reference to the doctrine of the separation of powers earlier in this chapter).[13] He or she is a senior member of the cabinet, speaker of the House of Lords and head of the judiciary—and sometimes performs this last mentioned function by sitting in the House of Lords as a Lord of Appeal, i.e. as a judge (*Chapter 12*). A main task of the Lord Chancellor is to ensure the efficient administration of justice and the courts. The post also carries responsibility for promoting certain reforms to the *civil* law.

As part of these duties, the Lord Chancellor is responsible for the selection and appointment, or recommendation for appointment, of virtually all judges, judicial officers and magistrates in England and Wales (and in Northern Ireland). He or she has general responsibility for the Court of Appeal, the High Court, the Crown Court[14] and magistrates' courts—and for the county courts[15] and administrative tribunals. All courts except magistrates' courts are administered through an agency of the Lord Chancellor's Department called the Court Service and since autumn 2001 there have been formal links between that service and magistrates' courts in terms of a director level post (*Chapter 2*).[16]

The Lord Chancellor's responsibility for training judges and magistrates is discharged via a Judicial Studies Board and extends to the whole of England and Wales, except that in Lancashire, Greater Manchester and Merseyside magistrates are (seemingly for purely historical reasons) appointed and trained by the Chancellor of the Duchy of Lancaster. The Lord Chancellor also has responsibility for the appointment of Queen's Counsel (QCs), i.e. progression of barristers or solicitors to the rank of leading counsel, and for the Legal Services Commission and thereby the Criminal Defence Service (*Chapter 12*).

## Parliamentary Secretary

Since 1992, a junior minister with the rank of Parliamentary Secretary has been appointed to the Lord Chancellor's Department to represent that department in the House of Commons.

## Lord Chancellor's Department

Although the office of Lord Chancellor (above) is much older, the Lord Chancellor's Department (LCD) dates from the appointment of the first permanent secretary in the nineteenth century. In its current guise, the department—which employs around 10,000 people—is responsible to the Lord Chancellor for the efficient administration of justice in England and Wales, working to support the Lord Chancellor. In the context of criminal justice this includes, e.g. oversight of the courts and strategic planning for court services, including those for the calling and swearing in of jurors (*Chapter 3*) and state funded representation via the CDS (above). The department also has a Human Rights Unit whose main responsibility is to ensure successful implementation of the Human Rights Act 1998. The unit also maintains and develops the UK's arrangements under various human rights treaties.

---

[13] It is difficult to understand how the tri-partite aspects of the role of the Lord Chancellor are continuing to survive into a human rights era.

[14] Both the High Court and Crown Court are always referred to in the singular.

[15] Civil courts dealing with such matters as debt recovery, lesser civil claims and family matters.

[16] The proposals contained in the White Paper *Justice for All* (*Chapter 15*), if implemented, will lead to changes in the general framework within which all criminal courts operate.

**The Home Secretary**
The office of Secretary of State, like that of the Lord Chancellor, is of ancient origin. It was formalised in 1377 and its holders became powerful figures under the Tudors. In 1782 the office was divided between the Secretary of State for the Home Department (or Home Secretary) and the Secretary of State for Foreign Affairs (Foreign Secretary). The Home Secretary is responsible for criminal justice policy and criminal law reform—as juxtaposed to matters affecting judicial decision-making or the administration of the courts and which fall to be dealt with by the Lord Chancellor (above). He or she also occupies a key role in relation to policing, HM Prison Service, the National Probation Service and the Youth Justice Board (see later chapters) as well as other quite separate responsibilities including for immigration and deportation.[17]

The Home Secretary is assisted by a number of junior ministers, including a minister for Crime Reduction, Policing, Community Safety and Young People and a minister for Criminal Justice, Sentencing and Law Reform—as well as a Parliamentary Under-Secretary for Community and Custodial Provision (see, generally, *Chapters 13* and *14*).

In recent years and post-Human Rights Act 1998 the Home Secretary has found himself in conflict with the judiciary on a number of occasions concerning who should set tariffs for life sentence prisoners (*Chapter 14*).

**The Home Office**
The Home Secretary is supported by the Home Office which, in particular, develops and—once passed by Parliament—implements new criminal justice legislation, including the creation and updating of offences, procedures, and the framework within which sentences are passed by courts. The Home Office is the government department responsible for internal affairs in England and Wales, has 'a specific aim of working closely with the LCD and CPS to deliver justice through effective and efficient investigation, prosecution, trial and sentencing and support for victims' (*Justice for All*) and perceives its own purpose as being 'to work with individuals and communities to build a safe, just and tolerant society enhancing opportunities for all and in which rights and responsibilities go hand in hand, and the protection and security of the public are maintained and enhanced' (Home Office web-site[18]). It carries a wide range of responsibilities including for:

- criminal law (offences, bail, procedure and sentencing)
- crime reduction programmes, advice and support on crime prevention
- co-ordination within the criminal justice process
- mentally disordered offenders
- support for victims including via the charity Victim Support (*Chapter 18*)
- criminal injuries compensation
- community issues including volunteering, the family, animal procedures, coroners
- dangerous drugs and preventing drug misuse
- issues concerning terrorists and terrorism

---

[17] Many statutes give the Home Secretary power to make delegated legislation, usually of a procedural, regulatory or detailed technical nature.
[18] www.homeoffice.gov.uk

- immigration, asylum and applications for UK citizenship.

The Home Office also has general oversight of the police. HM Prison Service and the Youth Justice Board are executive agencies of the department headed by independent officials who are responsible to the Home Secretary. The National Probation Service (NPS) is a directorate of the Home Office. A former responsibility for investigating miscarriages of justice passed from the Home Office to the Criminal Cases Review Commission in 1995 following the Royal Commission on Criminal Justice two years earlier.

Home Office functions are accompanied by an extensive, ongoing programme of research conducted through a Research Development and Statistics Department (RDSD). Every year the Home Office publishes the *Criminal Statistics* showing the numbers of offences committed and sentences imposed as well as numerous other research studies, statistics and associated materials (see, e.g. the documents on race and criminal justice mentioned in *Chapter 16*).

## THE CRIMINAL COURTS

Everything said about the criminal courts of England and Wales in this book must also be understood in the light of proposals contained in the White Paper *Justice For All* outlined in *Chapter 15* and the move towards overall strategic management or direction via the Court Service. References to such possible changes apart, the courts are described in their existing mode, which is likely to continue until at least 2005. They are:

- magistrates' courts: *Chapter 2*
- the Crown Court: *Chapter 3*
- the High Court, Court of Appeal and House of Lords (with a note on the European Court of Human Rights): *Chapter 4*; and
- the youth court (a part of the magistrates' court with special responsibility for people below the age of 18 years and which can only now be understood alongside the wide-ranging remit of the Youth Justice Board): *Chapter 5*.

There are also Courts Martial (military courts for service personnel), but these perform a specialist role beyond the scope of this book.

## OTHER CRIMINAL JUSTICE AGENCIES

Apart from the courts of law, the other main participants in the criminal justice process can be summarised as follows:

- the **police** who are preventers, detectors, investigators and prosecutors of crime (in that they initiate most prosecutions even though all but minor cases are later taken over by the CPS, below). Traditionally, police forces (now often called police services) have had an 'administration of justice department' or 'bench office' to deal with court process but the move is towards co-location with the CPS in joint Criminal Justice Units. The police also appear in court as expert witnesses and to give evidence in other capacities and aim to provide a high quality of care to witnesses. Key police personnel include investigating officers, local custody officers and gaolers. Some aspects of police work are provided on a nationwide basis. Certain police forces, of which the Transport Police is perhaps the most visible, have more limited or specialised powers. See, generally, *Chapters 6 and 11*

- the **Forensic Science Service** an executive agency which provides scientific support to the police (usually) and expert evidence in court (*Chapter 11*)
- the **law officers** of the Crown: the Attorney General and Director of Public Prosecutions (DPP), the head of the CPS (below and see *Chapter 12*) who is accountable to the Attorney General (whose authority is also needed for certain prosecutions)
- the **Crown Prosecution Service** (CPS) which is an independent agency responsible for most prosecution decisions once a case has been started. [19] This includes deciding on the appropriate charge—and reviewing the case file both at the outset and on a continuing basis by applying twin 'evidential sufficiency' and 'public interest' tests. The CPS can take over, discontinue or withdraw proceedings (and it must assume responsibility for virtually all police prosecutions other than some minor ones). The CPS employs solicitors and barristers although certain cases can be conducted by designated case workers who need not be so qualified: *Chapters 7 and 12*
- other **law enforcement agencies** including: the Serious Fraud Office (SFO) a non-ministerial department that investigates and prosecutes serious or complex fraud and whose director is accountable to the Attorney General (above); Customs and Excise; Department of Social Security; Health and Safety Executive; Trading Standards and Consumer Protection departments, TV Licence Records Office (TVLRO); the National Society for the Prevention of Cruelty to Children (NSPCC) and Royal Society for the Prevention of Cruelty to Animals (RSPCA): *Chapter 11*
- the **Criminal Defence Service** which provides state funded legal representation under the auspices of the Legal Services Commission: *Chapter 12*
- **legal representatives,** i.e. solicitors and barristers who can appear for either side—prosecution or defence—in a criminal case and subject to rules about rights of audience: *Chapter 12*
- the **National Probation Service** (NPS) described by the Home Office as 'an enforcement service' and which provides a range of services to the courts as well as generally seeking to prevent and reduce offending by carrying out community punishments and supervision and attempting rehabilitation of offenders. Probation officers are subject to National Standards such as those for the 'Supervision of Offenders in the Community'; the 'Preparation of Pre-sentence Reports' (PSRs): written assessments of offenders and their offending which contain key information for courts to consider before sentencing in all the more serious cases; and for 'Release on Licence', i.e. release from prison under the early

---

[19] Apart from certain lesser matters where the police have responsibility throughout.

release scheme. Probation officers are officers of the court but work quite independently of it. Probation facilities, or those arranged by the NPS, such as probation centres, probation hostels and work schemes in the community, enable courts to use community sentences—as well as conditional bail which may require someone to reside in a hostel pending the hearing of a case by the court. Probation officers also work alongside prison officers with regard to bail support schemes, resettlement, sentence planning and release: *Chapters 8, 9* and *13*

- the **Youth Justice Board** and local **youth offending teams** (YOTs), and **youth offending panels** (or referral panels) which are responsible for many 'first-time' juvenile offenders once the Crime and Disorder Act 1998 is fully operative. *Chapter 5*
- a **Sentencing Advisory Panel** an independent public body charged by the Home Office with encouraging consistency in sentencing and which *Justice for All* proposes replacing with a Sentencing Guidelines Council
- **local authorities** who play a lead role alongside the police in Crime and Disorder Reduction Partnerships and who have a range of community safety, crime prevention and prosecution responsibilities, e.g. the enforcement of bye-laws, consumer protection legislation, school attendance, the appointment of youth offending teams and the formulation of an annual youth justice plan: *Chapters 5* and *13*. They also bring civil care proceedings in respect of children subject to abuse or neglect, and have responsibility for vulnerable adults and a statutory duty to exercise their various functions in ways which will help to prevent or reduce crime.[20]
- **HM Prison Service** (HMPS) which operates in 136 establishments to carry out orders of the courts by providing a secure, controlled and safe environment for people sentenced to custody including healthcare services and basic education. This HMPS aims to achieve through a wide range of prison, young offender institution (YOI) and detention and training regimes for different age groups and categories or types of offender (ranging from adults in local prisons who are serving short terms of imprisonment to life sentence and other long-term prisoners and other serious offenders, together with provision for young offenders and juveniles): *Chapter 14*. Prisons also hold people who are on remand awaiting trial (i.e. where they are unconvicted and presumed innocent) (*Chapter 8*) or sentence (*Chapter 9*). In all cases prisoners must be escorted to courts for relevant proceedings (see also under *Private sector,* below).
- the **Assets Recovery Agency** created by the Proceeds of Crime Act 2002 to trace and recover criminal gains: see end of chapter.
- **HM Coroner** who is responsible for investigating suspicious or unexplained deaths
- **doctors** and **psychiatrists** who work either in prison healthcare centres or in the community and who are often called upon to provide reports on the physical or mental condition of an offender or alleged offender whether for court or other assessment purposes: *Chapter 13*

---

[20] Section 17 Crime and Disorder Act 1998. For an added dimension see *Crime and Banishment: Nuisance and Exclusion in Social Housing* (1999), Burney, E, Winchester: Waterside Press.

- the **Parole Board** which is an independent executive non-departmental public body charged with the responsibility of making risk assessments to inform decisions about the release and recall of long-term prisoners and life-sentence prisoners: *Chapter 14*
- the **non-statutory** or **voluntary sectors** which provide an extensive range of services to courts, prisons, the NPS and other criminal justice agencies and individuals including nationwide undertakings such as the crime reduction charity Nacro, Victim Support, the Court Witness Service and the National Neighbourhood Watch Association: *Chapter 13*
- the **private sector** which provides a range of services under contract to statutory agencies, such as drug or alcohol treatment schemes, prison building, finance and management (i.e. what are called 'private' but more accurately 'contracted out' prisons), prisoner escort services (which now transport virtually all prisoners to and from court on behalf of HM Prison Service, above).

## OTHER PARTICIPANTS

In addition courts and other criminal justice services will be particularly concerned with the interests of:

- **defendants** in criminal cases, including ensuring that all people charged with a criminal offence receive fair treatment and are not disadvantaged, discriminated against or marginalised
- **witnesses** and other people who assist the process of justice who must be treated in a proper manner. As already indicated above, there is now a nationwide Court Witness Service for all levels of criminal court and a fresh impetus is envisaged by *Justice for All* · *Chapter 12*
- **victims of crime** who although not directly involved in criminal proceedings, except as witnesses, must be kept informed about their cases and whose obvious interest in the outcome of a criminal justice decision should always be kept in mind. The independent charity Victim Support provides information and support to victims and runs the Court Witness Service, above. The year 2001 saw a *Practice Direction: Victim Personal Statements* issued by Lord Woolf, Lord Chief Justice which is serving to alter the previous imbalance whereby the victim of a crime could become a mere bystander in subsequent criminal proceedings: *Chapter 18*
- **the press, media** and **general public** whose entitlement, in normal circumstances, to observe the workings of justice and to be able to understand the process of justice should never be lost sight of: see *Open court*, below.

### Member organizations
A range of member organizations operate in and around the criminal justice process and pursue strategies with a view to influencing that process, and which impact on it from time-to-time. Most such organizations fall within the ambit of the voluntary sector already mentioned. A distinction is sometimes drawn between campaigning or reform organizations such as the Howard League,

Prison Reform Trust, Liberty and Justice and those organizations that offer to provide a service such as the various drugs charities or providers of accommodation, work placements or offending behaviour programmes. Some do both. The term 'partnership' often connotes the idea of a statutory agency such as HM Prison Service[21] or the NPS working alongside one another.

## INSPECTORATES

Increasingly the criminal justice process has come to rely on inspectorates of which there are currently the following:

- HM Inspectorate of Constabulary
- HM Crown Prosecution Service Inspectorate
- HM Magistrates' Courts Inspectorate
- HM Inspectorate of Prisons
- HM Inspector of Probation.

Under the proposals in *Justice for All*, the Magistrates' Courts Inspectorate will become part of a new independent inspectorate with jurisdiction to examine the administration of the Crown Court. The responsibilities of the inspectorates are noted in the text at appropriate points. There is also a Prisons and Probation Ombudsman (*Chapters 13* and *14*).

## SOME GENERAL CONSIDERATIONS

Certain general considerations arise in relation to all criminal cases and can be dealt with conveniently at the outset.

**Open court**
Under national law, members of the public are entitled to observe court proceedings, subject to there being available space and no interference. In exceptional circumstances criminal courts can sit *in camera* (i.e. completely in private), e.g. in the interests of national security or where life and limb are genuinely at stake—albeit rare events in practice.

Another scenario is where there is evidence which—although it is not used by the prosecutor—must be disclosed and it is claimed that the information is sensitive due to the way in which it was obtained (such as by way of a police undercover operation) or where the nature of policing itself affects national security. A court might decide that the proper course is to deal with the question of disclosure in private or without material being read out and even, in extreme instances, without the sensitive material being made known to the defendant or his or her legal representatives at all (and due not least to human rights considerations there is a heavy presumption against this highly exceptional course).

---

[21]   See *Prisons and the Voluntary Sector: A Bridge into the Community* (2002), Bryans S, Martin C and Walker R, Winchester: Waterside Press.

One common statutory situation where a court hearing is held in private is when a magistrates' court is considering whether to issue a warrant of further detention during a police investigation (i.e. before anyone has been charged with an offence) under the Police and Criminal Evidence Act 1984 (PACE) although, in such a case, the suspect will usually be present: see further in *Chapter 6*.

Youth courts (*Chapter 5*) are *not* open to the general public as a matter of entitlement but the press can attend (below). However, there has been a more sympathetic view towards admitting victims and other people with a legitimate interest in observing the proceedings in recent years.

## Press restrictions

Broadly speaking, the press can report whatever they wish of court proceedings except in those few situations where an Act of Parliament restricts this, or allows the court to do so, e.g. committal proceedings before magistrates (*Chapter 8*) (when only a bare outline of the case can be reported unless the accused person applies for this restriction to be lifted because, say, he or she may hope that other witnesses will come forward to support his or her case); or where publication is postponed by court order to avoid a 'substantial risk of prejudice to the administration of justice'.

Other legal restrictions on what can be reported exist in relation to the youth court, committal proceedings, children (when the court can make a direction preventing identification whenever a child appears in court in whatever capacity) and a limited range of other matters.

Seats are normally reserved for the press in courtrooms (the 'press bench') and representatives are entitled to be present except in those rare instances when proceedings are held *in camera*, above.

## Contempt of court

Both the Crown Court and magistrates' court have power to punish for contempt. This extends to anyone who wilfully insults the court, a judge magistrate, juror, officer of the court, lawyer or witness—whether in court or whilst going to or returning from court. Similarly, if anyone wilfully interrupts court proceedings or misbehaves in court. Offenders can be detained until the end of the proceedings and, if the court thinks fit, can be committed to custody (limited in the case of magistrates to committal for up to a month) or can be fined (again limited in magistrates' courts to £2,500) or both. Committal to custody can be revoked at any time, e.g. where the offender asks to apologise (thus showing contrition and 'purging' his or her contempt).

## Photography

Photographing, drawing[22] or tape-recording proceedings is punishable as a contempt of court (above)—but a court can give leave for the use of a tape-recorder, e.g. to an advocate who wishes to record complex evidence for transcription. The Crown Court takes its own contemporaneous note, often nowadays employing modern technology (which will ultimately lead to the note being displayed on computer terminals in a broad range of cases).

---

[22] Sketches of proceedings seen in newspapers or on television news bulletins are created outside the courtroom from memory by an artist who was in court to observe events.

## Presumption of innocence

It is almost trite to state that in England and Wales an accused person is presumed innocent unless and until proved guilty—following a decision by a jury or magistrates. This is now reinforced by Article 6 of the European Convention. The presumption affects the way people are dealt with at all stages of the criminal process and unless and until their status changes from *accused person* to *offender* as a result of conviction.

## Previous convictions

Historically, it has been the case that an accused person's previous convictions are not admissible in evidence to prove guilt in relation to a later trial for another offence [23] Exceptions to this rule have included the situation where the accused attacks the character of witnesses for the prosecution or wrongly asserts his or her own good character. Somewhat controversially, the White Paper *Justice for All* (*Chapter 15*) proposes that the court should be allowed to be informed of a defendant's previous convictions 'where appropriate', i.e. where relevant to the charge which the accused person now faces.

## Double jeopardy

A legal rule that goes back many century is that whereby someone who is convicted or acquitted of an offence may not be tried again for the same matter called *autrefois convict* and *autrefois acquit* respectively. In recent years the latter has been notoriously linked to the Stephen Lawrence case (*Chapter 16*). The rule is said to be grounded in finality of proceedings, a further argument being that if an investigator or prosecutor knows that he or she may have further 'bites at the cherry' he or she will prepare less thoroughly (and thus less fairly) at the outset. But with advances in technology including DNA testing and the ability to examine documents and materials more closely it has become possible to open old files many years on and long after someone has been acquitted quite unjustly. Controversially, the White Paper *Justice for All* (*Chapter 15*) thus proposes that the double jeopardy rule be abolished in relation to serious cases and where 'compelling new evidence comes to light'.

## Burden and standard of proof

In a criminal case the *burden* lies with the prosecutor to establish an accused person's guilt to the required *standard*—i.e. beyond reasonable doubt. The classic statement is that of Lord Sankey in *Woolmington v. DPP* (1935) AC 462:

> Throughout the web of the English criminal law one golden thread is always to be seen—that is the duty of the prosecution to prove the prisoner's guilt subject to what I have already said as to the defence of insanity and subject also to any statutory exception . . . If, at the end of and on the whole of the case, there is a reasonable doubt, created by the evidence given by either the prosecution or the prisoner . . . the prosecution has not made out the case and the prisoner is entitled to an acquittal . . . No matter what the charge or where the trial, the principle that the prosecution must prove the guilt of the prisoner is part of the common law of England and no attempt to whittle it down can be entertained.

---

[23] 'Give a dog a bad name and hang him' as it is sometimes put.

Just occasionally, however, the law does reverse the normal onus of proof and the defendant must establish something, e.g. where this is exclusively within his or her own knowledge or control such as the fact that he or she held a licence or was covered by insurance—things that it is virtually impossible to draw proper conclusions about unless the person who is accused provides an answer. The standard of proof in these exceptional instances—where the defendant has to prove something—is always the lesser 'balance of probabilities'.

### Right to silence

For many years it has been a feature of criminal justice in England that an accused person enjoys a right to remain silent. But whereas in the past that was always the end of matters—the underlying principle being that it is for the prosecutor to prove all the ingredients of an allegation without resort to the fact that an accused person declined to give an explanation—since 1995 it has been possible for inferences to be drawn where an accused person remains silent (which is still his or her right) either before or at the trial. See further in *Chapter 15*.

### Trial by peers

Trial in the Crown Court by a jury of ordinary people selected at random (*Chapter 3*) or by lay magistrates (*Chapter 2*) is sometimes described as trial by peers, the principle—said to stem from Magna Carta—being that people accused of crime should, so far as the central question 'guilty' or 'not guilty' is concerned, be dealt with by ordinary members of the community, not by the state or a professional judiciary. The one existing exception to this is that around 100 district judges (paid professionals) sit to hear cases in magistrates' courts. The White Paper *Justice For All* proposes inroads into the principle so as to allow trial in the Crown Court by a judge alone in certain situations and also makes proposals which would widen the make up of the jury (see *Chapters 3* and *15*). Law and sentencing have always been regarded as the legitimate and exclusive province of judges.

### Due process

The principle of 'due process' is less well developed in the UK than, say, in the USA—but nonetheless the requirements are such that people can only be interviewed, arrested, tried and sentenced if fair and correct procedures are followed at each stage. Similarly, public officers, whether judges or administrators must not abuse or misuse their powers: something which can be tested in the High Court by way of judicial review (*Chapter 10*) and which is now also protected by a raft of human rights considerations. In most instances, a material failure to follow correct procedure will prevent a conviction or constitute grounds for an appeal—unless, e.g. it is possible to deal with the case without resort to the evidence or other matter affected by the irregularity.

### Three categories of offence

It is impossible to fully understand the criminal justice process without knowledge of the three categories of offence and the court towards which each category is directed. All criminal cases—from unlawful parking or murder—start out in the magistrates' court (*Chapter 2*). But a distinction must first be drawn between allegations which magistrates can actually try (i.e. decide upon guilt or innocence, then pass sentence) and those where they can only deal with certain preliminary stages before the matter proceeds to the Crown Court (*Chapter 3*) for trial on indictment as it is known. The three categories are:

- summary offences
- either way offences; and
- indictable[24] only offences.

### Summary offences
In the normal course of events, summary offences can *only* be tried—and, if convicted, the offender can *only* be sentenced—by magistrates. Everyday examples of summary offences (sometimes called 'purely summary' or 'summary only') are:

- speeding and other road traffic offences such as careless driving, defective brakes, lights or steering, driving with excess alcohol in the blood or urine, and taking a vehicle without consent
- no television licence
- lesser public order offences
- common assault
- criminal damage—depending on the value of the damage (currently below £5,000)
- certain social security offences
- offences against local bye-laws.

Most summary offences are dealt with by summoning the alleged offender to court. If the defendant pleads guilty, the case may take only a few minutes to complete. Lesser offences are often dealt with by way of a written plea of guilty (subject to appropriate procedures being invoked by the prosecutor: see *Paperwork Cases* in *Chapter 8*). A plea of 'not guilty' attracts all the protections, rights and procedures of the criminal law. The trial of a purely summary offence must observe the same general rules of procedure and evidence as a trial for the most serious of matters. Maximum penalties for summary offences are laid down by the Act of Parliament creating the offence. This is often a fine although some more serious summary offences attract imprisonment.

There are moves, strengthened by *Justice for All,* for many lesser offences to be removed from the courts and turned into matters which can be dealt with by way of a fixed penalty (as can many minor matters already including road traffic offences and breach of certain bye-laws).

### Either way offences
The next level of offence is styled 'triable either way'—often simplified to 'either way'. Such offences can be tried either in the magistrates' court or in the Crown Court. The choice depends on the outcome of a procedure known as mode of trial (or 'choice of venue', or 'determining venue'). This is described in *Chapter 8.* Commonplace either way offences are:

---

[24] Technically, the umbrella classification 'indictable' includes both indictable only and either way matters—hence the sub-classifications 'indictable *only*' and 'either way'. The significance of this is for the experts and beyond the scope of this work.

- theft
- handling stolen property
- deception
- burglary (unless 'aggravated', e.g. with a firearm or weapon)
- criminal damage where the value is £5,000 or more
- assault occasioning actual bodily harm (abh)
- possession or supply of certain prohibited drugs.

Quite apart from mode of trial, either way offences may involve procedures known as 'plea before venue', 'committal for trial' and 'committal for sentence', all of which are outlined in *Chapter 8*.

### Indictable only offences
'Indictable only' offences *must* be tried in the Crown Court before a judge and jury. Such cases are now sent to the Crown Court from the outset once the accused has appeared in the magistrates' court on remand: *Chapter 3*. Examples of indictable only offences are:

- murder and other homicides
- rape
- robbery
- aggravated burglary (e.g. with a weapon)
- blackmail
- conspiracy by two or more people to commit a criminal offence.

### Reasons for decisions
Under statute—and whilst it is the exception rather than the rule—there is an obligation on a court to give reasons in some situations, e.g.:

- where a court does not award compensation or reparation (*Chapters 5, 18*)
- when sending someone to prison (*Chapter 9*)
- when not activating a suspended sentence (*Chapter 9*)
- when refusing bail or granting conditional bail (*Chapters 6 and 8*).

Human rights obligations have extended the situations in which reasons need to be given by decision-makers generally, so that, in effect, an explanation must be provided which is sufficient to allow a party to understand the outcome of a case or determination, or any material point or issue which arises during the progress of a case or whilst a court is considering a particular issue. Article 6 of the European Convention includes a requirement for 'judgements to be pronounced publicly'. This has been interpreted in case law as meaning that reasons should be given and announced for *most* decisions. The duty to give reasons extends to other decision-makers in some situations, e.g. where a police custody sergeant refuses to allow bail to someone who has been arrested, whilst human rights considerations often require procedures to be adequately explained.

### Criminal law and procedure
The criminal law is contained principally in Acts of Parliament, and in Rules and Regulations—also known as Statutory Instruments (SIs) or delegated

legislation—so far as procedures and certain technical details are concerned. Some aspects of the criminal law stem from the common law (the most striking instance being the offence of murder) and rulings of the higher courts. *Practice Directions* are also issued from time to time, usually, in relation to criminal procedures, by the Lord Chief Justice.[25] *Justice for All* proposes new codes of criminal procedure, evidence and sentencing as well as the codification of the criminal law.[26]

Where a point is a difficult one—or argued in depth by the lawyers in a case—they are likely to refer the court to the report of a ruling of the higher courts and to ask it to consider the comments of the judges. Such reports—known as 'law reports'—are normally authenticated by a barrister and often contain what are loosely referred to as 'precedents' (which is what a judicial ruling establishes). Law reports are published in various formats and series. Those in regular use in the criminal courts include: the *All England Law Reports; Weekly Law Reports; Criminal Appeal Reports* (including a series which deals exclusively with sentencing); *Justice of the Peace Reports;* and *Road Traffic Reports*. Practitioners also keep abreast of developments via shorter law reports which appear daily in *The Times* and *Independent*.

# FAIRNESS AND HUMAN RIGHTS

Traditionally, criminal courts have been guided by principles grounded in ideas of 'natural justice'. The twin pillars of natural justice are: no-one can be a judge in his or her own cause; and always hear both sides. The first of 'pillar' emphasises the need for courts to be impartial. If bias exists on the part of the judge or magistrate he or she is disqualified from sitting to hear the case—except when bias can properly be waived by the parties. A *financial* interest in the outcome of a case cannot be waived and neither should someone adjudicate if there is a close personal relationship or other interest. The second requirement of natural justice is that each party must be given a full and proper opportunity to put his or her case and with proper explanations by the court. This aspect of the rule is sometimes put by saying that the court must act fairly.

### The European Convention
Seemingly, considerations of natural justice are now subsumed within the fair trials provisions of Article 6 of the European Convention On Human Rights. One of the most important changes in over a century to the English legal system took place in October 2000 when the Human Rights Act 1998, in effect, incorporated the European Convention On Human Rights and Fundamental Freedoms into the laws of the UK and made those rights directly enforceable in UK courts.[27] Convention rights can be absolute, qualified, or limited.

---

[25] Two key annual texts for practitioners in the Crown Court and magistrates' court are, respectively, *Archbold's Criminal Pleadings* and *Stone's Justices' Manual.*

[26] Flowing from the Auld report. Codification of the criminal law has been mooted for centuries: a very substantial undertaking, but mentioned 'throwaway-style' in the White Paper. See also *Crime, State and Citizen: A Field Full of Folk* (2001), Faulkner D, Winchester: Waterside Press, pp. 169-170.

[27] For an overview see *Human Rights and the Courts: Bringing Justice Home* (1999), Ashcroft P *et al*, Winchester: Waterside Press.

Absolute rights cannot be restricted in any circumstances. Limited rights occur where the rights themselves set out the circumstances in which the right may be infringed. Qualified rights occur where rights, prohibitions and freedoms in the Convention contain qualification clauses. An example of an absolute right is that in Article 3 not to be subjected to torture, or inhuman or degrading treatment or punishment. Examples of limited rights are the right to liberty and security in Article 5, which states that 'Everyone has the right to liberty and security of person' and that 'No-one shall be deprived of his liberty' except as described in the article, including 'lawful detention . . . after conviction by a competent court' or under various forms of 'lawful arrest or detention'. An example of a qualified right is the right to respect for private and family life in Article 8 which can, e.g. be restricted by the state in the interests of preventing disorder or crime.

**Right to a fair trial**
Central to the work of the criminal courts is the right to a fair trial. Article 6 provides, among other things, that everyone charged with a criminal offence has certain minimum rights, including to be informed promptly, in a language he or she understands and in detail, of the nature and cause of any accusation against him or her; to have adequate time and facilities for the preparation of a defence; to defend himself or herself in person or through legal assistance and, if without sufficient means to pay for this, to be given it free when the interests of justice so require; to examine and call witnesses; and to have the free assistance of an interpreter where necessary. The concept of a fair trial is much wider than establishing guilt or innocence by way of a trial in court and can pervade the whole of the criminal process, from investigation right through to sentence and including, e.g. in relation to prison discipline (*Chapter 14*).

## PUTTING THE PROCEEDS OF CRIME TO WORK

There are various methods by which a convicted offender can be required to make reparation or pay compensation to a victim or be deprived of the proceeds of crime (see *Chapters 9* and *18*). The Proceeds of Crime Act 2002 establishes an Assets Recovery Agency to investigate and recover wealth accumulated through criminal activity, consolidates and strengthens existing powers of confiscation, introduces a new power of civil recovery, extends investigation powers and tightens up existing money laundering legislation.

What is particularly interesting is the way in which proceeds of crime will be made to work for aspects of the criminal process. According to a Home Office announcement at the time the Proceeds of Crime Act received the Royal Assent a range of projects across England and Wales were set to receive a share of £2.8 million from the recovered assets fund bringing the total amount awarded for this purpose since the scheme began to £3 million. This, it was stated

. . . will fund a wide variety of crime reduction initiatives . . . [and] a wide variety of projects. These include setting up a drug treatment clinic, launching a domestic violence awareness campaign, developing a street wardens scheme, the provision of specially equipped vehicles to tackle car thieves, and educating parents about the dangers of drugs.

# CHAPTER 2

# Magistrates' Courts

For the most part, magistrates' courts are served by ordinary members of the public who sit on the bench two or three times each month as a form of voluntary public service. Magistrates, or 'justices of the peace' (JPs) (terms which are synonymous), are chosen by the Lord Chancellor for their character, integrity and judgment. They are lay magistrates, i.e. not professionally trained or skilled in the law[1]—other than that which they learn through mandatory training in their role as a JP: *Chapter 12*—and they are not paid, except for their expenses plus a modest allowance if earnings are lost by attending at court. Lay magistrates receive legal advice from professionally qualified lawyers: justices' clerks and other court legal advisers. As well as around 29,000 lay justices there are some 100 district judges (magistrates' courts),[2] salaried professionals who are empowered to sit in alone and pass judgement.

## Justices of the Peace
The description 'justice of the peace' first appeared in the fourteenth century, although its origins can be traced back to the keepers of the peace appointed by Simon de Montfort in 1264. The Justices of the Peace Act 1361 built upon emerging powers to arrest suspects and investigate offences. Three or four of 'the most worthy in each county' were commissioned to dispense justice locally. Powers to punish offenders were added before the end of that century. Property qualifications were abolished in 1905 in favour of seeking out people with the personal qualities and suitability for the role. Since then, the bench has gradually become broad based, more representative of the community that it serves and it is now more balanced as between social background, age and gender.[3]

## District judges
As already indicated district judges are professional lawyers and are empowered to sit in judgement on their own. They are located mostly in London and other urban centres—but district judges have also been appointed to serve most counties on a shared basis, as between several petty sessions areas (PSAs: below). A district judge can be called in by any lay bench, e.g. at times of abnormal pressure or to deal with an unusually complex, sensitive, challenging or (for lay justices) time-consuming case. He or she has all the powers of a lay bench and will tend to work quickly by comparison having no need to retire for 'private consultation' (although he or she may sometimes reserve giving a decision for reflection or legal research).

---

[1]  Similarly in the Crown Court (*Chapter 3*) 12 ordinary members of the public—the jury—determine guilt or innocence.

[2]  Formerly known as stipendiary magistrates.

[3]  For information about the appointment of magistrates and their training see *Chapter 12*.

## Justices' clerks and the justices' chief executives

The system of summary justice relies for its efficacy on the unique nature of the relationship between lay magistrates and their legal advisers. The chief legal advisers are the justices' clerks, whilst day-to-day advice in the courtroom is generally provided by one of a team of court legal advisers. The adviser is not party to the decision of the court and legal rules dictate what advice should be offered and when the adviser should intervene, or visit the magistrates in their private retiring room.

For many years, the justices' clerk was also the manager of the court—but under the Police and Magistrates' Courts Act 1994 (as amended), each magistrates' courts committee (MCC) must appoint a justices' chief executive to take overall responsibility for the administration of the magistrates' courts in its catchment area. Outlines of the respective roles of the justices' clerk, justices' chief executive and MCC appear in *Chapter 12*. The administration of magistrates' courts involves many tasks beyond the activities which take place in the courtroom. Overall some 9,800 people are employed by MCCs across England and Wales.

# SUMMARY JUSTICE

Magistrates' courts[4] are courts of 'summary jurisdiction', a term which connotes a prompt and relatively inexpensive response to crime: the meting out of early sanctions and the provision of hopefully swift remedies (including compensation to victims of crime) for comparatively minor offending behaviour. Summary justice tends to be dispensed at a brisk pace compared with the business of other courts in the criminal courts hierarchy, in some instances in the absence of the offender under procedures allowing a written plea of guilty (*Chapter 8*). Many summary offences amount to little more than 'transgressions' and some cases occupy only minutes in court. But magistrates also deal with many matters which are serious, complex and of considerable import something which is likely to expand given proposals in *Justice for All* (*Chapter 15*) which notes that 'the principal function of magistrates' courts is to provide the forum in which all criminal prosecutions are initiated and most decided'.

# JURISDICTION

The word 'jurisdiction' is used to describe the extent of authority to deal with cases. In the criminal context, the responsibilities of magistrates' courts include:

- dealing with around 97 per cent of all prosecuted crime in England and Wales, from start to finish—the remainder being sent by magistrates to the Crown Court for trial or sentence. Virtually all criminal cases begin in the magistrates' court, even though 'indictable only' matters (such as murder,

---

[4]  For a comprehensive account see *Introduction to the Magistrates' Court* (2001), edn. 4, Gibson B, Winchester: Waterside Press.

rape and robbery: see *Chapter 1*) must now be sent straightaway by magistrates to the Crown Court

- taking mode of trial decisions in relation to either way offences (*Chapter 1*)
- deciding in contested cases (i.e. where there is a plea of 'not guilty') whether an accused person is guilty or not: *Chapter 8*
- sentencing offenders (with powers of up to six months' imprisonment for a single offence in many instances or 12 months in aggregate when sentences for two or more either way offences (*Chapter 1*) are imposed to run consecutively to one another (i.e. one following on from the other)). A list of available sentences appears in *Chapter 9*. The White Paper *Justice For All (Chapter 15)* proposes, in broad terms, a doubling of magistrates' powers to 12 months per offence.
- authorising further detention by the police of a suspect under the Police and Criminal Evidence Act 1984 (PACE): *Chapter 6*
- deciding whether someone ought to be released on bail or kept in custody pending the next stage of criminal proceedings: *Chapter 8*
- dealing with applications affecting property seized by the police and over which there may a dispute concerning possession or ownership
- issuing warrants of arrest or to search premises or seize illicit money, goods or substances
- dealing with people below the age of 18 in a special youth court: *Chapter 5*
- discharging a range of linked administrative duties, either at court or in some instances in a magistrates' private home.

Magistrates' jurisdiction is sometimes limited in time, e.g. proceedings for a purely summary offence must be commenced within six months of that offence being committed or coming to the notice of the prosecutor and certain errors can be corrected by the court itself within 28 days.

## LOCAL JUSTICE

Magistrates' courts are essentially courts that deal principally with matters arising locally so that the precise workload will vary with the make-up of the area. There are some 500 court centres in England and Wales, serving cities, towns and rural communities—and they are grouped under 42 administrative centres or MCCs (above). There is now a strategic link to the Court Service. *Justice for All* proposes that the administration of magistrates' courts be integrated within a new overall management arrangement for criminal courts, albeit that this is unlikely to have any widescale impact on the need for local units of operation and the discharging of justice by magistrates locally. A busy city or urban court is likely to see a greater proportion of serious crime ('heavy crime') than a court in a remote rural area (although serious offences can arise anywhere). A 'motorway court' will see a high percentage of road traffic cases; ports and airports generate Customs and Excise prosecutions and cases involving smuggling or drug-trafficking; and courts in country areas deal with breaches of livestock and similar regulations and poaching. Where the workload of a magistrates' court is of sufficient size cases may be streamed into 'remand courts', 'traffic courts', 'not guilty (or "trial") courts', 'non-police courts' (i.e.

courts dealing with what are often termed private prosecutions: see *Chapter 7*) etc, whereas the daily list (or 'agenda') in a single courtroom at a centre with a more modest throughput may contain all these varieties of case and more.

Special or 'occasional' courts may be held out-of-hours as necessary to deal with applications, e.g. for remands in custody/bail (*Chapter 8*), warrants of further detention (*Chapter 6*) or to deal with a large number of arrests following law and order disturbance. An Extended Court Sitting Hours project is being piloted in London and Manchester to see what might be achieved by courts operating outside their general sitting hours to deal with normal business.

**Petty sessions areas**
The geographical unit of operation is the petty sessions area, or PSA. The PSA is the basic measure of territorial jurisdiction although magistrates can deal with many matters wherever committed, including either way matters (*Chapter 1*).

## HEARINGS BEFORE MAGISTRATES

Lay magistrates normally sit 'in threes' (the legal maximum: the minimum is two magistrates except where powers are conferred on a single justice: below) to decide the outcome of cases. Special rules apply to youth courts: *Chapter 5*.

**Decisions by a single justice**
As already indicated, some decisions can be taken by one lay magistrate. An example is whether to allow bail or to place an alleged offender in custody (called a 'remand': *Chapter 8*). Saturday 'stand-by' courts often have just one magistrate. Cases might then be adjourned until the following Monday morning to be dealt with during normal business hours by a full court. A range of 'out of court' duties, such as signing documents, can be carried out by a single justice. Again, as already indicated, a district judge can always sit on his or her own.

**Evidence, argument and representations**
Like the jury in the Crown Court, magistrates listen to evidence and argument (sometimes called 'representations' or 'speeches'). They can adjourn to discuss matters in their private retiring room. If legal advice is required, they can call upon the court legal adviser for this part of their discussion. An explanation must be given of any advice received in private and the parties must have an opportunity to make relevant points (see further *Practice Direction (Justices: Clerk to Court) 2000: Chapter 12*). The final decision is then announced in court by the chairman. The court must give reasons or explanations in ordinary language in a range of situations (*Chapter 1*). Straightforward cases are often dealt with without adjourning. The chairman consults with his or her colleagues on the bench and announces their decision there and then. Conversely, a complex case might need to be considered for a substantial period of time in private. The trend is to conduct business in open court whenever possible.

Since 2000 all state-funded representation ('legal aid') (*Chapter 12*) in magistrates' courts is free of charge regardless of the means of the defendant.

# CHAPTER 3

# The Crown Court

The Crown Court sits at some 90 locations across England and Wales to deal with indictable and either way offences (*Chapter 1*). It replaced the former Assizes and Quarter Sessions in 1974 following a comprehensive review by Lord Beeching which led to the Courts Act 1971. For the future, the exact nature of its jurisdiction, methods and procedures is likely to be determined by the outcome of proposals contained in the White Paper, *Justice for All* (*Chapter 15*).

The Crown Court is usually named after its geographical location, e.g. Liverpool Crown Court, Leeds Crown Court, Winchester Crown Court—although jurisdiction is nationwide[1] and each court centre may deal with cases from beyond its normal catchment area under standing arrangements to transfer cases for reasons of local sensitivity, security or convenience to the parties and witnesses. Strictly speaking, all locations are part of '*the* Crown Court'—i.e. a single entity—and each venue a 'Crown Court centre'.[2] Typically, the premises will be fairly prestigious and often a local landmark—but equally they can be modern, functional, somewhat anonymous looking and designed to be ultra cost-effective. The Central Criminal Court (or 'The Old Bailey': after its London address) is part of the Crown Court and deals with cases arising in central London together with a variety of—often high profile or locally sensitive—cases transferred to it from other parts of the country.

## JURISDICTION

In broad terms, the Crown Court deals with those more serious offences, the two or three per cent of prosecuted crime, that filters beyond the magistrates' court (*Chapter 2*). There are several strands to its jurisdiction:

- dealing with criminal cases before a judge and a jury, i.e. involving
  —very serious offences which are triable only on indictment such as murder, manslaughter, rape or robbery (*Chapter 1*). These cases are now sent straight to the Crown Court as soon as the accused person has been charged with the offence and has appeared in the magistrates' court. There are no committal proceedings before examining justices (*Chapter 8*).[3]
  — either way matters where the magistrates' court has declined jurisdiction or the accused person has elected trial by jury (when there are committal proceedings: *Chapters 1* and *8*)

---

[1]  And in some cases extra-territorial, i.e. it can deal with certain offences where the events in question occurred or began outside England and Wales: see later in the text.

[2]  Or in some cases nowadays a 'combined courts centre'. i.e. a location where, say, magistrates' courts (*Chapter 2*), the High Court and county court also use the same facilities and hold their sittings.

[3]  *Justice for All* could lead to the abolition of committal proceedings in all cases.

— summary matters which can properly be dealt with at the same time as either of the above, i.e. where the same defendant is involved

— allegations of 'grave crimes' made against people below the age of 18 where these must be committed to the Crown Court for trial or in those discretionary situations where the youth court has declined jurisdiction (*Chapter 5* and below)[4]

- committals for sentence by magistrates' courts in respect of either way offences, i.e. cases where the offender was tried and convicted in the magistrates' court but where the magistrates consider that their power to impose up to six months imprisonment per offence (or 12 months in aggregate) are insufficient[5]

- appeals against conviction or sentence by magistrates, or against both of these. Such convictions may be in respect of summary or either way matters (see generally *Chapter 10*).

In contrast to the position in the magistrates' court where a time limit affects summary cases (*Chapter 2*), the jurisdiction of the Crown Court is not limited in time and it often deals with cases many years after the offence was committed, especially since the onset of DNA testing which has led to an increasing number of serious crimes being solved (and miscarriages of justice being corrected) 20 or more years after the events concerned and also under war crimes legislation which, by definition, may envisage a long period between offence and prosecution. There is, however, a common law principle and nowadays human rights considerations (see Article 6 of the European Convention On Human Rights noted in *Chapter 1*) whereby a long-delayed trial may be unfair.

In terms of the place where an offence is alleged to have been committed, the jurisdiction of the Crown Court extends across England and Wales. It can also deal with offences committed in territorial waters, on British ships, with treason, the murder of a British subject and certain other offences wherever allegedly committed.

## COMMITTAL FOR TRIAL

The process via which cases reach the Crown Court is known as committal for trial.[6] As already indicated, where an offence is *indictable only* the case is sent straight to the Crown Court at the outset. With either way offences (*Chapter 1*) there will be a committal if the magistrates' court has determined that trial at the Crown Court is more appropriate or the defendant has elected (i.e. chosen) trial by jury[7]—when proceedings before the magistrates' court turn into proceedings

---

[4] Similarly this will change if proposals in *Justice for All* are implemented (*Chapters 5* and *15*).

[5] *Justice for All* proposes the abolition of committals for sentence (*Chapters 9* and *15*).

[6] See footnote 3.

[7] This stage of the proceedings in the magistrates' court is known as 'mode of trial', i.e. the magistrates must determine which mode is more suitable (sometimes called 'determining venue'). As part of moves aimed at avoiding delay and encouraging a timely guilty plea (for which credit should be given: see *Chapter 9*), the accused person can, before the mode of trial stage is reached, indicate that he or she wishes to plead guilty (known as 'plea before venue'). In the event of a

with a view to committal for trial at the Crown Court. In cases of serious fraud or certain offences against children a special process known as 'transfer for trial' comes into play so that supporting evidence does not have to be submitted or rehearsed at the magistrates' court level.

At a committal for trial the magistrates are styled 'examining justices', i.e. they examine the evidence to see whether there is a case for committal. However, ever since 1967 there has been a general power to conduct a 'paper committal' without consideration of the evidence and the vast majority of committals are now of this kind. Where there is a paper committal the defendant must be legally represented, agree to the procedure and indicate that he or she does not wish to make a submission that the written statements and other documents (all of which must be served on him or her in advance) plus any exhibits (each of which must be identified) do not disclose sufficient evidence for the case to be committed to the Crown Court for trial by jury. Committal may be on the charge initially put to the accused or on any amended or substituted charge disclosed by the evidence.

In due course, the accused will be required to answer to the indictment (below). If he or she is allowed bail but fails to appear at the Crown Court, a bench warrant can (and usually will) be issued by a judge. The warrant may be with or without instructions for the further release of the accused person on bail, but will usually be 'without bail'.

## VOLUNTARY BILL OF INDICTMENT

It is possible for cases to start out in the Crown Court rather than in the magistrates' court—by way of a voluntary bill of indictment, i.e. where a written application, supported by other documentation, is made direct to a High Court judge who may order a trial in the Crown Court. In cases where magistrates have refused to commit or transfer a case to the Crown Court this is the only route that remains open to the prosecutor if he or she wishes to pursue the matter.

## JUDGE AND JURY

The business of the Crown Court is arranged according to the upper level of seriousness of criminal offences with which a given Crown Court centre is scheduled to deal and, correspondingly, the level of judge who normally presides at that particular centre or to deal with a particular court list. The most serious cases are dealt with by a 'first tier' Crown Court and normally before a High Court judge. The bulk of offences—second and third tier matters—are dealt with by circuit judges or recorders.[8]

Where the accused person pleads 'guilty' the matter is dealt with by the judge alone, who will pass sentence, often after receiving pre-sentence reports (PSRs) from the National Probation Service (NPS) (*Chapters 9* and *13*). Where

---

guilty plea the magistrates can then decide whether to sentence the offender themselves or to commit him or her to the Crown Court for sentence (see text).

[8] A part-time judge. Descriptions of judicial personnel are contained in *Chapter 12.*

there is a plea of 'not guilty' a jury will be sworn in and a trial will take place before judge and a jury.[9] The jury is made up of 12 ordinary members of the public empanelled at random from the electoral roll. The same jury may deal with several cases in succession where these are short and heard across a relatively brief span of time, but otherwise there is a fresh jury for each case. Given that a criminal trial may involve complex issues of law, fact or mixed law and fact, trial by jury—dispensing justice through the deliberations of inexperienced lay people—is achieved by separating out functions as follows:

- **The judge** has general charge of the course of the trial and deals with all matters of a legal nature, such as purely technical submissions or legal argument (often in the absence of the jury so that they do not hear of or their discussions do not become tainted by such matters, which are not part of the evidence in the case or do not become so unless the judge allows this: below). The judge is responsible for ruling on the admissibility of evidence, and on the practices and procedures of the Crown Court— and also for deciding certain questions of mixed fact and law such as whether or not the jury should hear about an alleged confession said to have been made by the accused person but which it is now claimed was obtained by duress or oppression, or whether other evidence should be ruled out as prejudicial or unfair. The judge must withdraw a case from the jury if there is insufficient evidence to support a conviction.

  Before the start of a case, the judge is responsible for matters of a preliminary nature and can make orders affecting the progress of the case—known 'directions' (usually at a preliminary or pr-trial hearing which may be in chambers with only the lawyers present).

  At the conclusion of a jury trial, the judge is responsible for summing up to the jury, i.e. reminding them of (or 'taking them' through) the evidence and directing the jury members as to its potential effect, and warning to consider the weight of particular pieces of evidence. At the very end of a trial, after the jury has deliberated in private (below), he or she will ask the foreman of the jury whether the jury has considered its verdict, whether it is unanimous and whether it finds the accused person guilty or not guilty. In the event of a conviction, the judge will pass sentence as already outlined in relation to a plea of 'guilty', above.

- **The jury** decides whether the accused person is 'guilty' or 'not guilty' by considering and weighing the evidence, in effect by looking at all factual matters which are relevant to whether the accused committed the offence for which he or she has been indicted and any admissible expert opinion (such as in relation to forensic or medical evidence).

  Subject to procedural safeguards, the judge can accept a majority verdict (below) and depending on the charge or charges a jury can return an 'alternative verdict': *Chapter 8.* How juries arrive at their verdict is unknown apart from the occasional snapshot of information which

---

[9]   *Justice for All* proposes that trials could take place before a judge alone in certain circumstances: see later in the text and *Chapter 15.*

emerges when a juror speaks out in breach of his or her obligations: jury deliberations are confidential and no first-hand research is allowed.

As mentioned in *Chapter 1*, trial by jury constitutes 'trial by peers' (said to be guaranteed by Magna Carta). Proposals contained in the White Paper *Justice for All* would, if implemented, affect this by allowing trial by judge alone where the accused requests this or in serious and complex fraud trials, some other complex and lengthy trials or where the jury is at risk of intimidation—along with a range of other possible changes set out in *Chapter 15*.

## ARRAIGNMENT

An accused person is 'arraigned' in the Crown Court (as opposed to being 'charged' before magistrates), i.e. the clerk of the Crown Court calls upon the accused by name, reads over the indictment (see next heading) and asks whether he or she pleads 'guilty' or 'not guilty'. According to the answer, the court will proceed to trial (below and *Chapter 8*) or sentence (*Chapter 9*) as appropriate.

## THE INDICTMENT

'Indictment' is the name given to the formal document in which the allegation or allegations against an accused person appearing in the Crown Court is or are set down in writing. Indictments may contain several allegations: 'counts' (or 'counts in the indictment') as they are known, but an individual count can only allege a single offence. Several people can be charged in the same indictment. These basic rules are supplemented by many others such as those affecting the circumstances in which offences or offenders can be tried alongside one another (called 'joinder'). Drawing up indictments is a skilled legal task usually for prosecuting counsel. The final indictment may need to be settled with the defence and in certain situations an application may need to be made to a judge to rule on matters which remain in dispute.

## TRIAL

The accused person is asked 'How do you plead?' (to 'enter a plea') to each count in the indictment in turn. The data indicate that many cases translate into guilty pleas at the point where the accused person is arraigned, but that until this point in time he or she may prefer to maintain his or her innocence (which may be to an extent tactical, stemming from a desire to be classified as a remand prisoner whilst awaiting trial rather than as a convicted prisoner with fewer privileges, or because he or she gambles on a 'cracked trial' the name given to a case which folds for want of a witness or because other evidence does not materialise). Various initiatives have emerged to counter this such as the plea before venue procedure[10] and the sentencing rule that an offender should be given credit for a

---

[10] See the explanation given at footnote 7.

timely guilty plea (*Chapters 9* and *15*). Every attempt is made by the Crown Court to expedite cases, but in some areas of the country it is still possible to spend a long period (a year to 18 months) on remand awaiting trial. Both the Auld report and *Justice for All* (*Chapter 15*) seek to structure this through a scale of discounts which would be made known to all defendants and which would replace the present, somewhat vaguer, arrangements.

Trials are governed by rules of procedure and follow the general pattern outlined in *Chapter 8*.

## VERDICT

The outcome of a criminal case falls into two stages, verdict and (if 'guilty') sentence. The basic rule is that the verdict of the jury must be unanimous. However, it is possible for the judge to accept a majority verdict provided that at least ten of the 12 jurors are of the same mind. This can only occur after the jury has been allowed time for consideration (at least two hours, or longer in a complicated case) to arrive at a unanimous verdict, but the judge is satisfied that this cannot be achieved. Verdict is discussed further in *Chapter 8*.

## SENTENCING POWERS

The powers of the Crown Court range up to life imprisonment, which is mandatory for murder and under the so-called 'two strikes' law[11] introduced by the Crime and Disorder Act 1998, and discretionary for a first offence, e.g. of manslaughter and rape. Many of the more serious offences carry a maximum sentence of 14 years in prison.

Sentences may be made so as to be consecutive to one another (i.e. where one starts to run when another ends) or concurrent (when they are served simultaneously)

The Crown Court has a wide range of powers with regard to ancillary orders—including to order compensation to be paid to victims of crime and the confiscation and forfeiture of property or assets where these represent the proceeds of crime.[12] The principles which affect sentencing decisions and the range of sentences, orders and related powers are outlined in *Chapter 9*.

## APPEAL

Appeals from decisions of the Crown Court in criminal cases—whether against conviction, sentence, or both—are heard by the Court of Appeal (Criminal Division). There is a further appeal to the House of Lords in certain circumstances: *Chapter 10*.

---

[11] i.e. an offender who commits certain serious offences for a second time must normally be given a life sentence.

[12] Now reinforced by the Assets Recovery Agency (ARA) created under the Proceeds of Crime Act 2002 (*Chapters 1* and *18*).

# PEOPLE UNDER 18 AND 'GRAVE CRIMES'

As indicated earlier in the chapter there are currently provisions whereby people below the age of 18 may—instead of being dealt with by the youth court—be committed to the Crown Court for trial in respect of what are known as 'grave crimes'. The practice of dealing with children in an adult forum, which has been criticised and in relation to which the United Kingdom has been found wanting by the European Court of Human Rights, is likely to alter as a result of proposals contained in *Justice for All* under which serious allegations against juveniles would be heard by a judge and magistrates sitting in the youth court.[13] These matters are further dealt with in *Chapter 5*.

Grave crimes apart, generally speaking, people below the age of 18 accused of criminal offences are dealt with in the youth court. However, it is possible for them to be dealt with either in the magistrates' court (*Chapter 2*) or in some cases at the Crown Court as a result of being charged alongside or in connection with an adult. As far as possible, such cases are in practice separated out wherever possible, so that the juvenile is tried or dealt with separately by the youth court. But this is not always possible and sometimes the interests of justice will require that an adult and a juvenile are tried together by the same court and at the same time, although the presumption should be against this course unless truly necessary.

# RIGHTS OF AUDIENCE

In general terms, rights of audience (i.e. the right to address the court on behalf of a client) in the Crown Court are restricted to barristers (sometimes called 'counsel') and those solicitors in private practice who are licensed to practice in that court.

Barristers retained by the Crown are known as 'Treasury counsel'. Senior barristers or Queen's Counsel (QCs) appear in the more serious cases.

The Courts and Legal Services Act 1990 enabled a wider range of people to acquire rights of audience in the Crown Court—either generally or in a given case, whilst European obligations may have a significant future impact on the structure of the legal profession and consequently rights as a whole. A general note about barristers and solicitors is contained in *Chapter 12*.

# ADMINISTRATION OF THE CROWN COURT

The Court Service is an executive agency of the Lord Chancellor's Department (LCD) and is responsible for running most of the courts (and tribunals) in England and Wales, i.e. the Crown Court, county courts, and the appeal courts

---

[13]  Already, the Crown Court makes special arrangements to 'tone down' the experience for juveniles of appearing there, such as adopting less formal courtroom arrangement, removing wigs and sitting on one level.

(*Chapter 10*).[14] The agency provides the necessary services to the judiciary and court users to ensure its impartial and efficient operation and plays an important part in implementing the Lord Chancellor's aim of a modern justice system.

## Crown Court circuits

For administrative purposes the Crown Court is divided into circuits serving different regions of the country and based closely on the historic Assize or Bar circuits which preceded the creation of the Crown Court.

## Administrators and chief clerks

The administrative work of the Crown Court is discharged by staff from the Court Service. Each Crown Court circuit is headed by an administrator and each Crown Court centre by a chief clerk who is responsible, among other things, for the general management, the listing and scheduling of cases, swearing-in of jurors and the care of witnesses[15] (subject in the case of any judicial aspects to the direction of the judge). In court, a member of his or her staff acts as a court clerk, calling on cases, swearing in jurors and witnesses, reading the indictment to the accused and generally dealing with day-to-day matters affecting the course of a case.

Unlike the situation in the magistrates' court (*Chapter 2*), the court clerk does not have to be a lawyer (though some are), nor does he or she perform advisory, legal or judicial functions in relation to the trial (there being no need with a professional judge). Some tasks of a judicial or quasi-judicial nature are however performed by clerks in the Crown Court, such as taxing bills of costs (i.e. the assessment of claims by legal representatives where costs have been ordered by the judge to be paid from public funds or between the parties).

## Summoning Jurors

Formerly, jurors were summoned to attend at the Crown Court by the chief clerk of the court centre concerned. There is now a Central Jury Summoning Bureau (CJSB) that is designed to improve the management of the jury process. Similarly, web-based services enable jurors to respond online and also provide information about the court process, including the role of jurors (as to which see *Chapter 12*). Coupled with this, the Local Authorities Secure Electronic Register project (LASER) ensures the CJSB has access to up-to-date records for this purpose.

## The Crown Court user group

As noted in *Chapter 1*, user groups or similar liaison devices are widely used as a way of interacting with other criminal justice agencies. Such groups are made up of regular participants in the criminal justice process locally. A Crown Court user group is often chaired by a circuit judge and will, e.g. include representatives of the Crown Court administration, the Bar and agencies such as the police, CPS, Law Society (solicitors), magistrates' courts, NPS and HMPS. Such groups function alongside and in addition to area committees of the Criminal Justice Consultative Council.

---

[14] The exception is the magistrates' courts but even then there are links at director level. *Justice for All* is likely to lead to the integrated approach already mentioned in *Chapter 2*.

[15] A nationwide Court Witness Service offers support to witnesses: *Chapter 1*.

# CHAPTER 4

# High Court, Court of Appeal and House of Lords

## With a Note on the European Court of Human Rights

Most criminal cases end with conviction and sentence, or acquittal, in either the magistrates' court or Crown Court as described in the last two chapters. However, there are various routes by which a case may go to appeal beyond these courts—to the High Court, Court of Appeal and House of Lords.[1] These higher courts have no 'first instance' jurisdiction except the House of Lords in the case of a peer of the realm (i.e. a member of that house) who may opt to be tried by the House (i.e. by his or her peers). In modern times, members of the House accused of criminal offences have always opted to be tried by the ordinary courts.

**The European Court of Human Rights: A Note**
Implementation of the Human Rights Act 1998 (*Chapter 1*) has had a number of indirect effects on appellate processes in the United Kingdom. If an existing national ruling is incompatible with the Convention national courts must seek to remedy this when dealing with a relevant case. In effect English judges and magistrates should accommodate European jurisprudence. In particular, the Convention is regarded as a 'living instrument' allowing the law to adapt—without fresh legislation—over time. This, taken together with the need for courts in England and Wales to reflect Convention rights, may be at odds with the doctrine of precedent (see later in this chapter). In a sense, European law takes precedence in that both national statute law and national case law should be interpreted compatibly with European law, not simply in the way it would have been by reference to the doctrine of precedent alone. Rulings of national courts can be challenged in the European Court of Human Rights in Strasbourg either by an individual (who should normally look to national remedies first) or by way of a reference to that court by a national court (usually in practice a reference by a higher court to which an individual has appealed). Further, any court (but again in practice one of the higher courts) can make a declaration of incompatibility in relation to UK primary legislation. This, in effect, obliges Parliament to consider 'fast track' amending legislation.

## HIGH COURT

The High Court deals principally with the more important civil disputes. It has three divisions: the Queen's Bench Division (QBD), Chancery Division and

---

[1]  For the appeal process see *Chapter 10* and for judicial personnel *Chapter 12*.

Family Division. It is centred in London at the Royal Courts of Justice in The Strand (often referred to simply as 'The Strand'), but may also sit at selected locations throughout England and Wales. In terms of its criminal jurisdiction, the QBD is the most significant division. It is presided over by the Lord Chief Justice and, although it has a broad remit to deal with civil actions for damages arising, e.g. from breach of contract and libel, commercial disputes and Admiralty cases, a 'Divisional Court' of the QBD deals with appeals from magistrates' courts and Crown Courts by way of case stated.

Additionally, the High Court has a general supervisory function in relation to a wide range of courts, tribunals and bodies or individuals performing public functions—including the criminal courts and the actions of government ministers. This function, known as 'judicial review', is designed chiefly to ensure that decisions made by these bodies or individuals do not exceed the powers given by Parliament and that they act reasonably and in full and proper accordance with the law (including now human rights law: above and *Chapter 1*). This jurisdiction is exercised principally by means of three prerogative orders, *prohibition, certiorari and mandamus*.

The above appeal processes are described in *Chapter 12*. The High Court is administered by the Court Service in a similar way to that outlined in *Chapter 3* in relation to the Crown Court.

## COURT OF APPEAL

As its name might imply, the Court of Appeal deals exclusively with cases on appeal. It has no first instance jurisdiction. Also commonly referred to as 'the appeal court', it comprises two divisions, criminal and civil. It is again housed in the Royal Courts of Justice in The Strand but can sit elsewhere although this is a somewhat rare occurrence. A judge of the Court of Appeal is called 'Lord Justice'. The jurisdiction of the court is divided as follows:

- *Criminal Division*
  The Court of Appeal (Criminal Division) hears appeals from people convicted and sentenced in the Crown Court. Its senior judge is the Lord Chief Justice who is responsible for the way the court is run and likely to set the tone of the court and the judiciary's stance towards the criminal law and criminal policy during his or her period of office. He or she may issue *Practice Directions* to be followed by other criminal courts.[2] Leave is required before there can be an appeal.

- *Civil Division*
  In contrast, the Court of Appeal (Civil Division) is headed by the Master of the Rolls and hears appeals from the High Court and county courts.

---

[2] The intriguing history of the office of Lord Chief Justice is described in *Lions Under the Throne* (1983), Mockler A, London: Muller.

Both divisions of the Court of Appeal may refer cases involving points of law to the House of Lords (below).

Quite apart from the fact that it is in the Court of Appeal where the criminal law itself falls to be tested (e.g. the extent and definition of the law of murder, the applicability and breadth of a particular defence to a criminal charge), a main significance of the Court of Appeal (Criminal Division) for the criminal justice process is that the court gives rulings following appeals against sentence (see, generally, *Chapter 9*). Often described as judicial guidance on sentencing, such rulings inform, and in many instances liberate or constrain, the sentencing practices of the Crown Court and magistrates' courts. Key rulings of this type are referred to as 'guideline judgements' (or 'sentencing guidelines'[3]). These and other rulings of the court are published in the law reports (*Chapter 1*) and become a central and particularly influential component of the law.

The system whereby other informal sentencing guidelines—devised beyond the courts proper and which develop by a mix of routes, including since 1999 a Sentencing Advisory Council—would be refined if proposals in *Justice for All* are implemented (*Chapters 9 and 15*).

## HOUSE OF LORDS

The House of Lords is the final national appeal court for both criminal and civil cases from the courts of England and Wales. Appeals to the House are dealt with by an Appellate Committee ('Judicial Committee' in other contexts) which is presided over by the Lord Chancellor who sometimes sits as a judge in that court. Leave is required before there can be such an appeal, either leave from the court below or the Appellate Committee itself. Scottish criminal cases have no such right of appeal.

The Appellate Committee is comprised of Law Lords (otherwise called Lords of Appeal in Ordinary). On their appointment Law Lords become life peers (so that when they retire as Lords of Appeal they remain members of the House of Lords and can continue to take part in its debates). In most cases they are existing members of the judiciary when first elevated to the House of Lords. The rule of practice is that they are either former holders of high judicial office or former practising barristers of at least 15 years' standing. There are eleven Law Lords. As members of the House they are appointed to the Appellate Committee (and 'Judicial Committee') to carry out the judicial functions of the House.

The Appellate Committee sits apart from the main business of the House of Lords in what many people find to be a somewhat undersized, if intimate, committee room (there have been proposals to remove this to The Strand, above, or a purpose built venue). There is a convention that Law Lords do not engage in political debate except where this is of direct judicial concern. They were notably active in the debates which led to the Police and Magistrates' Courts Act 1994 during which the government was obliged because of that involvement to abandon certain proposals in the original Bill touching on issues of judicial

---

[3]  Contrast other 'informal' guidelines such as those of the Sentencing Advisory Council mentioned in the text and the *Magistrates' Courts Sentencing Guidelines: Chapter 9*.

independence. Law Lords also tend to become actively involved in the main chamber of the House when Criminal Justice Bills or those concerned with constitutional matters are being debated.

Rulings of the House of Lords—judgements of the Law Lords—are known as 'speeches' and are of great import in relation both to the development of the law and day-to-day proceedings of the lower courts. They are a major source of the common law (i.e. judge made law as opposed to statute law) and have a comparable impact to Parliamentary legislation. But the underlying principle is that judges interpret or apply existing law rather than make new laws, so that the committee will only go so far along this route. Thus, e.g. when in 1995 the House of Lords had to deal with the question whether the longstanding *doli incapax*[4] rule should be abolished, it declined to alter the rule whilst at the same time acknowledging the need for a review of the law. Such a fundamental alteration, it stated, was something more appropriately dealt with by Parliament itself. The rule was then abolished by Act of Parliament.[5]

### Privy Council

A judicial committee of the Privy Council (PC) (the Appellate Committee in another guise, but possibly supplemented by foreign judges) sits as a final court of appeal from some Dominion territories, or former such territories that have opted to continue with this last avenue of appeal as an adjunct to their own national arrangements. Rulings of the PC are 'persuasive' under the English doctrine of precedent (next heading) rather than binding.

# THE DOCTRINE OF PRECEDENT: A NOTE

Rulings of the higher courts are published in the law reports (*Chapter 1*) in the form of verbatim accounts of the judgements or speeches (in the case of the House of Lords) of the judges, including any dissenting opinion. This comprises a vast databank from which lawyers seek to understand the precise nature of the law on a given topic.

In summary, the lower courts (Crown Court and magistrates' courts) are bound by, i.e. must follow, the ruling of a higher court, whilst within the upper courts hierarchy of House of Lords, Court of Appeal and High Court, a lower court is bound by the ruling of a higher court. The entire process is somewhat more subtle than this, in that certain rulings may be persuasive only and part of the daily routine of lawyers involves identifying and distinguishing cases which are not precisely in point, or to which a legitimate exception can be argued in the light of the exact circumstances of the present case, subsequent events, legislation and general developments in the law. Further, a great deal may

---

[4] Whereby, in the case of a defendant below the age of 14, the prosecutor had to establish—over and above the normal ingredients of an offence—that the defendant knew that what he or she was doing was 'seriously wrong'.

[5] Historically speaking, there have been instances where the committee did, in effect, alter the criminal law (e.g. somewhat notoriously by 'creating' the crime of conspiracy to corrupt public morals, and by holding that marital rape was a criminal offence when not regarded thus previously). Scope for judicial creativity will have become narrower due to Article 6 of the European Convention: 'no punishment without law' (*Chapter 1*).

depend on the status, judicial and professional standing, reputation and perceived thoughts of the court (or individual judge) whose opinion is under scrutiny. Lawyers 'cite' rulings or extracts from ruling in court in support or opposition to a given proposition.

To this already complex—if for lawyers fascinating—process must now be added the fact that the outcome of applying the doctrine of precedent is affected by the European Convention On Human Rights and considerations such as those noted earlier in the chapter.

# CHAPTER 5

# The Youth Court

Young people aged ten to 17 charged with criminal offences must normally appear and be sentenced in the youth court rather than the adult magistrates' court or Crown Court.[1] They are subject to the emergent youth justice arrangements described in this chapter. The investigation, processing and outcome of cases involving people below 18 years of age follows a similar pattern to that in relation to adults, subject to additional safeguards, procedures and sentencing powers. Thus, e.g. there are special provisions in the PACE Codes of Practice for investigating police officers (*Chapter 6*), including a duty to ensure that someone concerned with the welfare of the juvenile is informed and to secure the involvement of an 'appropriate adult'.

At the time of writing various changes are still being implemented whereby most first-time juvenile offenders will not be prosecuted or, when prosecuted, not be sentenced in the conventional sense. They will be dealt with in one of two ways: by the police under a statutory scheme of reprimands and warnings (replacing the former system of cautions which still remains for adults); or, where they do appear in court, by way of a referral order—which the youth court is obliged to make—under which their offending will be confronted via an intervention plan devised by a youth offending panel. There is also a strong emphasis on restorative justice (see *Chapter 18*). Underlying English child law are many further considerations stemming from international treaties and obligations such as the International Convention On the Rights of the Child as well as the European Convention On Human Rights (*Chapter 1*). Although the latter does not contain any provisions dedicated expressly to juveniles it is important to remember that it applies equally to adults and children.

## WELFARE AND PREVENTING OFFENDING

The conventional wisdom involves recognising that many young people pass through a difficult stage in their lives and are apt to challenge or test out authority. Sometimes this brings them into conflict with the criminal law. Traditionally, youth justice has represented one of the more enlightened aspects of criminal justice. Long before the present emerging arrangements there was a history of local projects and initiatives designed to cater for young people in trouble with the criminal law as they matured into adults and to pe-empt unsuitable punishments or those which might hinder their natural development

---

[1] Juveniles can appear in the adult magistrates' court, e.g. for remand when no youth court is sitting, or if charged jointly with an adult. If convicted by the adult court it has sentencing powers limited to a discharge, fine or a parental bind over. It can also make a referral order (see text). Otherwise, offenders under 18 years of age convicted in the magistrates' court must be remitted to the youth court for sentence. Someone under 18 may, where appropriate, be sent to and appear in the Crown Court for trial if charged with an adult or in respect of certain 'grave crimes' (see later in the chapter).

or damage them in later life. An early example was the work of Mary Carpenter in the nineteenth century; the process was continued in the Children Act 1908 and the formation of the Home Office Children's Department in 1914; and this approach found statutory recognition in the welfare principle in section 44 Children and Young Persons Act 1933 which continues to operates in all courts (whether, e.g. the person concerned appears as a defendant or as a witness):

> Every court in dealing with a child or young person who is brought before it either as an offender or otherwise shall have regard to the welfare of the child or young person.

The welfare principle must now be reconciled with the principal statutory purpose of youth justice laid down by the Crime and Disorder Act 1998, which is to prevent offending. Both must then be applied in conjunction with the just deserts sentencing philosophy of the Criminal Justice Act 1991 as described in relation to adults in *Chapter 9*.

# OVERALL SCHEME FOR YOUTH JUSTICE

The modern-day arrangements for youth justice stem largely from the Crime and Disorder Act 1998. Like many modern criminal justice statutes this Act has been phased in piecemeal and with provisions being piloted in various parts of England and Wales. A central purpose of the Act is to tackle crime and disorder and help towards creating safer communities.[2] The Act established a Youth Justice Board for England and Wales to oversee and co-ordinate arrangements for youth justice (apart from judicial aspects). Additionally, section 39 places a duty on local authorities with social services and education responsibilities to establish one or more youth offending teams (YOTs: see later in the text) for their area. The Act reflects several underlying themes, i.e. that:

- the principal purpose of the youth justice system is to prevent offending (above)
- action must always be taken without delay
- the police and local authority—together with the whole community—must establish a local partnership to prevent and reduce crime
- local authorities and other public bodies must consider the crime and disorder implications of all their decisions. Chief officers of police, probation boards and health authorities are required to co-operate; and
- there is a strong emphasis is on parental responsibility.

### Youth offending teams (YOTs)

YOTs concentrate on specialist professional work with young offenders including writing pre-sentence reports (PSRs) (below). YOTs (and YOT members through their own agencies) also co-ordinate youth justice services locally including community sentences, rehabilitation schemes, crime prevention initiatives and bail schemes. They also adminster the youth offending panel in relation to the

---

[2] For a fuller outline see *Child Law* (2001), Powell R, Winchester: Waterside Press.

referral order already mentioned. Reprimands and warnings (see next heading) are the exclusive province of the police. Each youth offending team (YOT) should include a:

- social worker
- probation officer
- police officer
- someone nominated by the health authority in the local authority area; and
- someone nominated by the local authority's chief education officer.

The team may also include individuals from other agencies and organizations if considered appropriate. Apart from its central linking role, a YOT must carry out any functions assigned it pursuant to an annual Youth Justice Plan which each local authority with social services and education responsibilities must formulate and implement.

### Reprimands and warnings

Under the Crime and Disorder Act 1998 the former non-statutory system of police cautions and informal warnings (juvenile cautioning schemes comparable to those which apply to adults: *Chapter 6*) was replaced by a statutory scheme of police reprimands and warnings. In broad terms:

- a *reprimand* does not involve any other form of statutory intervention; but
- a *warning* is accompanied by intervention to reduce the likelihood of re-offending. There can normally be only one warning and this generally acts as a bar to a conditional discharge in any later court proceedings for a fresh offence within two years. Once the police decide to issue a warning, the YOT has a core role in devising the intervention plan.

Both reprimands and warnings are administered by the police usually with the parents present (wherever possible).

### The referral order

At the time of writing, YOTs across England and Wales were well-advanced in appointing and training youth offending panels in readiness for the duties and responsibilities described under the next heading. A referral order is the immediate recourse for courts in relation to most 'first-time' juvenile offenders, i.e. juveniles convicted of an offence for the first time. Only where the case is suitable for a discharge or, at the opposite extreme, a custodial sentence will the court sentence in that way at the outset. In all other cases a referral order must be made.

### Youth offending panel

This panel (sometimes called the referral order panel)[3] operates under the auspices of the local YOT and is comprised of YOT members and other people specially appointed to the panel, either generally or in an individual case. Its

---

[3] The terms 'referral panel' and 'youth offending panel' seem to be interchangeable.

responsibilities include devising an intervention plan for the juvenile, and counselling him or her with the aim of preventing future offending. This may, in appropriate cases, involve input by the victim and other measures, such as the making of reparation, as part of a restorative approach (see, generally, *Chapter 18*). The idea is in the grand tradition of diversion from the main criminal process which has always been a strong feature of youth justice, albeit in this instance linked into that process and to other powers of sentence where the offender fails to respond to the opportunity offered by the intervention plan or continues to commit criminal offences.

# THE YOUTH COURT

The youth court was established in 1992 to replace the former juvenile court (established in 1908).[4] It deals almost exclusively with *criminal* cases and operates under the administrative umbrella of the magistrates' court and local magistrates' courts committee (MCC) (*Chapter 2*). It is also subject to the same general laws, but these are overlaid with special codes of jurisdiction, practice and procedure, and there are special sentencing powers.

Each sitting of a youth court must include both a man and a woman magistrate unless this is impracticable—and there is a minimum requirement of three magistrates (as opposed to two in the adult court). Youth courts are not open to the public.[5] Members of the press *are* admitted, but it is an offence to publish the identity of a juvenile unless the court specifically authorises this in an individual case.

### The youth court panel[6]
Youth court magistrates belong to a statutory youth court panel and receive special training. Except in London (where youth court magistrates are appointed direct to the panel) magistrates are appointed from the general body of existing JPs locally and also continue to serve in the adult court. The panel appoints its own chairman and deputy chairmen and also meets for training purposes and to keep up-to-date with developments, local YOT arrangements and youth justice practice. The Judicial Studies Board and Youth Justice Board have issued a *Youth Court Bench Book* (2001) with a view to assisting in this process.

### Children and young persons
The youth court deals with:

- children: aged ten to 13 years inclusive; and
- young persons:[7] aged 14 to 17 years inclusive.

---

[4]  When the former care jurisdiction of the juvenile court moved to the family proceedings court.

[5]  An aspect which has become the subject of human rights arguments based on the more general principle of open court (*Chapter 1*). A more sympathetic approach concerning admission to proceedings has emerged towards victims and interested community representatives, perhaps due to restorative thinking and other international obligations.

[6]  The 'youth court panel' should not be confused with the 'youth offending panel' (i.e. the referral order panel).

[7]  'Young person' may sometimes sound odd, but is used by statute—and thus in other parts of this work for precision. Young persons may be 'children' in other statutes: see *Child Law*, footnote 2.

The age of criminal responsibility in England and Wales remains at ten years despite competing arguments about whether it should be raised or lowered.[8] Generally speaking the youth court deals with all criminal offences, whatever their level of seriousness. However, there is power to commit a young person (i.e. someone aged 14 or over) to the Crown Court for trial in respect of certain grave crimes (next section). A power to commit to the Crown Court for sentence in other situations was removed by the Crime and Disorder Act 1998.

### 'Grave crimes'

A youth court can—*at the outset of a case*—and in respect of certain serious (what are termed 'grave') crimes, such as rape, wounding, aggravated burglary or sexual assault, decline altogether to deal with the matter and commit the accused to the Crown Court for trial. The nature of the individual offence, the age of the offender and other relevant considerations are weighed by the youth court to determine whether it should exercise this power pursuant to section 53 Children and Young Persons Act 1933. Certain cases *must* be sent to the Crown Court under this provision, i.e. where homicide (murder, manslaughter, causing death by dangerous driving, etc.) is involved.

In the Bulger case,[9] the grave crimes provisions attracted criticism from the European Court of Human Rights in that the formal setting of the Crown Court was held not to be appropriate when dealing with young children, however serious the allegation (murder in that instance). The European Court concluded that there was a lack of effective participation engendered by the procedures and practices adopted in the Crown Court whereas the position should be such as to promote the child's ability to understand and take account of his or her intellectual and emotional capacities. Overall the procedure was unfair pursuant to Article 6 of the European Convention (*Chapter 1*). Since that time, the Crown Court has adopted procedures designed to reduce formality when dealing with juveniles. The White Paper *Justice For All* (*Chapter 15*) proposes that such serious allegations be heard by a judge and magistrates sitting in the youth court.

### Remand

As with adults, children and young persons can be arrested and detained by the police (*Chapter 6*) and remanded by the courts when a case is adjourned (*Chapter 8*), but must be granted bail subject, broadly speaking, to the same criteria as adults (though these may, in practice, be interpreted more sympathetically in view of a juvenile's age or lack of maturity etc.). However, there is one anomaly in that defendants aged 17 and over (NB *not* 18 and over: the standard age for the adult court) who are remanded into custody go to a prison or remand centre[10] whereas a refusal of bail to someone below the age of 17 normally operates as a remand to local authority accommodation.

---

[8] It is one if the lowest ages of criminal responsibility in Europe. Below ten years of age a juvenile must be dealt with via parental or local authority care or supervision under the welfare provisions of the Children Act 1989 and associated measures, or he or she can be made the subject of a child safety order in the family proceedings court.

[9] *T. v. United Kingdom* and *V. v. United Kingdom* (1999) 30 EHRR 121.

[10] i.e. to all intents and purposes a prison, but for unconvicted or unsentenced male prisoners aged 17 to 21. Women of any age can be held in a remand centre.

Where a juvenile *is* remanded to local authority accommodation, that authority can seek permission from the court to use secure accommodation or, if the juvenile is 15 or 16 and *male*, the court itself can remand him in HM Prison Service custody if strict criteria are satisfied. Further details of the juvenile remand provisions are beyond the scope of this introductory work.

### Pre-sentence reports (PSRs)

PSRs are prepared by YOT members, who are also responsible for other written assessments such as those made to courts and youth offending panels in relation to referral orders. Reports on juveniles are something of a specialism, not least because there is often a wider family dynamic, which may be fragile and insecure and in many instances reveal a broken home or disturbed background. Much work with juveniles involves trying to repair such damage, building or restoring self-esteem, and encouraging life choices that do not involve resort to crime. Where the offender is still at school, relevant information may often be available from teachers and will usually be incorporated into the PSR.

The power to deem a PSR to be unnecessary (*Chapter 5*) applies to offenders below the age of 18 in a modified form. A PSR can *only* be dispensed with before passing a custodial sentence or one of the more intrusive community sentences on a juvenile if there is an earlier report which the court can consider. However, good practice in relation to people in this age group—whose lives and circumstances can change rapidly—means that a fresh report is usually obtained.

### Youth court sentencing powers

Youth court sentencing demands a different mind-set to that for the adult court due to the mix of welfare, crime prevention and seriousness factors noted earlier. It also requires specialist knowledge and preferably experience. The general youth court sentencing criteria apart the following points should be noted:

*Fines on juvenile offenders*
Fines are subject to maximum cash limits of £250 (children) and £1,000 (young persons). Parents or guardians ordered to pay their children's fines—see *Parental responsibility* below—are assessed on the basis of their own means, not those of the child (but the juvenile maxima still apply).

*Compensation*
This has the same ceiling as in the adult magistrates' court, i.e. £5,000 per offence and with TICs (*Chapter 6*) capable of being taken into account when arriving at the appropriate figure. Again parents can or must be ordered to pay any compensation ordered according to the child's age: see *Parental responsibility* below.

*Reparation order*
This is an order requiring the offender to make reparation, as specified in the order, to the victim of his or her crime or to the community at large. The order sets out the nature of the work envisaged which may be for no more than 24 hours duration to be completed within three months of the order. A responsible officer—usually from the YOT—oversees the order. Victim-based reparation may only be required with the express consent of the victim and may include a letter

of apology and, where appropriate, meeting face-to-face. The government's faith in restorative approaches (*Chapter 18*) is reflected in the requirement for the court to indicate why it has not made a reparation order where it had power to do so.

### Community penalties

The main community penalties such as the community rehabilitation order (CRO) and community punishment order (CPO) outlined in *Chapter 9* in relation to adults are also available in the youth court—but for 16 and 17 year olds only (see *Table 1* on page 53 for the full list and age ranges). Flexibility exists because all offenders under 18 years of age may be placed under local authority supervision rather than that of the YOT although as YOTs develop this may come to be a comparative rarity. Conditions may be attached to such supervision orders akin to those applicable to community rehabilitation orders. One particular possibility is supervision with a number of conditions attached making up a programme of activities etc. for the juvenile offender.[11] One sentencing device which uses conditions attached to supervision or community rehabilitation orders to maximum effect is what is known as intensive supervision and surveillance.[12]

Notionally, the purpose in having a wide range of options is to allow courts, in consultation with YOTs, to select the most suitable sentence according to the maturity and circumstances of the offender and the facilities and arrangements available locally. However, there are many people who would argue that a proliferation of sanctions can lead to overload in sentencing terms and to what is known as 'up-tariffing'—sentencing at a higher level than is truly appropriate in the hope that better and more resources will be applied to improve the chances that a juvenile will be diverted from crime. This, of course, is fine until the juvenile offends again, or fails to comply with the conditions imposed, and is then sentenced at a yet higher or more intensive level—leading to escalation.

The Criminal Justice Act 1998 added action plan orders to the community sentencing armoury of the youth court, and also drug treatment and testing orders (DTTOs). The former enables the YOT to construct a programme of action to tackle offending behaviour; whilst the latter leads to regular testing for unlawful substances. In all cases the offence must be serious enough for a community sentence: *Chapter 6*.

### Custody

The detention and training order (D&TO) provides a single custodial sentence for ten to 17 year olds. It is currently available for people from 12 years of age upwards. The D&TO can be made in respect of 15 to 17 year olds for any imprisonable offence which is so serious that only a custodial sentence can be justified (see, generally, *Chapter 9*). Twelve to 14 year olds can also receive a D&TO if, in the opinion of the court, they are persistent offenders and have committed an offence that also satisfies the same basic threshold criteria for a custodial sentence. Both the youth court and the Crown Court can impose a D&TO, the length of the sentence being determined by the court in precise bands fixed by the 1998 Act. Thus the D&TO can be for four, six, eight, ten, 12,

---

[11] Traditionally called intermediate treatment (IT), though this term seems to have fallen out of use.

[12] Similar approaches are also used in relation to bail and post-custody supervision.

18 or 24 months only. The sentence must not exceed the maximum term fixed by statute for the offence in question in the case of an adult.

Under the D&TO half the sentence is served in custody and half in the community but the precise variety of secure accommodation to which an offender is sent and detained in is a decision for the Youth Justice Board, not the court. Accordingly, a child may be placed and kept in a young offender institution (YOI) or other form of secure accommodation such as a local authority secure unit. All these facilities are known collectively as the 'secure estate' for which the Youth Justice Board is the commissioning authority. Once the juvenile has served half the term of the order he or she will be released subject to supervision in the community. If release requirements are not complied with, the youth court may, on application, fine the offender or return him or her to custody for up to three months or the remainder of the D&TO.

Youth court sentencing powers are set out *Table 1* on page 53.

# PARENTAL RESPONSIBILITY

Youth justice law and practice stresses the key importance of parental responsibility, particularly in relation to younger or less mature offenders.

Courts *may* require parents or guardians of 16-year-olds and 17-year-olds to attend court and to pay financial penalties imposed on their children. Similarly, they *may* bind over parents or guardians of offenders aged 16 and 17 to take proper care of and to exercise proper control over the offender. They can also bind over the parent or guardian to ensure that the young person complies with the requirements of a community sentence. However, the court is not, with this age group, under a duty to exercise these powers as it is in relation to offenders below 16. With such younger offenders it *must* exercise its powers to require parents or guardians to attend court or to pay any financial penalties unless the parents or guardians cannot be found or it would be unreasonable to do so—and, similarly, it *must* bind over the parent or guardian if it is satisfied that this would be desirable in the interests of preventing further offending.

### Parenting orders
Under the Crime and Disorder Act 1998, magistrates' courts can make a parenting order under which parents or guardians receive instruction and guidance in parenting skills under the auspices of the local YOT.

# THE FUTURE OF YOUTH JUSTICE

As already indicated, the present arrangements are of quite modern origin and are still to be fully implemented. However, general changes proposed in *Justice for All* would, if fully implemented, alter the underlying sentencing framework and criteria. There are also proposals that what are currently 'grave crimes' should be tried by a judge and magistrates in the youth court, subject also to possible reclassification of the offences to which this procedure would apply. The central proposals are set out in *Chapter 15*.

## Table 1: Sentencing Powers of the Youth Court[13]

| SENTENCE | AGE LIMITS | MINIMUM | MAXIMUM |
|---|---|---|---|
| Absolute discharge | None | n/a | n/a |
| Conditional discharge | None | None | 3 years |
| Fine | 10-13 | None | £250 |
|  | 14-17 | None | £1,000 |
| Compensation | None | None | Up to £5,000 per offence |
| Reparation order | 10-17 | Aggregate 24 hours | |
| Attendance centre order | 10-15 | 12 hours (or less) | 24 hours |
|  | 16-17 | 12 hours | 36 hours |
| Action plan order | 10-17 | 3 months available | |
| Drug treatment and testing order (DTTO) | 16-17 | 6 months | 3 years |
| Supervision order | 10-17 | None | 3 years |
| Community rehabilitation order (CRO) | 16-17 | 6 months | 3 years |
| Community punishment order (CPO) | 16-17 | 40 hours | 240 hours |
| Community punishment and rehabilitation order (CP&RO) | 16-17 | CS 40 hours | 100 hours |
|  |  | CP aspect 3 years CRO aspect 12 months | |
| Curfew order | 10-17 | None | 6 months |
|  |  | (or if under 16 three months) | |
| Parental bind over |  | Up to £1,000 | |
| Parenting order | None | 12 months (3 months counselling) | |
| Detention and training order (D&TO) | 10-17 | 4 months | 24 months |
|  |  | (certain set periods only: see text) | |

---

[13] Sentences are often subject to qualifications, criteria, limitations, restrictions, special procedures and further explanations.

# CHAPTER 6

# Investigation, Arrest and Charge

The criminal justice process begins when a crime comes to the notice of the authorities, e.g. when it is experienced or discovered by the victim and reported to the police. But formal action can only be taken when the process of investigation and detection leads to the identification of a suspect and ultimately to the suspect being charged with a criminal offence.

The White Paper *Justice for All* sets out various ways in which the Government intends to facilitate and improve this aspect of the criminal process, i.e. by 'giving the police and prosecution the tools to bring more criminals to justice' and with a central aim of 'getting things right at the start'. This implies continuing improvements in technology, information databases and other methods of identifying suspects as well as better case preparation. Some of the advances in technology now available to the police and modern police operating methods are noted in *Chapter 11* together with a description of the nature and organization of the modern-day policing function, including developments contained in the Police Reform Act 2002.

Police duties of crime prevention and crime reduction involve a range of working partnerships with local authorities and others (*Chapters 11* and *17*) whilst the prosecution of offenders—when crime does occur—is, at the outset, a matter exclusively for the police. This task is increasingly aided by improved links with the Crown Prosecution Service (CPS) (*Chapter 7*) that anticipate the need for sound and reliable evidence in court and possible defence challenges to the charge itself and to the procedures used at the investigation and arrest stages. Moves towards compatible technology, virtual case files, harmonised systems and improved communications are designed to make the charging or summoning of offenders the first step in a co-ordinated system of record-keeping across the criminal process. A Case Preparation and Progression Project has been established that brings together all the participants in the pre-trial process. The aim is 'to provide a smoother, more efficient passage of cases through the courts, which reflects and meets the needs and rights of all participants'.

## DETECTION

Crimes may be detected in a variety of ways including:

- information or a lead from the victim or a member of the public
- the offender being caught in the act or in 'hot pursuit'
- an admission by a suspect during questioning (known as 'a confession' and to which special rules of evidence and procedure apply)
- an informal admission to some other private individual rather than to the police or other person in authority

- following detailed analysis of forensic, circumstantial, video, computer or other evidence including by the Forensic Science Service and other experts (*Chapter 11*).

Some crimes are cleared up when an offender who is charged with or convicted of one offence openly admits to other offences. Where there are several similar offences, the accused may be charged with some of them whilst, at his or her request, others are taken into consideration (known as TICs: *Chapter 9*) when sentence is passed. Traditionally, an offence has been described as 'cleared up' where:

- someone ('the accused' or 'the defendant') has been charged or a summons has been issued—although the defendant will not necessarily have been convicted
- someone has been cautioned (or in the case of a juvenile warned or reprimanded)
- the offence is admitted and could be taken into consideration (above) when the offender is sentenced; or
- in some cases where no further action is taken even though there is sufficient information to implicate a suspect. A case might not be proceeded with, e.g. because the offence is admitted in a prison interview by somebody who is already serving a substantial custodial sentence for another offence, or because the offender is under the age of criminal responsibility, suffering from mental disorder, or the victim or other key witnesses would be unable to give evidence.

The Home Office describes the difference between crimes recorded by the police and crimes cleared up as 'the justice gap'.[1] *Justice for All* states that:

> . . . the gap between recorded crime and the number of offenders brought to justice needs to be reduced. Our priority must be bringing more criminals to justice . . . Less than half the public believe that the CJS is effective in bringing people who commit crimes to justice. While crime overall has fallen since 1997, the fear of crime is still too high: according to the *British Crime Survey*, over 22 per cent of people have a high level of concern about violent crime and many also worry about less serious types of crime . . . Unfortunately, too many people do escape justice. This is the 'justice gap', namely the number of offences recorded by the police and the number of offences where an offender is brought to justice. During 2001-2002 recorded crimes totalled 5.5 million. The police only successfully detected 23 per cent of these offences, that is 1.29 million.

The White Paper also expresses concern about the under-reporting of racist crime and domestic violence. It catalogues the total number of all arrest outcomes as follows: charge or summons (0.78 million), caution (0.21 million),

---

[1] In the glossary to *Justice for All*, the term 'justice gap' is used to describe the difference between crimes *committed* and crimes cleared up *by conviction*, which in fact connotes something quite different and which has traditionally been known as the attrition rate (which the glossary appears to equate with the justice gap also). It has been claimed that as few as two or three per cent of crimes are cleared up if all offences, including those which go unreported, are counted.

TIC 0.11 million; no further action (0.2 million).[2] Some offences have better clear-up rates due to a high likelihood of the victim being able to identify the offender or the offence may directly implicate him or her. The victim of an offence must be informed when that offence is cleared up and in what manner.

# THE COURSE OF AN INVESTIGATION

As indicated above, improving detection and ultimately conviction rates with the underlying aim of long-term crime prevention and crime reduction is an essential tenet of present-day criminal policy and this begins with sound investigation techniques. There is an increased reliance on monitoring groups of offenders, e.g. via Multi-agency Protection Panels (MAPPs). MAPPs seek to identify and manage dangerous and high profile offenders in local communities in a concerted effort to stop them committing further crimes. In addition there is a Persistent Offender Task Force comprising senior representatives from the agencies and which is linked to a Persistent Offender Project aimed at 'catching, bringing to justice and rehabilitating offenders who are responsible for a disproportionate amount of crime'. This project is running for three years as a first step towards the Labour Government's manifesto commitment in 2001 to 'double the chance of persistent offenders being caught and punished by 2011'. Along similar lines, the Street Crime Initiative aims to identify and implement ways of effectively tackling street crime via targeted police operations and cross-agency activity. Other largely police-led partnership initiatives are mentioned in *Chapter 17* which looks at how the strategy is to have agencies working together at various points in the criminal process.

An investigation may involve interviewing many prospective witnesses and assembling other evidence such as exhibits, documents, forensic evidence and expert reports. Relevant information must only be obtained within the law and special legal provisions come into play as soon as there is a suspect—breach of which may result in evidence later being ruled inadmissible by a court. The provisions of the Police and Criminal Evidence Act 1984 (known as 'PACE') (below) are now reinforced by the European Convention On Human Rights and in particular the fair trial provisions of Article 6 (*Chapter 1*).

### Arrest, search and seizure

The police enjoy wide powers of arrest[3] and search in respect of people suspected of criminal offences either under the general law or in relation to particular kinds of offence. The Police National Computer (PNC) records information on people arrested and prosecuted for criminal offences. The police can take possession of property where they believe it to have been the subject of a criminal offence such as stolen goods or prohibited drugs, and also items used or intended for use in committing an offence such as weapons, tools, keys, appliances, getaway vehicles, account books and forged documents—or any other item which might become evidence or which it is unlawful to possess.

---

[2]  *Justice for All*, extracts from paras 1.4 and 1.5.
[3]  Under the Police Reform Act 2002, community support officers (CSOs) will be able to detain an individual pending their arrest by the police.

Procedures exist through the magistrates' court concerning the return of legitimate property where ownership is later disputed, whilst the courts have powers to order restitution or compensation to a victim of crime and to order items such as drugs or firearms to be forfeited and destroyed. Where capital assets are involved the situation may lead to a confiscation order and the involvement of the Assets Recovery Agency (see, generally, *Chapters 9* and *18*).

In many instances, the police require a warrant from a magistrate before they can enter property to search, e.g. for stolen goods or drugs—but powers also exist to seize property where they are already lawfully on premises or the circumstances justify an immediate or emergency response. Where a warrant *is* required, the application must be made on oath and must normally be authorised by a senior police officer before being made.

### Arrestable offences and serious arrestable offences

Certain offences are 'arrestable' generally—irrespective of any free-standing power to arrest in relation to a given offence—i.e. principally those which attract a maximum sentence of imprisonment of five years or more. Where offences are arrestable other powers go hand-in-hand with this fact. Various police powers rest on the investigation or charge being in respect of a 'serious arrestable offence'. This term applies first to certain offences listed in the Police and Criminal Evidence Act 1984 (PACE) which are always serious. In addition, any other arrestable offence may be regarded as serious if its commission has led, or is intended or likely to lead, to serious harm to the state or to public order; serious interference with the administration of justice or the investigation of offences; the death of, or serious injury to, any person; or substantial financial gain or loss to any person.

### Bail by a police officer

During an investigation, someone arrested by the police may be granted bail by a police custody officer to re-appear at a police station—or, after being charged with a criminal offence, to appear before a magistrates' court at a fixed time and place. The police can grant conditional bail.[4] The Bail Act 1976 and human rights considerations oblige the officer concerned to make a record of any such decision and, if requested to do so by the person in relation to whom the decision was taken, to provide a copy of this record to him or her. Similarly, where bail in criminal proceedings is granted by endorsing a court warrant of arrest that is 'backed for bail': see, generally, *Chapter 8*.

### PACE and the PACE Codes

Investigation and arrest fall within an array of legal provisions and approved practice created by PACE and the Codes of Practice made pursuant to that Act. There is provision throughout the PACE procedures for the detained person (or his or her legal representative) to make representations to decision-makers. PACE or the Codes have the following effects at key points in the process of investigation, arrest and charge:

---

[4] Currently only *after* the accused has been charged. *Justice For All* proposes that the police should be allowed to impose bail conditions *before* charge. To save time, they are to be given power to grant 'street bail' for some minor offences, i.e. without first taking the suspect to a police station (*The Guardian*, 18 September 2002). There is a strong emphasis on reducing offending on bail.

*Procedure on arrest*

Where someone is arrested or taken into custody by a constable he or she must be taken to a police station as soon as reasonably practicable (except when already there). Certain statutory powers of arrest are exempt. This must be a 'designated police station' (see later in this chapter) if it appears that it may be necessary to keep the person in police detention for more than six hours—unless the constable will be unable to take the individual to a designated police station without injury and lacks the necessary assistance. Delay is authorised in certain instances. The person must be released if the constable becomes satisfied that there are no grounds for keeping him or her under arrest.

*At the police station*

If someone attends voluntarily at a police station or other place for the purpose of what is perhaps euphemistically termed 'assisting the police with their enquiries' or accompanies a constable without being arrested, he or she is entitled to leave at any point unless arrested—when he or she must be informed at once of the arrest and the reason for it. Someone brought to a police station under arrest or who is arrested at the police station should be informed by the custody officer of the following rights and of the fact that they need not be exercised immediately, i.e.:

- to consult the PACE Codes of Practice
- to have someone informed of his or her arrest. A person arrested and held in custody is entitled on request to have a friend, relative or other person who is likely to take an interest in his or her welfare told, as soon as practicable, that he or she has been arrested and is being detained. An officer of at least the rank of superintendent may authorise delay in the case of someone in police detention for a serious arrestable offence (above) where he or she has reasonable grounds for believing that release would lead to interference with or harm to the evidence relating to such an offence, interference with or physical injury to other persons, to the alerting of other suspects not yet arrested, or would hinder the recovery of property. Special provisions apply to terrorism offences.
- to consult a solicitor. Someone who is arrested and held in custody in a police station or other premises is entitled on request to consult a solicitor privately at any time. Consultation must be permitted as soon as practicable except to the extent that delay is permitted. An officer of at least the rank of superintendent may authorise delay in the case of a serious arrestable offence if he or she has reasonable grounds for believing such consultation would have an effect similar to that described in the last paragraph. The right is to consult privately, but an assistant chief constable or commander may authorise consultation only in the sight and hearing of a qualified officer of the uniformed branch. Again, special provisions apply to terrorism offences.

**Police detention of suspects**

Where someone is arrested without a court warrant but the custody officer at the police station to which he or she is taken considers that there is insufficient evidence to charge that person and is not prepared to hold that individual for questioning, or cannot legally do so, the custody officer must release him or her. But this may be on bail subject to a requirement to return to a police station at some later date (above). Likewise, if a custody officer is conducting a review of detention (below) and he or she concludes that detention without charge can no longer be justified, the suspect must be released with or without bail.

### After 24 hours

Similar decisions must be made at the end of 24 hours detention without charge. The basic rule is that someone must not be kept in police detention for more than 24 hours without being charged (and, as indicated earlier, must be released before that time if there is no longer any justification for holding him or her). This 24 hour limit may be extended up to 36 hours by a senior police officer but only in the case of a serious arrestable offence. A police officer of the rank of superintendent or above who is responsible for the police station may authorise a person to be kept in police detention for the period up to 36 hours if he or she has reasonable grounds for believing that:

- detention without charge is necessary to secure or preserve evidence or to obtain evidence by questioning the suspect;
- the offence is a serious arrestable offence; and
- the investigation is being conducted diligently and expeditiously.

When detention for less than 36 hours is authorised a further period expiring not later than the end of the initial 36 hours may be authorised, provided the same conditions are still satisfied.

### Beyond 36 hours: further detention following an application to the court

Where continued detention to authorised by a senior officer, the detained person must still be released with or without bail at the expiry of 36 hours unless an application is made to a magistrates' court—sitting 'otherwise than in open court'—and this results in a warrant of further detention being issued. Such a warrant allows the police to continue to detain the suspect. Warrants of further detention can be issued for up to 36 hours at a time, provided that the suspect is not detained for longer than 96 hours overall. He or she must then be charged or released—although if released a fresh arrest is possible, e.g. if new evidence emerges, and provided the provisions are not actively circumvented or abused.

Application must be made by a constable on oath, supported by information specifying the offence, the general nature of the evidence on which the suspect has been arrested, what inquiries have already been made and what further inquiries are proposed, plus the reasons for believing continued detention is necessary. The court must be satisfied that there are reasonable grounds for believing that further detention is justified by virtue of the same criteria that govern the exercise of the superintendent's discretion (above). Application may only be made:

- before the expiry of 36 hours
- where it is not practicable for the magistrates' court to sit at the end of 36 hours but the court will sit during the six hours following the end of that period, before the expiry of those six hours.

This six hour period of leeway is not limited to the situation where the 36 hour period expires and no court is sitting at all. Magistrates also have discretion during the course of a court sitting whether to hear such an application straightaway or to wait, provided that they do so for no longer than six hours. The PACE Codes of Practice recognise the impracticability of a court being convened outside the hours of 10 a.m. and 9 p.m.

Where the court is not satisfied that further detention is justified it must refuse the application (but can adjourn within the initial 36 hours). If the application is refused the arrested person must be charged forthwith or be released with or without bail. However, he or she need not be released by the police before the expiry of 24 hours detention, or of any longer period for which continued detention has been authorised by a superintendent, i.e. up until the end of the initial 36 hours.

Where application is made after the expiry of 36 hours and it appears that it would have been reasonable for the police to have made the application within that time, the court must dismiss the application.

## AFTER CHARGE

Once someone has been charged[5] with an offence at a police station, the police custody officer must decide whether to bail the accused (above) for appearance at court or to arrange for him or her to be brought before a court within 24 hours for the court to take that decision.

If someone is charged with an offence the custody officer must order release from detention with or without bail unless one of a number of grounds is satisfied, e.g. that his or her name or address cannot be ascertained; that the custody officer has reasonable grounds for believing that the person will abscond, commit an offence or interfere with the administration of justice if released; or that detention is necessary for the person's own protection or, if a juvenile,[6] continued detention is in his or her own interests.

Anybody who, after being charged with an offence, *is* kept in police detention or detained by a local authority must be brought before a magistrates' court. If he or she is brought before a court for the petty sessions area in which the police station is situated this must be as soon as practicable and in any event not later than the first sitting after being charged with the offence. If no magistrates' court is due to sit on the day when he or she is charged, or the next day, the custody officer must inform the local clerk to the justices who must consider whether or not to arrange for a court to sit then or within a brief statutory timescale.

## CUSTODY OFFICERS AND THEIR DUTIES

Certain police stations must be designated by the chief officer of police to be used for detaining arrested people and one or more custody officers must be

---

[5]  *Justice for All* proposes 'as soon as practicable' giving the CPS responsibility for determining the charge in cases other than for routine offences or where the police make a holding charge.

[6]  For this purpose meaning anyone under the age of 18.

appointed for each designated police station. The custody officer must be of at least the rank of sergeant; but a non-involved officer of any rank may perform the function if a designated custody officer is not readily available.

It is the duty of the custody officer to ensure that all people in police detention are treated in accordance with PACE and the Codes of Practice. Special provisions cover the situation where an arrested person is taken to a police station that is not a designated police station and concerning transfer between police stations. Where someone is arrested for an offence or returns to a police station to answer to bail, the custody officer must, as soon as practicable, determine whether he or she has sufficient evidence to charge that person with the offence. If there *is* sufficient evidence, the suspect must be either charged or released without charge—with or without bail. Following a charge, the custody officer must order release either with or without bail of anyone arrested without a warrant other than in limited circumstances.

### Review of police detention
The circumstances of people in police detention must be periodically reviewed by a review officer who is, in the case of a person arrested and charged, the custody officer, and in the case of a person arrested but not charged, a non-involved officer of at least the rank of inspector. PACE sets out a timetable and the detained person or his or her solicitor is entitled to make representations at appropriate points.

### Juveniles
If an arrested person is a juvenile, the custody officer must, if practicable, ascertain the identity of the person who is responsible for his or her welfare and inform that person that the juvenile has been arrested, and the reason why he or she is detained. If the juvenile is known to be subject to a supervision order, reasonable steps must be taken to notify the supervisor. The custody officer must also, as soon as practicable, inform an 'appropriate adult' of the grounds for detention and the juvenile's whereabouts and ask the adult to come to the police station to see the juvenile. In practice, the local youth offending team (YOT) (*Chapter 5*) will be alerted in any event.

By 'appropriate adult' is meant the parent or guardian; or, if the juvenile is in care, the relevant care authority or voluntary organization; or a social worker; or, failing any of the above, a responsible adult who is not a police officer or police employee. The appropriate adult may or may not be a person responsible for the juvenile's welfare—and has an important role in advising and observing for fairness. This aspect is also nowadays conducted in conjunction with the local YOT.

A custody officer who authorises an arrested juvenile to be kept in police custody must ensure that, after being charged, the arrested juvenile is moved to local authority accommodation unless he or she certifies either that it is impracticable to do so or, in the case of a juvenile aged 12 or over, that no secure accommodation is available and keeping the juvenile in other local authority accommodation would not be adequate to protect the public from serious harm from him or her.

When the question of charge and bail arises then again the local YOT has a frontline role in terms of bail information and where appropriate bail support (terms outlined in *Chapter 8*).

**Mentally handicapped and mentally disordered suspects**
Similar 'appropriate adult' procedures apply in relation to mentally handicapped and mentally disordered people suspected of committing criminal offences.

## REVIEW BY THE CROWN PROSECUTOR

The next stage in the criminal justice process is for the file to be reviewed by a Crown prosecutor (where this has not already occurred simultaneously with the investigation). The police and CPS have been increasingly located in joint Criminal Justice Units (CJUs) across England and Wales a process that *Justice For All* indicates will continue until all 42 administrative areas are served in this way. Either before or after the CPS review of the case file, a decision may be made to caution the offender or to refer him or her to another agency rather than to bring a prosecution or to continue with criminal proceedings. All these items are considered in the next chapter.

# CHAPTER 7

# The Decision to Prosecute

With the general run of criminal offences the decision whether or not to prosecute is initially one for the police.[1] To all intents and purposes this coincides with the decision to charge a suspect (*Chapter 6*) or to 'lay an information' at a magistrates' court as a prelude to a summons (*Chapter 8*). But from this point onwards the decision whether a prosecution should continue or be discontinued becomes one for the Crown Prosecution Service (CPS), an independent agency whose head, the Director of Public Prosecutions, is accountable to the government's chief law officer, the Attorney General. The nature, organization and structure of the CPS is described in *Chapter 12*.

The Serious Fraud Office (SFO) discharges a wider role in that within its field of operations it has both an investigation and prosecution function—albeit often triggered by information from the police. The SFO is a non-ministerial department accountable through its director to the Attorney General.

## CONSENTS

Certain offences can only be prosecuted by or with the consent or approval of the Director of Public Prosecutions (which since the formation of the CPS can in practice usually be supplied by any Crown prosecutor) or the Attorney General, called a *fiat*. These requirements do not prevent investigation, detention and arrest (*Chapter 6*) or in most cases charge and remand on bail or in custody (*Chapter 8*).

## REFERRAL AND CAUTIONING SCHEMES

The police are *not obliged* to prosecute when a suspect is identified. They always have a discretion whether to prosecute or not.[2] Quite apart from decisions not to prosecute (or to take 'no further action'), an offender can be referred to another agency or cautioned. There are a number of arrest referral schemes targeted on different kinds of offenders, usually involving partnerships between the police and other agencies including drug actions teams (see, generally, *Chapter 17*). These are multi-agency groups set up to co-ordinate local action on drug misuse and bring together senior representatives of various public services including health and social services (in addition to the

---

[1]   Or in other cases for the enforcement agency given that responsibility by Parliament, e.g. Customs and Excise (and see the further examples in *Chapter 1*). Generally speaking, there is also a right to bring a purely private prosecution: see later in this chapter. *Justice for All* proposes 'as soon as practicable giving the CPS responsibility for determining the charge in cases other than for routine offences or where the police need to make a holding charge'.

[2]   *R v. Metropolitan Police Commissioner, ex p. Blackburn* [1968] 2 QB 118. Nowadays the 'Lambeth Experiment'—a 'softly, softly' approach to simple possession of certain drugs—comes to mind.

usual criminal justice agencies). These and other schemes (e.g. those concerned with mental disorder) seek to identify a range of vulnerable and other people who should be referred for help, treatment, advice or participation in a particular programme and where prosecution would serve little, if any, worthwhile public interest. Referral may or may not be linked to the offender being cautioned or given a deferred caution (below) according to the circumstances.

### Cautioning

The police may choose to formally caution on offender (or, in the case of a juvenile, to warn or reprimand him or her within the terms of the statutory scheme introduced by the Crime and Disorder Act 1998: *Chapter 5*). Adults may be cautioned provided there is sufficient evidence for a conviction, the offender admits his or her guilt and consents, and it is not necessary in the public interest to institute criminal proceedings. This is a formal warning administered by a senior police officer in uniform, normally at a police station. A caution gives the offender a chance to demonstrate his or her capacity for lawful behaviour and reform without being blighted by a criminal record. It can be effective in the sense that comparatively few of those cautioned re-offend.

From the 1980s onwards Home Office guidance encouraged greater use of cautioning and the number of offenders dealt with in this way increased rapidly. However, following a change of policy, a circular issued 1994 sought to reduce the level of cautioning, in particular by discouraging the use of 'repeat cautions', i.e. those where the offender has already been cautioned in the past. Cautioning is nowadays governed by nationwide guidelines (although these can be supplemented locally) and in practice applies to a range of lesser matters.

Where the CPS are advising the police the *Code for Crown Prosecutors* sets out guidance for Crown prosecutors. In relation to adult cautions and under the heading 'Police Cautions', it includes the following guidance:

6.11 . . . The police make the decision to caution an offender in accordance with Home Office guidelines.

6.12 When deciding whether a case should be prosecuted in the courts, Crown prosecutors should consider the alternatives to prosecution. These will include a police caution. Again the Home Office guidelines should be applied. Where it is felt that a caution is appropriate, Crown prosecutors must inform the police so that they can caution the suspect . . .

The code then deals with the situation where this proves abortive, in effect by requiring the prosecutor to review the case afresh and in the light, e.g. of any refusal by the individual concerned to accept a caution.

Proposals in *Justice for All* would generally enhance the role and input of the CPS at the prosecution decision-making stage. The White Paper also proposes a structured form of caution called a 'conditional caution' in which the CPS might, in certain 'borderline cases', decide that the public interest and the interests of justice may be better served if an offender agrees to be given a caution with conditions that may include a requirement, e.g. to compensate the victim or to undergo treatment or training. Failure to comply with the conditions would result in prosecution.

### Deferred cautions

The decision whether or not to caution can be linked to an arrangement whereby the offender is required to take part in a scheme or programme designed to prevent his or her offending in the future, known as a 'deferred caution'.[3] Such schemes focus principally on drug users arrested for possessing small amounts of Class A or Class B drugs and usually for personal use.[4] The offender is not cautioned but placed on police bail, and the decision whether or not to caution is deferred for a short period of time to allow the offender to obtain help from a specialist drug agency. If the offender engages with that agency in a satisfactory way and shows good progress the police will take no further action. If not, the offender will be cautioned or prosecuted as appropriate.

### Relevance of cautions to future cases

Cautions are cited in court if the offender commits a further offence for which he or she is prosecuted, and may have an effect on sentence where the subject matter of the caution or cautions is relevant to the present conviction (see, generally, *Chapter 9*). A caution might, e.g. tend to show that the offender understood the wrongfulness of particular conduct, having been warned by the police about similar behaviour in the past.

### Diversion generally

Cautioning is one means of diversion from the formal criminal justice process. Since the 1980s criminal justice strategies have to varying degrees involved diverting offenders away from court and into informal community networks.[5] Diversion schemes often involve putting right damage caused or taking some remedial action as a condition of non-prosecution, and in this sense can be viewed as restorative in nature (*Chapter 18*). By analogy, under a vehicle rectification scheme an offender might be allowed the opportunity to repair his or her vehicle so as to bring it within the law within a certain time and then to return with it to a police garage for inspection. The referral order scheme for juveniles appearing in court for the first time (*Chapter 5*)—although technically a prosecution—builds on the diversionary thinking of past decades.[6]

## CROWN PROSECUTION SERVICE (CPS)

The CPS is responsible for most public prosecutions in England and Wales and may take over any private or other prosecution. It has a legal duty to do so in

---

[3] The present deferred caution should be contrasted with the proposed conditional caution above.

[4] The Criminal Justice and Court Services Act 2000 gives the police power to drug test detainees in police custody. The measure is being piloted in nine areas.

[5] The term 'diversion' is also sometimes used where there *is* a prosecution: to describe the channelling of offenders into community-based sentences instead of custody.

[6] As to which see, e.g. *Growing Out of Crime: The New Era* (1992, reprinted 2002), Rutherford A, Winchester: Waterside Press.

relation to proceedings started by the police—widely defined by statute. In many instances the CPS is consulted *before* proceedings are begun, particularly if legal technicalities or other complexities are involved or the case involves a suspect who is particularly vulnerable.

The governing provision is the Prosecution of Offences Act 1985 under which, among other things, the DPP must issue a *Code for Crown Prosecutors* 'giving guidance on general principles to be applied by them'. The code thus sets out the basic principles which Crown prosecutors must apply when they come to consider individual cases.

### The *Code for Crown Prosecutors*

The code is a public document. Although written for members of the CPS, it is widely used by other lawyers and agencies such as the police in order to understand the way in which the CPS makes decisions.[7] The code begins with a number of general statements and principles as follows:

#### 1. Introduction

1.1 The decision to prosecute an individual is a serious step. Fair and effective prosecution is essential to the maintenance of law and order. Even in a small case a prosecution has serious implications for all involved—victims, witnesses and defendants. The Crown Prosecution Service applies the Code for Crown Prosecutors so that it can make fair and consistent decisions about prosecutions.

1.2 The code helps the Crown Prosecution Service to play its part in making sure that justice is done. It contains information that is important to police officers and others who work in the criminal justice system and to the general public. Police officers should take account of the code when they are deciding whether to charge a person with an offence.

1.3 The code is also designed to make sure that everyone knows the principles that the Crown Prosecution Service applies when carrying out its work. By applying the same principles, everyone involved in the system is helping to treat victims fairly and to prosecute fairly but effectively.

#### 2. General Principles

2.1 Each case is unique and must be considered on its own facts and merits. However, there are general principles that apply to the way in which Crown prosecutors must approach every case.

2.2 Crown prosecutors must be fair, independent and objective. They must not let any personal views about ethnic or national origin, sex, religious beliefs, political views or the sexual orientation of the suspect, victim or witness influence their decisions. They must not be affected by improper or undue pressure from any source.

---

[7] Copies of the *Code for Crown Prosecutors* can be obtained from the CPS, 50 Ludgate Hill London, EC4M 7EX or can be viewed at the CPS web-site www.cps.gov.uk

2.3 It is the duty of Crown prosecutors to make sure that the right person is prosecuted for the right offence. In doing so, Crown prosecutors must always act in the interests of justice and not solely for the purpose of obtaining a conviction.

2.4 It is the duty of Crown prosecutors to review, advise on and prosecute cases, ensuring that the law is properly applied, that all relevant evidence is put before the court and that obligations of disclosure are complied with, in accordance with the principles set out in this code.

2.5 The CPS is a public authority for the purposes of the Human Rights Act 1998. Crown prosecutors must apply the principles of the European Convention On Human Rights in accordance with the Act.

### The continuing duty to review cases

The High Court has held (in a judgement in a civil case) that the CPS owes a duty of care to people who are subject to its decisions. The high standards demanded by the duty to review cases and to make effective decisions as to whether a case should continue or be discontinued are encapsulated as follows:

### 3. Review

3.1 Proceedings are usually started by the police. Sometimes they may consult the Crown Prosecution Service before starting a prosecution. Each case that the Crown Prosecution Service receives from the police is reviewed to make sure it meets the evidential and public interest tests set out in this code. Crown prosecutors may decide to continue with the original charges, to change the charges, or sometimes to stop the case.

3.2 Review is a continuing process and Crown prosecutors must take account of any change in circumstances. Wherever possible, they talk to the police first if they are thinking about changing the charges or stopping the case. This gives the police the chance to provide more information that may affect the decision. The Crown Prosecution Service and the police work closely together to reach the right decision, but the final responsibility for the decision rests with the Crown Prosecution Service.

### The twin test

Crown prosecutors apply an 'evidential test' and a 'public interest' test. The relevant parts of the code read as follows:[8]

### 4 Code Tests

4.1 There are two stages in the decision to prosecute. The first stage is **the evidential test**. If the case does not pass the evidential test, it must not go ahead, no matter how important or serious it may be. If the case does meet the evidential test, Crown prosecutors must decide if a prosecution is needed in the public interest.

4.2 This second stage is **the public interest test**. The Crown Prosecution Service will only start or continue with a prosecution when the case has passed both tests . . .

---

[8]  The emphases appear in the original.

The evidential test is explained in more detail in section 5 of the code and the public interest test in section 6. The evidential test is sometimes explained by saying that for a prosecution to be launched or continued there must be a realistic prospect of conviction, which, under the latest version of the code means that it must be more likely than not that a prosecution would be successful. The Crown prosecutor must consider what the defence case may be, and how that is likely to affect prosecution—including whether the evidence can be used in court and whether it is reliable.

As to the public interest test:

6.2 The public interest must be considered in each case where there is enough evidence to provide a realistic prospect of conviction. A prosecution will usually take place unless there are public interest factors tending against prosecution which clearly outweigh those tending in favour. Although there may be public interest factors against prosecution in a particular case, often the prosecution should go ahead and those factors should be put to the court for consideration when sentence is being passed.

6.3 Crown posecutors must balance factors for and against prosecution carefully and fairly. Public interest factors that can affect the decision to prosecute usually depend on the seriousness of the offence or the circumstances of the suspect. Some factors may increase the need to prosecute but others may suggest that another course of action would be better.

The code then lists some common public interest factors, both for and against prosecution, which it states are not exhaustive. Crown prosecutors must decide how important each factor is in the material circumstances of each case and go on to make an overall assessment, including the interests of the victim. The code proceeds as follows:

**Some common public interest factors in favour of prosecution.**

6.4 The more serious the offence, the more likely it is that a prosecution will be needed in the public interest. A prosecution is likely to be needed if:

a a conviction is likely to result in a significant sentence;

b a weapon was used or violence was threatened during the commission of the offence;

c the offence was committed against a person serving the public (for example, a police or prison officer, or a nurse);

d the defendant was in a position of authority or trust;

e the evidence shows that the defendant was a ringleader or an organizer of the offence;

f there is evidence that the offence was premeditated;

g there is evidence that the offence was carried out by a group;

**h** the victim of the offence was vulnerable, has been put in considerable fear, or suffered personal attack, damage or disturbance;

**i** the offence was motivated by any form of discrimination against the victim's ethnic or national origin, sex, religious beliefs, political views or sexual orientation, or the suspect demonstrated hostility towards the victim based on any of those characteristics;

**j** there is a marked difference between the actual or mental ages of the defendant and the victim, or if there is any element of corruption;

**k** the defendant's previous convictions or cautions are relevant to the present offence;

**l** the defendant is alleged to have committed the offence whilst under an order of the court;

**m** there are grounds for believing that the offence is likely to be continued or repeated, for example, by a history of recurring conduct; or

**n** the offence, although not serious in itself, is widespread in the area where it was committed.

**Some common public interest factors against prosecution**

6.5 A prosecution is less likely to be needed if:

**a** the court is likely to impose a nominal penalty;

**b** the defendant has already been made the subject of a sentence and any further conviction would be unlikely to result in the imposition of an additional sentence or order, unless the nature of the particular offence requires a prosecution;

**c** the offence was committed as a result of a genuine mistake or misunderstanding (these factors must be balanced against the seriousness of the offence);

**d** the loss or harm can be described as minor and was the result of a single incident, particularly if it was caused by a misjudgement;

**e** there has been a long delay between the offence taking place and the date of the trial, unless:

· the offence is serious;

· the delay has been caused in part by the defendant;

· the offence has only recently come to light; or

· the complexity of the offence has meant that there has been a long investigation;

**f** a prosecution is likely to have a bad effect on the victim's physical or mental health, always bearing in mind the seriousness of the offence;

**g** the defendant is elderly or is, or was at the time of the offence, suffering from significant mental or physical ill health, unless the offence is serious or there is a real possibility that it may be repeated. The Crown Prosecution Service, where necessary, applies Home Office guidelines about how to deal with mentally disordered offenders. Crown prosecutors must balance the desirability of diverting a defendant who is suffering from significant mental or physical ill health with the need to safeguard the general public;

h the defendant has put right the loss or harm that was caused (but defendants must not avoid prosecution solely because they pay compensation); or

i details may be made public that could harm sources of information, international relations or national security;

The code goes on to explain that deciding on the public interest is not simply a matter of adding up the number of factors on each side. Crown prosecutors must decide how important each factor is in the circumstances of each case and go on to make an overall assessment. It also stresses the relationship between the victim and the public interest:

6.7 The Crown Prosecution Service prosecutes cases on behalf of the public at large and not just in the interests of any particular individual. However, when considering the public interest test Crown prosecutors should always take into account the consequences for the victim of the decision whether or not to prosecute, and any views expressed by the victim or the victim's family.

6.8 It is important that a victim is told about a decision which makes a significant difference to the case in which he or she is involved. Crown prosecutors should ensure that they follow any agreed procedures.

There are also special considerations in relation to youths and juveniles.

## DISCONTINUANCE

Various chapters of this book contain references to cases being discontinued by the CPS. Discontinuance is a statutory function which enables the prosecutor to stop a prosecution after it has been started by the police and, subject to what is said below, at any stage after that if the twin test referred to earlier in this chapter ceases to be satisfied under either limb. With this in mind, the Crown prosecutor must conduct regular reviews of the case file.

Discontinuance is available in all cases in magistrates' courts at any time before the defendant has pleaded guilty or the trial has started and, in some cases only, at the Crown Court before the indictment (*Chapter 3*) has been brought. In reviewing and deciding whether to discontinue a case, the Crown prosecutor is guided by the principles set out in the *Code for Crown Prosecutors*.

## PRIVATE PROSECUTIONS

Except where expressly prohibited by law or where the consent or authority of a designated official or body is required by statute, any citizen can bring a private prosecution, i.e. commence criminal proceedings. There are hazards however. Among other things, a private prosecutor risks costs being awarded against him or her if the prosecution fails; an attempt to lay an information may be rejected as vexatious or an abuse of the processes of the court; a badly judged citizen's arrest[9] may result in an award of damages; or the matter can be taken over by the CPS as explained earlier (and possibly be discontinued whatever the wishes of the private prosecutor). Nonetheless, a number of such prosecutions occur each year, often in respect of quite serious matters, and sometimes where the CPS has already advised the police against prosecution or declined to continue with the case. Modern times have seen private prosecutions result in convictions, e.g. for manslaughter, rape and serious offences involving the abuse of children.[10]

The costs of a successful private prosecution fall to be met from the public funds but there is nothing in the nature of state funded legal representation for an individual to bring a prosecution rather than to defend one (*Chapter 8*).

### 'Non-police' matters

In practice there are areas where the police tend to tread warily, but these have receded in recent years in relation, e.g. to domestic violence and harassment where there have been extensive efforts to ensure that perpetrators are brought to justice. As already explained, there are areas where responsibility is cast by statute on someone other than the ordinary police. Prosecutions by such officials or bodies—sometimes called 'non-police' prosecutions—may also find the label 'private prosecutions' being applied to them, albeit this concept differs from that where an ordinary private citizen brings proceedings.

---

[9] Private prosecutions are usually commenced by way of an information and summons (*Chapter 8*) and the individual will need to convince a magistrate or justices' clerk of the *bona fides* of the application. There are considerable additional hazards attached to a citizen's arrest—where the lawfulness test for an arrest by a private citizen is more arduous than for a police officer, who is entitled to act on reasonable suspicion.

[10] But not in the Stephen Lawrence case (*Chapter 16*) where a private prosecution was notoriously unsuccessful, thereby giving the alleged culprits immunity from prosecution under the double jeopardy rule (*Chapter 1*) and precipitating the controversial proposal in *Justice for All* that the rule be abolished in certain situations.

# CHAPTER 8

# Bringing a Case to Court

Criminal proceedings commence when either an information is laid and a summons is issued (see further below) or by way of arrest and charge as outlined in *Chapter 6*. In practice, all the more serious cases begin by this latter route. Following an investigation in accordance with PACE the accused person is charged by a custody sergeant and either bailed to appear at court or taken directly to court in custody.[1] In either case he or she will in due course be called upon to answer the allegation unless it is discontinued by the Crown Prosecution Service (CPS) (*Chapter 7*) or it is otherwise withdrawn or abandoned.

Court procedure is laid down by Act of Parliament, or in statutory instruments (also known as SIs, Regulations, Rules) drawn up in consultation with interested parties. Rules of court are supplemented by an inherent jurisdiction on the part of judges and magistrates to adapt their procedures to the ever-changing circumstances and needs of individual cases. All procedures must now take account of human rights considerations. There are various consultative committees whereby the interests of the judiciary and court users are taken into account including a Crown Court Rules Committee. *Justice For All* (*Chapter 15*) proposes a new, common, procedural code (together with a criminal evidence code and a Criminal Procedure Rules Committee)[2] as well as improvements to preparatory or pre-trial hearings with a view to making the management of individual cases more effective. One development has been a Trial Unit within the CPS (often with a police presence) which is responsible for the preparation of Crown Court prosecutions and which complements the Criminal Justice Units mentioned in earlier chapters in relation to the early stages of criminal proceedings and the magistrates' court.

## COMMENCING COURT PROCEEDINGS

Virtually all criminal cases start out in the magistrates' court and are either dealt with to their conclusion by that court or committed to the Crown Court for trial (*Chapter 3*) or sentence (*Chapter 9*). Indictable only matters (*Chapter 1*)—in essence the most serious offences—must nowadays be sent straightaway by magistrates to the Crown Court.[3]

### Information and summons[4]
An information may be oral or written (in practice both are nowadays generated by computer simultaneously). In substance, an information is an application for a

---

[1] Usually, if in custody, within 24 hours: Sundays and Bank Holidays excluded.
[2] As indicated in *Chapter 1* it also proposes the codification of the criminal law.
[3] Proceedings can start in the Crown Court by way of a voluntary bill of indictment (*Chapter 3*) but this is quite rare.
[4] *Justice for All* (*Chapter 15*), proposes that these procedures should be replaced by more functional arrangements and that the information as such should be abolished.

summons which, in turn, is an instruction to the accused person to attend court at a given time and place. An information must be laid (i.e. be placed) before a magistrate or justices' clerk for his or her decision whether a summons should be issued. This is a judicial decision—albeit that in practice vast numbers of run-of-the-mill summonses are issued every working day with minimal, if any, scrutiny unless there is some special reason for caution as sometimes in the case of a private prosecution (*Chapter 7*) or where an obscure or rarely prosecuted offence is alleged.

One situation in which an oral information frequently occurs is when the defendant is already present at a magistrates' court and the prosecutor wishes to alter the original allegation. Another is where a citizen 'walks in off the street' and makes an allegation, e.g. of assault by a neighbour, although in both this and the in-court example the allegation would, in practice, be written down by court staff. The informant might then be asked to sign the information and even, in the case of a private individual, be required by a magistrate to give evidence on oath in confirmation of the allegation (although neither writing, signing or sworn evidence is a strict prerequisite for a summons). More generally, computer input now equates to the old written information.

An information must contain the name of the informant, the name and address of the defendant, the allegation and enough details to indicate precisely what is being alleged, i.e. the date, place and nature of the alleged offence and in practice the statutory provision or common law rule which makes such events a criminal offence.

### Arrest and charge

The word 'charge' is often used loosely to indicate any situation where an allegation is put to a defendant whether by the police or other prosecutor before court or by a member of the court staff at a court hearing. This loose meaning also covers the situation where an information (as opposed to a charge proper) is read out to the defendant in court, i.e. the court legal adviser might well say to the defendant 'You are charged that . . . '. But when the word is used in its strict sense, this is to make a distinction between proceedings by way of information and summons and those by way of arrest and charge. The word 'charge' also distinguishes events at a magistrates' court level from those in the Crown Court where the terms arraignment and indictment are used (*Chapter 3*).

When the defendant is charged by the police, a 'charge sheet' is completed, a copy is handed to the accused person and another is sent to the magistrates' court. No summons is issued—this being superfluous as the defendant will have been released by the police on bail to appear at court at a fixed time and place, accompanied by written details, or have been brought directly to court.

### Warrant of arrest

An information must be in writing and be substantiated on oath where a warrant of arrest is being applied for rather than a summons. Such an application can only be made to a magistrate. Warrants with or without instructions to the police to bail the defendant to appear in court at a fixed time and place can be issued by magistrates, in a variety of situations:

- instead of a summons where the offence is imprisonable and a summons will not suffice (e.g. where the address of the alleged offender is unknown)
- where the defendant has failed to answer a summons
- where he or she has failed to surrender to bail, e.g. following being charged by the police and released on bail to attend court.

A warrant containing instructions to the police to release the accused person on bail after arrest is described as 'backed for bail'. As explained in *Chapter 3*, the Crown Court can issue a bench warrant where an accused person fails to turn up for his or her trial in that court. Both the Crown Court and the magistrates' court can issue a warrant where the accused person does not remain at court throughout the proceedings.

### Failure to surrender to bail

Any failure to surrender to bail (or to remain at court throughout the proceedings) is known as 'absconding' which, apart from leading to the likelihood of an arrest warrant (above) will also be a ground for refusing bail in the future: see under next heading. Failure to surrender to bail is a criminal offence in its own right. It is punishable by magistrates by a Level 5 fine (£5,000) or up to three months in prison and by an unlimited fine or up to 12 months in prison in the Crown Court. Magistrates have power to commit to the Crown Court for sentence (*Chapters 3* and *9*) for this offence.

## BAIL OR CUSTODY

Once charged, an offender must be released on bail by the police or be brought before a magistrates' court in custody—usually within 24 hours. *Justice for All* expresses concern about the extent to which some people commit further offences whilst they are on bail and puts forward a number of proposals designed to confront this, i.e. that the police be allowed to add conditions to a person's bail from the outset of an investigation and to 'weight the court's discretion against granting bail to a defendant who has been charged with an imprisonable offence committed whilst already on bail for another offence' and the piloting 'in high crime areas' of a presumption of remand to custody where the suspect tests positive for Class A drugs on arrest but refuses treatment. There are also plans to extend the prosecutor's right of appeal against the grant of bail (below) to cover all imprisonable offences. Already, when sentencing (*Chapter 9*), an offence must be treated as more serious if it was committed whilst the offender was on bail.

### Police bail

The police may bail a suspect to return to the police station for an investigation to continue (*Chapter 6*) or for appearance at court following his or her being charged by them. Police bail should normally be granted unless circumstances comparable to those that would justify a court in refusing bail exist (below). The police currently have power to grant bail with conditions attached once the accused person has been charged but, as indicated in *Chapter 6, Justice for All* proposes extending this so that it applies before charge also. Reasons must be given to the accused person for refusing bail.

### Court bail

The Bail Act 1976 guarantees a right to bail to people charged with a criminal offence, i.e. a right not to be held in custody unless one of several strict legal exceptions applies. Where the court does find that such an exception exists on the facts of a particular case the defendant is remanded into custody, usually for not more than eight clear days at a time before conviction. Longer remands in custody are possible, in certain circumstances for up to 28 days. After conviction and pending sentence (usually for reports to be prepared: *Chapter 9*), the limit on each such a remand is 21 days.

Someone who is refused bail can appeal to a judge of the Crown Court or a judge of the High Court if one is sitting at the local Crown Court centre. The prosecutor can appeal to the Crown Court against a grant of bail in certain cases.[5]

### Young people

People aged 17 to 20 who are refused bail are held in remand centres (in effect prisons for unconvicted or unsentenced male prisoners aged 17 to 21 or women of any age) or prisons. Below the age of 17, a refusal of bail operates as a remand to local authority accommodation but during the remand period, a court can order or authorise the use of secure accommodation. If the defendant is aged 15 or 16 and *male* a court can remand him to a remand centre or prison if strict statutory criteria are met.

### Grounds and reasons

Apart from in exceptional situations bail can only be refused if a court is satisfied that a statutory exception to the general right to bail exists. Exceptions are usually called 'grounds'. Thus, e.g. bail can be refused in relation to imprisonable offences before conviction if there are *substantial* grounds for believing that if given bail the defendant would:

- fail to surrender to custody (i.e. abscond)
- commit an offence
- interfere with witnesses.

The precise grounds vary according to whether the decision is being made before or after conviction and the scope for refusing bail is less where the offence itself does not attract imprisonment. However, defendants can be held in custody for any offence for their own protection (e.g. to prevent them being harassed, placed in fear or physically attacked, or where they are personally vulnerable) or where there has been a previous breach of bail by absconding and the court believes that the defendant would abscond again if given bail. Among other exceptions to the right to bail, an offender *need not* be granted bail if the offence is indictable (including either way matters) if he or she was already on bail for an earlier offence when the later offence was allegedly committed. *Justice for All* proposes to 'weight' the court's current discretion in favour of bail being refused in such circumstances.

---

[5]  Assuming that bail was opposed by him or her in the first place. Currently, the offence in question must be one punishable with imprisonment for five years or more or an offence of vehicle-taking. As already noted above, *Justice for All* would extend this to *all imprisonable offences*.

The Bail Act 1976 requires that where a court or constable grants or withholds bail a record should be made of that decision and the reason for it. Magistrates are obliged to announce the grounds for refusing bail in open court (e.g. that the defendant would interfere with witnesses) and, as a distinct item, their reasons for this conclusion (e.g. that the defendant has already made threats towards witnesses which events suggest should be taken seriously). This is now reinforced by fair trial considerations under human rights law (*Chapter 1*). A copy of the decision must be given to the defendant on request. In practice, pro forma are used with grounds and sample reasons pre-printed and with boxes available for ticking, crossing or adding to where the decision does not fit into a standard pigeonhole. However, the quasi-automated nature of recording much remand decision-making should not be allowed to obscure the fact that a full and proper exercise in judicial discretion—by listening to the facts and drawing only legitimate inferences from them—is essential before the record is made. Nonetheless, no particular standard of proof is required.[6]

Reasons must be given for *granting* bail in the case of murder and certain other prescribed offences; whilst bail cannot be granted at all in the case of a charge of murder or attempted murder, rape or attempted rape, or manslaughter if the defendant already has a conviction for one of these offences or culpable homicide.

### Repeat applications for bail

There are legal rules barring 'repeat applications' for bail, i.e. the same arguments being put forward by defendants over and again at subsequent remand hearings. Under national law courts are not obliged to listen to the same matters repeatedly although this statutory bar appears to have been applied in a relaxed manner since the Human Rights Act 1998. The bar does not, in any case, apply on a defendant's first two appearances.

### Custody time limits

There are limits on the total length of time for which a defendant may be held in custody before a case starts. Either way cases tried by magistrates must be begun within 70 days or in some cases 56 days.[7] Where a case is to be committed for trial, the committal process must be started within 70 days. A period of 112 days is then allowed between the date when magistrates send the defendant to the Crown Court and arraignment (*Chapter 3*). If a time limit expires, the defendant cannot be remanded in custody any longer for the offence in question. He or she can still be prosecuted, but must be released on bail pending further stages of the proceedings. Time limits can be extended by the court in an individual case for good cause.

### Conditional bail

Bail can be granted subject to conditions, e.g. to live at a given address; report to the police, say, 'between 6 p.m. and 8 p.m. every Monday, Wednesday and Friday'; not to associate with the victim or witnesses (called a condition of 'non-

---

[6]  Or for that matter evidence: although some evidence on oath is often given, especially where information is challenged, including evidence by the arresting officer.

[7]  Depending on whether mode of trial (see later in the text) has been determined within the first 56 days, when the limit telescopes down to the shorter of the two periods.

association'); or to stay away from a designated geographical location. Reasons must be given for conditions. Generally speaking, the police have power to grant conditional bail after charge, something that *Justice for All* would extend to earlier stages of an investigation. A defendant can be arrested, with or without a warrant of arrest, for breach of a condition, but this is not in itself a criminal offence (unlike absconding, above). Bail can then be revoked by the court to which the defendant is taken by the police.

### Sureties and securities

A frequently used pre-release bail condition is that the defendant put forward a responsible individual who is prepared to vouch for his or her appearance at the end of the remand period—known as a 'surety'. The surety agrees to forfeit a sum of money to the court if the defendant absconds. The sum is set by the court and can be forfeited in whole or in part.[8] Quite distinct is a 'security'. Here, the defendant deposits money or some other valuable form of security with the court as a guarantee that he or she will return to court on the due date. Despite the existence of this provision, English bail arrangements do not, as matter of course, involve deposits of money or valuables (in contrast, e.g. to the position in the USA where the requirement of a bail bond is commonplace).[9]

### Bail information and bail support

Bail information schemes operated, as appropriate, under the auspices of the National Probation Service, HM Prison Service or youth offending teams (YOTs) exist nationwide. These involve obtaining and verifying information about the defendant's circumstances which is relevant to the bail decision and providing this to the CPS and the defence. Possibilities for bail which were not investigated before an initial remand to custody are pursued during the first remand period, e.g. the existence of a fixed address (or sometimes a temporary address but well away from potential witnesses or local feeling), or of a surety, or whilst security is raised (above). The results are placed before the court at the next remand hearing. Many areas of the country operate bail support schemes to work with bailed defendants who might otherwise be at risk of offending if released into the community. Bail schemes may be linked into a range of referral schemes such as those designed to identify and assist people affected by drug misuse.

### Bail hostels

The NPS manages or arranges bail hostel or other accommodation for certain people who are on bail (and also combined community sentence and bail hostels for those on bail, a community rehabilitation order or post-custody supervision). The purpose of a bail hostel is to accommodate people who are awaiting trial or sentence and who require a high level of supervision in the community, not simply defendants who just need a roof over their heads.

---

[8]   Also known as a recognizance.
[9]   The security provisions are, however, frequently used if the defendant lives or may travel abroad. Their under-use in other cases may stem from the somewhat cumbersome nature, for courts, of retaining and accounting for valuables deposited which tend to work against the utility of the provisions.

# MODE OF TRIAL

Mode of trial[10] is a key feature of the early stages of the criminal justice process where the offence is triable either way (*Chapter 1*). A magistrates' court must decide whether—on the face of things—the case appears to be more suitable for trial by magistrates or trial at the Crown Court. In effect, the magistrates' court must predict the likely sentence if the accused person is convicted, i.e. whether or not it is within their maximum powers—at present of six months per offence or 12 months in aggregate (*Chapter 9*) but set to rise if proposals in *Justice for All* are implemented (*Chapter 15*). The defendant also has a free-standing right to claim trial by jury. There are thus the following stages:

- *Mode of trial: Stage 1 'The court decides'*
  The magistrates decide which mode of trial is more suitable by taking a
  provisional view on the seriousness of the offence and the differing powers
  of magistrates and the Crown Court to impose sentence if the defendant is
  convicted. This view is based on a summary of the case by the prosecutor
  and any representations which the defendant wishes to make (e.g. that
  although the offence appears to be serious it is one which raises no great
  complexities and is likely to be well within magistrates' maximum
  sentencing powers). No reference is made to the likely plea at this stage. In
  1995, the Lord Chief Justice issued *National Mode of Trial Guidelines*, which
  indicate factors magistrates should take into account, both generally and in
  relation to particular offences.[11]

- *Mode of trial: Stage 2 'The defendant elects'*
  If the magistrates decide that the offence is more suitable for trial by
  them (summary trial), the defendant still has a right to elect (i.e. choose)
  between trial by magistrates and trial by jury in the Crown Court. He or
  she is told of this right and cautioned by the court legal adviser to the
  effect that even if trial by magistrates is chosen there is nonetheless—in
  the event of conviction—a power to commit to the Crown Court for
  sentence if, at the end of the day, the magistrates' powers turn out to be
  insufficient. This will usually be because unanticipated information later
  emerges to justify this (including the defendant's previous record which
  is not normally seen by the court before the sentence stage) (*Chapter 9*).[12]

  - *Mode of trial: Criminal damage*
  Where the alleged offence is one of criminal damage and it is unclear
  whether the value of the damage is over £5,000, the court can offer to

---

[10] To complicate an already intricate picture, mode of trial can only be fully understood alongside the statutory 'plea before venue' procedure which precedes it. Here, the defendant can intimate a plea of 'guilty' from the outset. This allows magistrates to by-pass mode of trial and move direct to the sentencing stage—including, where appropriate, committing the offender to the Crown Court for sentence. In effect, *Justice for All* would sweep away all such preliminaries in favour of getting the defendant to the right level of court from the outset.

[11] These have not been updated since that time.

[12] The defendant's previous record might be seen at the start, for preliminary purposes, or in certain situations during a trial, if proposals in *Justice for All* are implemented.

treat the case as a summary matter. If the defendant rejects this it is treated as an either way offence.

The mode of trial provisions and the right to elect trial would all be affected by proposals contained in the White Paper *Justice For All*: see *Chapter 15*.

## COMMITTAL FOR TRIAL

Where the magistrates decide at *Stage 1* above that trial by the Crown Court is more appropriate or the defendant elects trial by jury at *Stage 2*, the proceedings turn into committal proceedings, i.e. proceedings with a view to sending the case to the Crown Court for trial by jury. 'Indictable only' offences (*Chapter 1*) *must* be tried in the Crown Court before a judge and jury and are now sent direct to that court once the accused person has appeared before magistrates invariably following arrest by the police. The committal process itself is outlined in *Chapter 3*.

## DISCLOSURE OF THE PROSECUTION CASE

Before a defendant is called upon to make any decision concerning mode of trial in respect of an either way offence, he or she is statutorily entitled to advance disclosure of the prosecution case. This is provided by the prosecutor setting out the main features of the case, usually in a written summary (it can, in appropriate cases, be disclosure of all the evidence available).

The advance disclosure provisions do not apply to purely summary offences or indictable only ones—although, in response to the fair trial provisions of the European Convention On Human Rights, prosecutors regularly provide details in such cases as appropriate. Generally speaking, the defence is under no legal obligation to disclose its hand in advance of the trial (except for the defence of 'alibi' in the Crown Court and cases involving allegations of serious fraud, disclosure of official secrets or relating to the running of companies: all matters beyond the scope of this handbook). *Justice For All* (*Chapter 15*) makes proposals whereby the issues in a case would be identified before a trial proceeds, connoting disclosure on the part of both the prosecution and the defence so as to assist in this process. Defendants would need to disclose the substance of any defence in advance of the trial or risk adverse comment to the jury. Initially, the prosecutor would need to supply the defence with copies of all material relevant to the offence or to the offender or to the surrounding circumstances of the case, whether or not it intended to rely on that material (with special rules, as there are now, for certain sensitive materials). Requests for further disclosure by the defence could then be made on the basis of likely relevance to the line of defence disclosed. This would be accompanied by new pre-trial procedures to assist in clarifying and defining the issues in the case before trial set out in *Practice Directions* and rules of court. At present no such obligations to 'co-operate' are placed upon the defence, although it is possible for courts to draw any legitimate—albeit somewhat unformulated and ill-defined—inferences from silence, either before or during the proceedings, on the part of the accused (*Chapter 1*).

# PRELIMINARY MATTERS

Depending on a myriad of considerations, there may be several stages (usually involving the defendant's attendance at court) between the start of criminal proceedings and the time when the he or she comes to enter his or her plea to an allegation. These depend on the nature of the offence, the precise circumstances and decisions made by the parties. In general terms, *Justice for All* seeks to rationalise these processes and stresses the key importance of effective preliminary hearings (see below). The proceedings follow a pattern determined by rules of court and supplemented locally by agreements (or 'protocols') botwoon oourto and the other agencies concerning, e.g. the expected maximum periods of time for completion of various tasks. Certain cases before magistrates may be 'fast-tracked' to an early first hearing and the defendant given the opportunity to enter a guilty plea at this stage if appropriate (which in turn will attract a sentencing discount: *Chapter 9*). There may also be criminal directions hearings at which administrative matters are considered such as the grant of state funded legal representation (*Chapter 12*) and the likely plea. A plea of guilty can be intimated at this early stage which, in the case of an either way offence, may obviate the need for the court to consider mode of trial (see footnote 10).

In the Crown Court, judges hold preliminary hearings and give directions concerning the course of a case and their expectations of the parties and of their legal representatives in preparing for trial. Legal arguments may also be indicated or rehearsed at this point and the need for any legal research identified. The whole purpose is to eliminate items which might delay or interrupt the proceedings once they reach a court hearing proper, with both justice and financial considerations in mind as matters of public interest. Attempts have been made to enhance this process via the CPS Trial Units already mentioned. *Justice for All* lays stress on the quality of preparation at all stages of the criminal process noting, as a key matter of concern—and as part of its analysis of 'what is not working'—that at present 'no-one has overall responsibility for making sure that the prosecution and the defence are ready to proceed and present their cases properly'.[13]

The proposals in *Justice For All* seek to ensure that all preliminary matters progress in a structured, balanced and expeditious way. The White Paper contrasts the existing largely voluntary nature of pre-trial arrangements with the statutory procedure in relation to serious fraud under which there is a pre-trial hearing, before the jury is sworn in, designed to assist the management of the case and which constitutes the start of the trial proper. This provision apart, there is, at present, no such compulsion in relation to criminal allegations generally. The challenge will be to expedite cases whilst protecting the interests of defendants, victims and justice.

---

[13] A conclusion with which many judges and magistrates might disagree, perhaps, the court having assumed this mantle for many years. What is in issue, maybe, is the effectiveness of that process.

## GUILTY PLEA

The procedures in all criminal courts following a plea of 'guilty' follow a similar pattern. The court moves directly to the sentencing stage (*Chapter 9*). The facts of the case are outlined by the prosecutor and the defendant is invited to add any explanation or make representations—known as 'mitigation'. Mitigation may relate to the *offence* (i.e. where the offender claims that it is less serious than might appear) or the *offender* (his or her personal circumstances are such that a less severe or different kind of penalty should be imposed than might otherwise be the case). Mitigation is usually put forward on the defendant's behalf by his or her barrister or solicitor. A list of any previous convictions is handed to the court, together with other 'antecedent' information and, where applicable, a list of offences which the offender is asking the court to take into consideration (TICs). (*Chapters 6 and 9*).

If the likely sentence is a community sentence or custody, the case will normally be adjourned (i.e. out back for a number of weeks, usually three weeks) for inquiries. In practice, pre-sentence reports (PSRs) (or specific sentence reports (SSRs)) are obtained from the NPS in all the more serious cases—and with the possibility of reports being required from other people such as doctors or psychiatrists (see, further, *Chapters 9 and 13*).

There may be applications for compensation to be paid to the victim and where appropriate the case file will include a 'victim personal statement' (*Chapters 9 and 18*). Additionally, there will be an application for a contribution towards the costs of the prosecution.

### Equivocal plea

A criminal court cannot accept an equivocal plea, i.e. one where the defendant pleads guilty but then adds something which indicates a defence to the allegation or that the plea is being made purely for reasons of convenience (such as 'Yes, I took the goods from the supermarket but I always intended to pay for them' or 'I just want to get it all over with'). The case is put back, normally to a new date, for the defendant to reconsider his or her position, take legal advice (or further legal advice), and, if necessary, for a trial to be held in which the evidence can be fully considered and tested by cross-examination. Equivocal pleas are usually identified at the mitigation stage.

### Credit for a guilty plea

A defendant is entitled to credit for having entered a guilty plea (see *Chapter 9*), something that *Justice For All* would place on a more formal, structured and open footing.

## WRITTEN PLEAS OF GUILTY

A special procedure exists in magistrates' courts under which written pleas of guilty can be accepted by the court and which has been refined and enhanced over the years since 1957 when it was first introduced. The procedure can be invoked by prosecutors in respect of certain summary offences only. Cases dealt with under this procedure are known as 'paperwork' cases.[14]

Such cases must be commenced by way of information and summons (above). The defendant must also be served with a 'statement of facts' which contains a written outline of the circumstances of the offence. If the defendant then pleads guilty in writing, the statement of facts is read out in court together with any written mitigation and financial information put forward in writing by the defendant—a special form being provided for this purpose. The court then sentences the defendant in his or her absence. An application for costs can be made in writing and notice can also be served to cite any relevant previous convictions.

The defendant does not have to plead guilty. This is made clear in the accompanying notice. There are also special procedures covering the situation where the defendant changes his or her mind about the plea, or turns up at court in person wishing to add to what has been set out in writing. There is also flexibility, in that the court can notify the defendant that the case will be dealt with at any time within a span of 28 days and a further procedure whereby the documentation served on the defendant can be used to prove the case in his or her absence if he or she fails to respond. Where the offence is a road traffic matter attracting endorsement of a driving licence, the defendant will also have to send his or her driving licence to the court for mandatory penalty points to be entered on it. If an equivocal plea is discerned in the written mitigation the case will be put back for the defendant to attend court.

Increasingly, many lesser offences are being disposed of by way of the fixed penalty system under which a 'ticket' is issued by a police officer, community support officer, traffic warden or other authorised person.

## NOT GUILTY PLEA

Broadly speaking, the procedure on a plea of 'not guilty' is the same whatever the level of the offence or court. The presumption of innocence applies to all criminal trials (now reinforced by Article 6 of the European Convention On Human Rights). Once such a plea is entered, the prosecutor must establish the allegation by evidence and to the required standard of proof, beyond reasonable doubt (*Chapter 1*). Failing this the accused must be acquitted. The underlying principles are the same for trial by magistrates and trial by jury in the Crown Court—but governed by separate statutory provisions and codes of procedure.

### Case for the prosecution
In the normal course of events, a criminal trial opens with the prosecutor outlining the case to the jury or magistrates. He or she will then call evidence to support the allegation. Usually, this will be the evidence of witnesses which is given on the religious oath of their own choosing—or on affirmation—called 'testimony'. Other forms of evidence include written statements (which are admissible provided certain formalities are complied with and the defence does

---

[14] Alternatively as 'section 12 cases' (after section 12 Magistrates' Courts Act 1980, which sets out the procedure); or MCA cases (after the Magistrates' Courts Act 1957 which first introduced it).

not object);[15] exhibits (such as weapons, drugs, stolen goods or forged documents); and any confession made by the accused person to the police in accordance with PACE (*Chapter 6*), or other admission, formal or informal.[16] There may also be forensic or other expert evidence. Experts apart, evidence must generally be confined to facts not opinions (it being a for the court to rule whether someone is an expert).

Criminal proceedings are adversarial in nature.[17] At the end of the evidence of each witness for the prosecution the defendant or his or her advocate can cross-examine, i.e. ask questions. A purpose is to challenge what has been said, to cast a different light on the evidence being given, to discredit the witness, to show he or she is unreliable, or sometimes that he or she is being deliberately untruthful. The prosecutor may re-examine the witness to clear up any new matters arising from cross-examination. The process is later reversed if there are defence witnesses, when the prosecutor is the one to cross-examine (below).

Witnesses are not normally allowed into court before they give evidence. An example where they might be allowed in earlier is where an expert witness is given permission to observe the evidence of other people so that he or she can comment on it during his or her own evidence and in the light of his or her expertise. All courts now benefit from the existence of the Court Witness Service operated by the charity Victim Support (*Chapter 18*).

## Refreshing memory

Testimony must be given from memory (and, indeed, gains strength from directness and accuracy of recollection)—but a witness can be given permission to refresh his or her memory from a note made at the time of the events under consideration (known as a 'contemporaneous note'). Police officers—who may attend many incidents in the course of their day-to-day duties—are routinely given permission by courts to refer to their notebooks under this rule although this can only occur after the officer has satisfied the court that the note was in fact made reasonably close to the time of the events and from his or her own recollection rather than, e.g. copied from a colleague's account.

## Withdrawal of the case from the jury

In the Crown Court, the judge may withdraw a case from the jury where he or she considers that there is no basis for a prosecution to continue.[18] There is no exact equivalent to this in the magistrates' court but the situation is analogous to the procedure in relation to no case to answer (below)—save that the judge's power extends to withdrawing the case at any time if it becomes clear that there

[15]  Written statements used in trials are often referred to as 'section nines' (after section 9 Criminal Justice Act 1982).

[16]  Controversy has been caused by 'cell confessions' to fellow prisoners under this head, principally because there is a natural suspicion of vested interest (e.g. ensuring early release). Contrast formal admissions which are made expressly for the purposes of the proceedings and normally vetted by a lawyer.

[17]  They are thus criticised by some adherents of restorative justice (*Chapter 18*) in that they are divisive and tend to generate conflict rather than solve problems and repair harm. There is 'no property in a witness', i.e. in principle they belong to neither party and can be called to give evidence by or for either.

[18]  *Justice for All* would allow the prosecutor a right of appeal against a decision to withdraw the case from the jury.

is no basis for continuing with the trial. The judge may also direct the jury to bring in a verdict of not guilty where, legally speaking, this is the correct course.

### No case to answer
Before a defendant is called upon to elect (i.e. decide) whether or not to give evidence there must be a *prima facie* case. There will be no case to answer where the prosecutor has failed to adduce any evidence whatsoever of an essential ingredient of the offence charged (such as no evidence that property which is the subject of an allegation of theft belonged to someone other than the accused person); or where the prosecution witnesses have been shown by defence cross-examination to be so unreliable that no reasonable court could convict on their evidence. The defence may make a submission of 'no case' at the conclusion of the evidence for the prosecution, or the judge or magistrates can (indeed should always) consider, of their own motion, whether there is a *prima facie* case. If not, the case ends there and then. The defendant is discharged and is normally entitled to costs from public funds. Otherwise, the trial continues and the defendant must decide whether or not to give evidence and call other witnesses to the facts or to his or her character.

### Case for the defence
The defendant in a criminal trial is not obliged to give evidence albeit that it is possible for inferences to be drawn if he or she remains silent either during the investigation (*Chapter 6* and *15*) or at the trial (subject to any human rights considerations). Nonetheless, he or she may choose to say nothing at all. The court will then decide the case on the prosecution evidence alone (and any inferences which it may legitimately draw from the defendant's silence). It may be, e.g. that there is a *prima facie* case but that the evidence is weak and, even without any explanation from the defendant would be incapable of satisfying the court beyond reasonable doubt. If the accused does give evidence then the procedure mirrors that outlined in relation to the case for the prosecution. The defendant gives evidence first (in the normal course of events), followed by any other defence witnesses. All will be liable to cross-examination by the prosecutor; this followed by any re-examination by the defendant or his or her legal representative.

Depending on the offence in question, the criminal law recognises a number of general defences such as self-defence, provocation and honest mistake.

### Speeches
As already indicated, the prosecutor will open his or her case with an outline of the allegations. The defendant or his or her representative is allowed a closing speech. This 'last word' in a criminal trial is regarded as a valuable right. But if the defendant puts forward legal argument, the prosecutor will be entitled to answer it, and also to counter any false or misleading impressions created by the accused person or his or her advocate such as an incorrect or misguided summary of the evidence, or pejorative remarks about the victim which the victim is otherwise unable to answer. [19]

---

[19] Variations are possible. These are beyond the scope of this handbook.

## Onus on the defendant

Just occasionally the law reverses the normal onus of proof and the defendant must establish something such as the fact that he or she holds a particular licence, permission or authority or that goods have been properly obtained and are not the proceeds of crime, matters which might appear otherwise from external appearances and which it would be impossible for the prosecutor to know the full truth of without putting the defendant to proof. In such cases the defendant is required to establish the relevant matter on a balance of probabilities (the standard of proof which ordinarily applies in civil cases).

## Verdict

The jury or magistrates must reach their verdict, i.e. determine whether or not the accused person is guilty, based only on the merits of the case. The process can be viewed as involving three steps:

- the court deciding what facts it will accept from the evidence. This will involve decisions not simply about which evidence is true and which false, mistaken or unreliable, but also questions about how much weight to give to individual pieces or strands of evidence.
- deciding whether the facts add up to the offence in question; and
- deciding whether, in all the circumstances, it is satisfied of guilt beyond reasonable doubt.

Alternative verdicts relating to other offences disclosed by the evidence may be returned in the Crown Court (and in limited situations in the magistrates' court). Thus, e.g. where someone is charged with murder the jury can bring in a verdict of manslaughter instead. The scope for alternative verdicts is a legal matter and rests on the nature of the original indictment or charge and the precise nature of the evidence in a given case. Broadly speaking, such verdicts relate to lesser offences of a similar kind encompassed by the same events.

In the Crown Court, the judge will review the evidence and direct the jury on the law (*Chapter 3*). In the magistrates' court this dual process is the responsibility of the magistrates who, technically speaking, 'direct themselves'. In practice any legal considerations are recognised to be the province and responsibility of the court legal adviser (*Chapter 2*).

Conviction leads to sentence. The position is then the same as when the accused enters a plea of 'guilty' (above) except that in the case of a trial the court is likely to have heard far more information about the case. The defendant will also have lost any advantage by way of a 'sentence discount' which might have been gained by a timely guilty plea (*Chapter 9*).

## Acquittal, *autrefois acquit* and *autrefois convict*

An acquittal (or 'dismissal' as it is more commonly called in magistrates' courts) results in the defendant being discharged. He or she will then normally be entitled to costs from public funds. Acquittal does not, strictly speaking, establish innocence—but, as the law stands, a defendant cannot be tried again for the self-same offence or matter—the rule against double jeopardy. This aspect has already been mentioned in *Chapter 1* along with the somewhat controversial proposal in *Justice for All* that this historic rule be abrogated in certain situations.

# CHAPTER 9

# The Sentence of the Court

Sentencing is perhaps the most visible aspect of law and order. It takes place against a background of public interest and concern about offending and often, nowadays, media comment. Criminal justice policy on sentencing is formulated by Acts of Parliament and promulgated via ministerial statements and departmental publications, guidance and information. To this must be added, in the current context, key proposals contained in the 2002 White Paper, *Justice For All*. In 2001 the Home Office published *Making Punishments Work: Report of a Review of the Sentencing Framework for England and Wales* (the Halliday report)[1] which recommended, among other things, a new sentencing framework which should do more to support crime reduction and reparation whilst meeting the needs of punishment. *Justice for All* builds on Halliday. In noting—under the heading 'What is not Working'—that there are 'extreme cases of variation in sentencing in England and Wales' the White Paper indicates that where a defendant is convicted, then, among other things, 'we will':

- focus on dangerous, serious and seriously persistent offenders and those who consistently breach community sentences;
- ensure that dangerous violent and sexual offenders can be kept in custody as long as they present a risk to the public;
- ensure tough, more intensive community sentences with multiple conditions like tagging, reparation and drug treatment and testing to deny liberty, rehabilitate the offender and protect the public; and
- ensure more uniformity in sentencing through a new Sentencing Guidelines Council.

It also proposes three new forms of sentence to be know as 'custody minus', 'custody plus' and 'intermittent custody' terms which are explained along with with notes on both the Halliday report and *Justice For All* in Chapter 15.

**The current arrangements in outline**
Within the legal framework for sentencing, it is the task of judges and magistrates to take into account all proper considerations, to reflect valid public concern and to deal with each case on its own individual facts and merits. The features of each case must be balanced with what are generally referred to as the general aims and objects of sentencing. As explained in *Chapter 4*, *Practice Directions*, guideline judgments and other rulings of the Court of Appeal play a significant part in this process. Sentences and orders in criminal proceedings fall into the following main categories:

---

[1] (2001) London: Home Office. After John Halliday, the senior official involved. The impact could be multi-dimensional in that the jurisdiction of different levels of court may also be affected by other proposals flowing from (but not wholly reflecting) suggestions in Lord Justice Auld's *Review of the Criminal Courts* (2001) *(Chapter 15)*.

- imprisonment (or detention in a young offender institution (YOI) for people aged 18 to 20 years of age) [2]
- community sentences including, e.g. the community rehabilitation order (CRO) and the community punishment order (CPO)
- fines
- compensation (as a penalty in its own right or in addition to punishment, as an ancillary order: see next point) and other orders affecting property
- ancillary orders such as those relating to court costs and disqualification, e.g. from being a company director, from driving, from keeping an animal.

## Maximum sentences

Maximum sentences are fixed by law. Thus, e.g. the Crown Court can, depending on the offence in question, sentence up to the following limits:

- life imprisonment: see below
- 14 years: for offences such as house burglary, blackmail and handling stolen property
- ten years: for offences such as non-domestic burglary, obtaining property by deception, criminal damage and indecent assault on a woman
- seven years: for offences such as theft and false accounting
- five years: as in the case of causing actual bodily harm
- two years: for offences such as carrying an offensive weapon and aggravated vehicle taking.

In the magistrates' court the maximum term of imprisonment for an individual offence is six months; or 12 months in aggregate where consecutive sentences are passed for two or more either way offences as described in *Chapter 2*.

It is common legislative practice for other powers to be fixed by reference to whether or not an offence is imprisonable[3] (e.g. the power to make an attendance centre order or a CPO). Likewise, certain warrants of arrest can only be issued if an offence is imprisonable. Rights to bail are affected in a similar way (*Chapter 8*).

Fines and compensation are generally speaking not limited by statute in the Crown Court, but fines imposed by that court must be reasonable and proportionate to the offence so as to comply with both national sentencing principles and human rights law. Fines and compensation each have a ceiling of £5,000 per offence in the magistrates' court (subject also, in the case of fines imposed by that court, to a table of ceilings set by five statutory fine levels: see later in the chapter).

## Life sentences

Life imprisonment is the *mandatory* sentence for offences of murder committed by people aged 21 and over.[4] In the case of offenders aged 18 to 20 the equivalent mandatory sentence is 'custody for life'; and when the offender is aged ten to 17 'detention during Her Majesty's pleasure'. Life imprisonment is also the

---

[2] YOI is scheduled to be replaced by imprisonment. The difference is likely to be more in the classification of the establishment where the sentence is served than in the nature and effect of the sentence itself.

[3] i.e. the fact that an offence attracts imprisonment not necessarily that it will be imposed.

[4] See also *Chapter 14* which contains a short note on life sentence regimes.

maximum penalty that a court may pass for a number of other serious crimes, including manslaughter, robbery, rape, buggery, various assaults and certain firearms offences—when it is known as a discretionary life sentence.

A life sentence is indeterminate. In the case of mandatory sentences of life imprisonment or custody for life the Home Secretary sets a 'tariff', i.e. the minimum term that must be served by way of punishment before the prisoner can be considered for release, following which release may be authorised only by the Home Secretary and following a favourable recommendation from the Parole Board. Where offenders receive discretionary life sentences or a juvenile receives a sentence of detention during Her Majesty's pleasure the trial judge specifies a 'tariff'—at the end of which the prisoner is considered for release on licence. In these cases the release decision is made by the Parole Board, which can direct the Home Secretary to release the prisoner on licence if it is satisfied that it is no longer necessary for the protection of the public that he or she should continue to be confined. Whilst in prison lifers are subject to a special HM Prison Service life sentence regime which includes ongoing risk assessment and, other things being equal, progress through various stages and categories of prison establishment.[5] On release a lifer remains on licence for the rest of his or her natural life and is liable to recall at any time.

### 'Natural lifers'

The vast majority of life sentence prisoners are eventually released on life licence as already noted above. However, a small number of mandatory lifers (the figure is thought to be around 25 people) have been told by the Home Secretary that they will, literally, spend the rest of their lives in prison. They include the serial killer Dr. Harold Shipman, the 'moors murderer' Myra Hindley, multiple murderer Rosemary West and kidnapper and murderer Michael Sams.

### 'Two strikes' compulsory lifers

Since 1998 under what is often called the 'two strikes' law presumptive or compulsory life sentences apply to certain offenders convicted of one of a range of serious offences for a second time. Although such sentences are sometimes called 'mandatory', they are administered as discretionary life sentences and are therefore to be distinguished from the mandatory life sentence for murder. Also, a two strikes life sentence may have a tariff which is set relatively low depending on the overall circumstances of the 'two strikes' in question.

## THE SENTENCING FRAMEWORK

The current sentencing arrangements stem from the Criminal Justice Act 1991[6] which enacted the first comprehensive English sentencing framework. It set out criteria and thresholds for different levels of sentence: discharges, fines and

---

[5]   For an overview see *Murderers and Life Imprisonment: Containment, Treatment, Safety and Risk* (1998), Cullen E and Newell T, Winchester: Waterside Press. The Home Secretary's power to set the tariff for mandatory sentences of life imprisonment and custody for life has several times been challenged, as yet unsuccessfully, in the ECHR, he having lost powers to the judiciary in comparable circumstances. Also suspect is the right to set a 'full life tariff' (see text).

[6]   Now consolidated in the Powers of Criminal Courts (Sentencing) Act 2000.

compensation, community penalties (where the offence is 'serious enough') and custody (where it is 'so serious that only a custodial sentence can be justified'), together with a discernible sentencing philosophy geared primarily to the seriousness of offences or, in the case of violent or sexual offences, the need to protect the public from serious harm from the offender.

In broad terms, sentences are measured in terms of their impact by the extent to which they restrict the liberty of the offender. In general—and consistently with the jurisprudence of the European Court of Human Rights—their impact must be commensurate with—or proportionate to—the seriousness of the offence under consideration, known as the 'just deserts' approach. As already indicated, where the offence is a violent or sexual offence, custody can also be used to protect the public from serious harm from the offender so that the offender can be held for longer than would have been justified by the seriousness of the offence alone.

The 1991 Act (as later amended) thus represented a considerable landmark. It contained not just a new framework but many new procedures and required new ways of thinking on the part of judges and magistrates. However, despite an at first progressive stance amongst some sections of the judiciary the then Conservative government[7] reversed major aspects of it in 1993. The sentencing climate then hardened throughout the remainder of the 1990s notably through the 'tough on crime' and 'prison works' stance of then Home Secretary, Michael Howard MP. One consequence was that the prison population rose by over 30 per cent to its present record level of around 71,500 (mid-2002). The Government has intimated that this could continue to rise: to 75,000 or more within five years.

## The sentencing framework in outline[8]

The present sentencing framework can be summarised as follows:

- **DISCHARGES**: where punishment is 'inexpedient'.
- **FINES**: where, by implication, punishment *is* expedient (but more severe punishment is inappropriate). The size of a fine must reflect the seriousness of the offence *and* the offender's financial circumstances.
- **COMMUNITY SENTENCES**: where the offence is 'serious enough'. The degree of 'restriction of liberty' must be commensurate with the seriousness of the offence *and* the particular order or orders which is or are suitable for the offender.
- **CUSTODY**:
  — where the offence is 'so serious' that *only* such a sentence can be justified; or
  — if the offence is a sexual or violent one (as defined by statute) and where 'only such a sentence would be adequate to protect the public from serious harm' from the offender; or
  — where the offender has refused to consent to (one of the few) types of community sentence which still require such consent.

---

[7] Which was itself responsible for the 1991 Act! For an analysis see *Crime, State and Citizen: A Field Full of Folk* (2001), Faulkner D, Winchester: Waterside Press; *Criminal Justice in Transition* (1994), Ashworth, A *et al*, Winchester: Waterside Press.

[8] Based on *The Sentence of the Court* (Revised reprint, 2002), Gibson B (ed.), Winchester: Waterside Press (which contains further details about many of the items covered in this chapter).

The *length* of a custodial sentence must be commensurate with the seriousness of the offence or, as appropriate, the need to protect the public from serious harm from a sexual or violent offender.

## GENERAL CONSIDERATIONS

Quite apart from statutory sentencing considerations, there are certain generally understood objects of sentencing that, historically speaking, have formed the backdrop to sentencing in so far as they are consistent with the relevant legislation. Different aspects come to the fore from time-to-time according to the judicial or political mood and some of them, or the inter-relationship between them, can be contentious. They include matters such as the need for punishment, retribution, rehabilitation, to protect the public, prevent crime, demonstrate public concern and deter offenders (perhaps the most controversial object of all in that the link between a sentence and the future behaviour of an offender, not to mention any link with the future behaviour of other people, is notoriously tenuous). With youth justice, the principal statutory purpose is now to prevent offending (which must be reconciled with other key aims: *Chapter 5*).

### Previous convictions
It is the practice *after* conviction[9] for the sentencing judge or magistrates to consider the offender's 'character and antecedents', including his or her previous convictions if any. These can be taken into account when assessing the seriousness of the present offence—as can failures to respond to previous sentences. It is over ten years now since the 1991 Act was implemented but there has never been a legal ruling on the scope of the previous conviction rules as established by that Act. The Magistrates' Association once advised its members that they:

> . . . should clearly identify which convictions or failures are relevant for this purpose and then consider what the effect of such convictions or failures is in relation to seriousness.

An example would be if they indicated a pattern of calculation or pre-meditation which would be an aggravating factor, or where a juvenile qualifies as a 'persistent offender' (see *Chapter 5*).

### Offences taken into consideration (TICs)
The prosecutor may also produce a list of TICs. The non-statutory practice of a defendant asking for outstanding offences—for which he or she has not been prosecuted—to be taken into consideration developed as a way of encouraging offenders 'to make a clean breast' of matters. Although not restricted in scope, applications are commonplace where the main prosecuted offences and the TICs are triable either way and similar in kind (in practice usually 'a string of similar

---

[9] Currently, previous convictions are only rarely admissible *before* conviction, e.g. where a defendant puts forward evidence of his or her own 'good character', or attacks the character of a prosecution witness. *Justice For All* proposes allowing such information to be given *during* a criminal trial 'where relevant': *Chapters 1* and *15*.

offences'). Endorsable motoring offences may become TICs if the principal offence carries a power to disqualify. The defendant is usually asked to sign a written list in which the TICs are set out. In the event of a refusal to accept them, the prosecutor must decide whether to bring charges or alternatively to let matters drop.

### Pre-sentence reports (PSRs)

In practice, a PSR is needed in all the more serious cases. Although a PSR can be deemed by the court to be unnecessary in an individual case, such a report remains desirable in most situations where imprisonment or the more severe forms of community sentence are a potential outcome. The main purpose of a PSR (together in some cases with a separate medical or psychiatric assessment) is to assist the court in arriving at an appropriate sentencing decision. PSRs are prepared by probation officers from the National Probation Service (*Chapter 13*)[10] in accordance with *National Standards*. Alternatively, courts may receive a specific sentence report (SSR), which is more focused and directed towards the suitability for the offender of a particular type of community penalty.

The court is required to give a copy of the report to the offender or his or her legal representative. The Crime (Sentences) Act 1997 provides for the disclosure of PSRs to prosecutors, the purpose being to assist prosecutors in their duty to challenge any misleading or inaccurate information put before the court, or any improper mitigation (*Chapter 8*). The information in a PSR is likely to include:

- an analysis of the current offence (or offences) and the circumstances leading up to it. This includes matters such as an assessment of the degree of premeditation, the impact of the offence on the victim, the offender's attitude to the offence, and any special circumstances (e.g. family crisis, alcohol, drugs, physical or mental health problems) which are directly relevant to the offending.
- relevant information about the offender, including an evaluation of his or her previous patterns of offending (if any), the results of previous sentences and any personal or social information which is relevant to past offending, to the likelihood or otherwise of reoffending or to any community sentence which the PSR proposes for consideration
- an assessment of the risk to the public of reoffending by the offender, including the likelihood of further offences, the nature and seriousness of such offences, the offender's capacity and motivation to change and the availability of programmes which could reduce the risk or impact of further offending.
- information about a suitable community punishment which could be passed on the offender if the court sees fit. Where this involves a community order involving supervision, the report contains an outline of the supervision plan including the aims of the programme, the methods to be used, the likely impact on offending and the steps to be taken if the offender does not comply.

---

[10] Or in the case of juvenile offenders by a member of a local youth offending team (YOT) (when stricter legal rules also exist concerning when PSRs can be dispensed with: *Chapter 5*).

## Charges left on the file

In the Crown Court charges are sometimes ordered by the judge to be left on file after the accused has been convicted of some but not all of the charges. Where, e.g. a substantial prison term is imposed for one or more offences and it would be pointless pursuing the remaining matters at that time these outstanding items are left in abeyance. If that person later successfully appeals against conviction the outstanding matters might then be revived.

## Mandatory seriousness factors

When sentencing, an offence must be treated as more serious if it was committed whilst on bail (*Chapter 8*) or it is a racially aggravated offence (*Chapter 16*)

## Discount for a guilty plea

Courts must normally give credit (or 'discount') for a timely plea of guilty of up to around one-third (a principal which would be built on and structured under the Auld proposals as refined in *Justice For All:* see *Chapters 1* and *15*).

## No separate penalty

In magistrates' courts the practice of imposing 'no separate penalty' (NSP) is regularly used. The device is employed when a defendant stands convicted of several offences but the totality of the offending behaviour can be dealt with by sentencing for the main offences and marking others NSP. This non-statutory approach might be used, e.g. where there is a catalogue of motoring or other minor offences, but where justice can be done by sentencing for just some of them.

# BINDING OVER TO KEEP THE PEACE

The ancient jurisdiction to bind over citizens can be used to mark behaviour which might lead to a breach of the peace—called 'preventive justice'. It stems from the Justices of the Peace Act 1361. Bind overs have, however, been somewhat curtailed by human rights considerations. No longer can courts bind over people *to be of good behaviour* but only *to keep the peace* and in clear and precise terms.[11] A bind over can be used on its own, or in conjunction with separate punishment for criminal offences. It can be made on application by a private individual (e.g. a neighbour or partner), or of the court's own volition, as where someone is acquitted of an offence but the evidence leaves cause for concern. The defendant is required to enter into a recognizance (an acknowledgement of indebtedness to the Sovereign in a sum fixed by the court). If he or she breaches the order during a period set by the court (often 12 months) the court may order forfeiture (also called 'estreatment') of all or part of the sum originally fixed. If someone refuses to be bound over they can be imprisoned under procedures akin to those for contempt of court.

---

[11] The need to rely on this longstanding if somewhat controversial power has receded since the Protection From Harassment Act 1997 under which the court, in addition to standard punishments, can make a restraining order, breach of which is a further criminal offence; and since 1996 a readily accessible family jurisdiction to make 'non-molestation' orders.

## COMPENSATION

By law, compensation to a victim of crime ('the aggrieved') must come before any punishment by way of a fine. It should also be an automatic consideration in all other cases. Compensation may be used in addition to any other method of dealing with the offender, or can stand alone as a sentence. Courts must give reasons for *not* awarding compensation where they could have done so: see *Chapter 18* where the Government's determination to place victims and witnesses at the heart of the criminal justice process, as stated in *Justice for All*, is also noted.

## DISCHARGES

Discharges can be used where punishment is 'inexpedient'.

### Absolute discharge
An absolute discharge signifies a technical offence or extreme triviality. It puts matters at an end, and involves the offender in no further obligations or liability—other than that it ranks (as all sentences now do) as a conviction for the purposes of a criminal record.

### Conditional discharge
An offender may be conditionally discharged for up to three years. The condition is that he or she does not commit another criminal offence in that period. The discharge will then lapse. If a fresh offence is committed during the period fixed by the court, the offender can be sentenced afresh for the offence in respect of which the conditional discharge was made. The offender will then face sentence for two matters, the old and the new. Conditional discharges also rank as convictions.

## FINES

As already indicated, fines are generally unlimited in the Crown Court. In the magistrates' court (where they are used for vast numbers of offences) the maximum amount of a fine is determined under the statute creating the offence by reference to the one of five levels, currently:

| | |
|---|---|
| Level 1 | £100 |
| Level 2 | £200 |
| Level 3 | £1,000 |
| Level 4 | £2,500 |
| Level 5 | £5,000 |

### Guideline fines
All magistrates' courts use sentencing guidelines. These are likely to be (or to be based on) the *Magistrates' Courts Sentencing Guidelines* published by the Magistrates' Association with input from a range of interested parties and endorsed by the Lord Chancellor. The current guidelines were issued in 2000 and

it can be anticipated that any future guidelines will be issued under the auspices or in conjunction with a national Sentencing Guidelines Council as proposed in *Justice for All* (*Chapter 15*). They concentrate on the seriousness of particular offences and usually suggest a penalty (or sentencing 'entry point') for an average offence of the type in question. The court should then weigh aggravating and mitigating factors in an individual case, including any special considerations relating to a particular offence, locally or nationally. Fines must *reflect* the seriousness of the offence and take account of the offender's financial circumstances where these are known.[12] Magistrates may make a financial circumstances order requiring the offender to disclose the necessary details. Failure to comply is an offence, as is making a false declaration.

## Enforcement

Financial orders, whether imposed in the Crown Court or magistrates' court, are enforced and collected by the magistrates' court and under the direction of the justices' chief executive of the relevant magistrates' courts committee (MCC) (*Chapter 2*). *Justice For All* proposes that fines which are not paid on time should attract a surcharge.

Enforcement is by way of a 'means inquiry', i.e. a court hearing to which the defaulter is summoned to give an explanation for non-payment. The main enforcement methods are: attachment of earnings order (AEO); distress warrant (i.e. sending in the bailiffs); money payment supervision order (MPSO); attachment of state benefits; and committal to prison.

Imprisonment in default can only be ordered where there has been wilful refusal or culpable neglect to pay—and, in effect, where the court has tried or eliminated for good reason all other methods and given the defaulter every opportunity to pay or to explain his or her default. The maximum term of imprisonment in default is directly related to the amount outstanding and ranges up to 45 days for fines imposed by magistrates' courts. Longer default periods can be used where the fine was imposed by the Crown Court in a substantial amount (up to ten years). Committal can be suspended on terms, e.g. £10 a week, in which case the warrant will not be issued unless there is further default in payment. If there *is*, the situation must be reviewed again by the court. Failing successful representations or explanations, the warrant committing the defaulter to prison can then be issued. Committal in default of payment is available where the offender is aged 18 or over, but defaulters under 21 year of age are currently detained in YOIs, as opposed to a prison.[13] There are well in excess of 20,000 committals a year for fine default, usually for short periods but a defaulter can, in effect, buy himself or herself out of prison by paying the balance due. There are generally only a small number of defaulters in prison at any one time solely for default and usually for what some commentators consider to be pointlessly short periods that are also disruptive in terms of the overall management of prisons.

---

[12] A statutory 'unit fines' system introduced by the Criminal Justice Act 1991 was abolished in 1993. In setting a unit fine, courts decided on a number of units (usually on a scale from one to 50) reflecting the seriousness of the offence and then calculated the value of each unit in line with the disposable income of an individual offender. The scheme became quite popular in its non-statutory pre-1991 format, but the statutory version attracted a criticism from the public and media following peculiar outcomes at some courts.

[13] See footnote 2.

# COMMUNITY SENTENCES

There are six community sentences in the case of an adult offender.[14] Before any of these can be used the offence must be 'serious enough' to merit this. The restriction of liberty imposed by the order or orders chosen must be commensurate with the seriousness of the offence and the order or orders must be the most suitable for the offender. The adult community orders are:

- community rehabilitation order (CRO)
- community punishment order (CPO)
- community punishment and rehabilitation order (CP&RO)
- curfew order (with or without electronic monitoring)
- attendance centre order (under 21 years only)
- drug treatment and testing order (under 18 years only).

Each of the main orders is governed by an NPS *National Standard*.

### Community rehabilitation order (CRO)
A CRO (formerly known as a probation order) can be made for from six months to three years in respect of an offender aged 16 or over. The statutory purposes are:

- to secure the rehabilitation of the offender
- to protect the public from serious harm from the offender
- to prevent the commission by him or her of further offences.

*Requirements*
The order places the offender under the supervision of a probation officer. Standard conditions are normally attached, e.g. to report to a probation officer and to receive visits from him or her at home. Extra conditions can be added and more sophisticated forms of CRO (sometimes called 'intensive supervision') involve extra requirements:

- *a requirement as to residence.* This could be:
  — residence in an approved probation hostel managed by the NPS or a voluntary organization
  — residence at a non-approved hostel or other institution such as a dependency clinic which may tackle drug and alcohol addictions (some of these are commercial ventures)
  — a requirement to reside where directed by the probation officer. This is likely to be in the offender's home area or at a private address which is considered suitable by the probation officer. The requirement will restrict the offender from moving without first seeking approval from the officer
- *a requirement to attend either a probation/rehabilitation centre or other specified activities for up to 60 days*
  — such a centre is a resource approved by the Home Secretary offering an intensive programme which addresses offending behaviour and its

---

[14] For the range of such sentences for juveniles see *Chapter 5.*

causes. Offenders are expected to attend for a full day (up to 60 days in all) to complete the programme

— specified activities are approved by the local probation board. Offenders can be required to attend, e.g. an alcohol education group, an offending behaviour group, an anger management group, a substance misuse group

— there is an exception to the 60 day maximum rule in the case of sex offenders, when there is no upper limit on the number of days for which attendance can be required (subject to this not exceeding the length of the CRO)

• *a requirement to receive treatment for a mental condition* This can only be used when the court has an assessment from a psychiatrist and treatment is available. Again, the requirement can be for the whole length of the order or for a part of this time as specified by the court

• *a requirement to receive treatment for drug or alcohol dependency.* This refers to day or residential facilities—usually for the seriously addicted. There is no restriction on the length of the requirement.

The emphasis is on confronting offending behaviour, i.e. getting the offender to face up to his or her own wrongdoings, and working to prevent future offending. There is also a restorative element (*Chapter 18*) in some situations, with offenders being encouraged to make reparation and to apologise to victims, usually in writing and only when it is appropriate for such contact, which is always carefully managed. An underlying rationale of many community penalties is that a change in behaviour requires effort and commitment on the part of the offender— something not easily generated by imprisonment. Another trend is for the NPS to become the manager of resources and facilities—forging partnerships with other people and organizations, including the private sector or voluntary sector—as opposed to being the sole provider (*Chapter 17*).[15]

*Breach of the order*
Breach by failing to comply with the terms of a CRO renders the offender liable to a fine, a community punishment order (below) or attendance centre order (under 21 year olds only: below), with the CRO continuing—or to the replacement of the CRO with a new sentence for the original offence. This decision will depend, e.g. on the seriousness of the breach, the attitude of the offender to the order and the supervising officer's report to the court. Special provisions apply where an offender breaches an order of another magistrates' court or of the Crown Court.

*Commission of a further offence*
A further offence committed during the operational period of the CRO does not, in itself, render the offender liable to re-sentencing for the offence for which the CRO was made. Everything depends on whether the supervised person is regarded, overall, as being in breach of the requirements of his or her CRO.

---

[15] See, generally, *Chapter 17*. For further information about the work of the NPS see *Introduction to the Probation Service* (1998), Whitfield D, Second edition, Winchester: Waterside Press; (2001) enhanced reprint with additional material by Nellis M.

## Community punishment order (CPO)

The CPO was introduced in 1973 (and until 2001 was known as community service[16]) as a form of punishment with in-built reparation. A CPO can be made in respect of an adult for between 40 and 240 hours to be completed within 12 months. The offender carries out unpaid work in the community, several hours per session. The offence must be 'imprisonable'. An assessment of the offender's suitability for the order from the NPS must be considered. Work has to be available.

### Breach of the order

The offender can either be fined for the breach or be re-sentenced for the original offence. In the first situation, the CPO continues.

## Community punishment and rehabilitation order (CP&RO)

The CP&RO (formerly called the combination order) combines between one and three years community rehabilitation with between 40 and 100 hours community punishment. This is the only way in which the two limbs of the order can be combined. The result is a high level of restriction of liberty, particularly if conditions are attached to the CRO part.

## Curfew

Courts can make curfew orders for between two and 12 hours in any day. In the case of an adult the maximum period of the order is six months. A curfew order may include requirements for securing the offender's whereabouts during curfew periods. This can involve fitting an electronic tag on the ankle or wrist and installing a monitoring unit, usually at the offender's home, known as 'tagging'.[17]

## Attendance centre order

This order is described under the heading *Young Offenders*, below.

## Drug treatment and testing order

The court can make a drug treatment and testing order for a period of between six months and three years. This sentence is intended for drug-related offenders and carries with it the power of regular sampling and—significantly—a review by the court at not more than three monthly intervals. The NPS, together with other suitable agencies, is responsible for supervising and implementing orders.

## IMPRISONMENT

Imprisonment has for many years been seen as a sentence of last resort.[18] Under the Criminal Justice Act 1991, the offence must be *so serious* that no other sentence

---

[16] And originally conceived as an 'alternative to custody': see *Paying Back: Twenty Years of Community Service* (1993), Whitfield, D and Scott, D, Winchester: Waterside Press. Coming full circle, the tenor of *Justice for All* is that community punishments can be reparative and an alternative to custody.

[17] See *The Magic Bracelet: Technology and Offender Supervision* (2001), Whitfield, D, Winchester: Waterside Press.

[18] Prison regimes are described in *Chapter 14* along with a short outline of the scheme for release whereby, after a period in custody, a portion of most prison sentences is served in the community.

can be justified. A special additional rule applies to most sexual or violent offences, where the court may also order a prison sentence—or one longer than is indicated by the seriousness of the offence—to protect the public from serious harm from the offender.[19]

An offender can also be imprisoned if he or she refuses consent to a community sentence which requires consent (though few now do) or in analogous circumstances on breach of a community order.

If imprisonment is used, the court must give its reasons for this. State funded legal representation (*Chapter 12*) must be offered and a PSR should normally be considered (but can be dispensed with if deemed unnecessary). Where there are several offences, separate terms of imprisonment for each offence can be made concurrent or consecutive and an earlier suspended sentence (below) being put into effect at the same time can be added to the total length of imprisonment imposed for current offences.

### Suspended imprisonment

Imprisonment may be suspended for between one and two years. The court must first be satisfied that *imprisonment* is appropriate—and then go on to decide that, in the circumstances, it is correct to suspend its operation. There must be 'exceptional circumstances' for the suspension. If the court suspends the sentence, it must consider imposing a fine (and effectively compensation) in addition. Reasons for imprisonment must first be announced, even though sentence is suspended, extra reasons being given for this.

If the offender commits another imprisonable offence within the operational period of the suspended sentence, that sentence falls to be activated. Normally it *will* be activated unless there is a cogent reason for not doing so. The reason must be announced by the court. The court can choose to: 'take no action' (an actual form of disposal); to alter the operational period (including, in effect, by re-starting it for a new two year period); or to activate the sentence for a shorter term than that originally imposed and suspended. An activated sentence can be made concurrent or consecutive to any other sentence of imprisonment.

### Committal to the Crown Court for sentence

Where magistrates consider that a sentence longer than six months (or 12 months in aggregate) is required the offender can be committed to the Crown Court for sentence, provided that at least one of the offences is triable either way. This may occur at the 'plea before venue stage' (see *Chapter 8*) or following conviction where the magistrates have adopted summary trial.[20]

## COSTS AND WITNESS EXPENSES

Costs including the expenses incurred by witnesses in attending court to give evidence may be awarded against either party according to the outcome of the

---

[19] *Justice for All* proposes a new sentence to ensure that dangerous violent and sexual offenders stay in custody for as long as they present a risk to society.

[20] Committal for sentence would disappear amongst the changes in jurisdiction and procedure envisaged by *Justice for All*.

case and events which occurred during the proceedings. Where a defendant is acquitted, or the case is withdrawn, abandoned or discontinued, he or she is normally entitled to his or her costs from public funds. Costs can be ordered to be paid by the CPS, police or other prosecutor in an appropriate situation. Conversely, a convicted defendant risks having to pay all or part the costs of the prosecution, including those of any civilian (as opposed to police) witnesses.

## OTHER ANCILLARY ORDERS

Apart from costs, other ancillary orders include such diverse matters as driving disqualification or the endorsement of penalty points on a driving licence; other disqualifications, e.g. from being a company director following a conviction for fraud; restitution orders in respect of stolen property; deprivation, forfeiture or confiscation orders with regard to a range of articles such as offensive weapons, drugs, forged documents and implements used to commit or attempt crime, or in some situations with regard to the proceeds of crime. Often, in the case of a foreign national, a sentence of imprisonment will be accompanied by a recommendation that thereafter the offender by deported to his or her own country. The final decision is then one for the Home Secretary.

## MODERN DEPARTURES

A trend is discernible in some modern legislation of dealing with given behaviour via civil and criminal powers enacted alongside one another or in a linked way. Thus, a restraining order can be made under the Protection From Harassment Act 1997 in either civil or criminal proceedings. This prohibits further specified conduct by the offender. Breach of a restraining order, whether originally made in criminal or civil proceedings, is a criminal offence.[21] Under the Football (Disorder) Act 2000 a criminal court must, in certain situations, make a criminal banning order where someone has been convicted of a football-related offence connected with a regulated football match (i.e. a match in England and Wales or abroad involving a team from the Premier League, Football League or Conference). However, the police can apply for a civil banning order where it appears to them that someone has at any time caused or contributed to any violence (not necessarily football-related) in the United Kingdom or elsewhere. Breach of either order attracts the same criminal sanction of up to six months' imprisonment or a fine of £5,000. The existence of criminal sanctions on breach of civil anti-social behaviour orders has already been mentioned in *Chapter 1*.

## MENTAL IMPAIRMENT

The mental impairment of an accused person can affect criminal proceedings at several points, including diversion from the criminal justice process altogether

---

[21]  Although it remains for the provision making breach of a restraining order made in civil proceedings a criminal offence.

into hospital or other facilities (*Chapters* 6 and 7). Similarly, an accused person may be unfit to plead, or raise the defence of insanity—either of which will normally result in him or her being detained without limit of time. Diminished responsibility, which may be transient, is a defence to murder and, if successful, reduces a conviction to manslaughter thereby giving the judge a discretion concerning the type and length of sentence (as opposed to a mandatory life sentence for murder: see earlier in the chapter). Mental health legislation allows courts to deal with cases in a variety of ways when problems arise from the defendant's mental state. This includes power to make hospital orders or guardianship orders (usually supervised by a local authority). Conditions of treatment for a person's mental state can also be attached to CROs (see above).

Reports are usually obtained from psychiatrists before a decision is made and a court considering sending someone to prison who appears to be suffering from mental disorder must obtain and consider such a report before making that decision. If an offender is sent to a hospital, a judge of the Crown Court can make an order restricting discharge by the authorities.

## DEFERMENT OF SENTENCE

Deferment is designed to deal with the situation where—because of what a court has discovered about the offender—it considers that it is proper to postpone the sentencing decision '(a) to have regard . . . to his conduct after conviction (including, where appropriate, the making by him of any reparation for his offence); or (b) to any change in his circumstances'. The defendant must consent to the deferment. The maximum period for which sentence can be deferred is six months. There is no power to remand an offender or make him or her subject to any requirements or restrictions during the deferment period and the court, in deferring sentence, cannot make ancillary orders except for an interim driving disqualification or a restitution order. In addition:

- deferment may only be used *once* in respect of any offence. There are no restrictions as to the kind of offence.
- the court must ensure that the offender understands exactly what is being proposed and to what he or she is being asked to consent. The general principle is that offenders have a right to know their fate as soon as possible after conviction.
- the interests of the victim must be considered. Postponing sentence may mean postponing formal compensation (although there has been a fresh emphasis on reparation since the Powers of Criminal Courts (Sentencing) Act 2000).
- the court must give reasons for the deferment.

Some specific object should be in mind, and whether or not this has been met will need to be assessed at the end of the deferment period. There is then normally a new PSR charting the offender's progress or otherwise.

# YOUNG OFFENDERS

Offenders aged 18 but under 21 are termed 'young offenders' or 'young adult offenders'. The underlying position in relation to the 18 to 20 age group is broadly the same as that in relation to offenders aged 21 and over as already set out above. There are the following main differences:

- *Detention in a young offender institution (YOI)* Offenders under 21 cannot be sentenced to imprisonment but can be ordered to be detained in a YOI. There is a minimum sentence of two months. As with imprisonment, magistrates' maximum powers are six months, or normally 12 months where there are two or more either way offences. There is power to commit to the Crown Court for sentence. The restrictions on custody are the same as for imprisonment. Again, magistrates must give reasons and explain these in ordinary language. The court must obtain a PSR (above) unless it considers this to be unnecessary (which, given the age of offenders in this category, would be unusual); and state funded legal representation must be offered. Detention in a YOI is scheduled to be replaced by imprisonment for those aged 18 to 20 inclusive.
- *No suspended sentence* It not possible to pass a suspended sentence of detention in a YOI (even though detention for non-payment of fine *can* be suspended).
- *Attendance centres* These are places where offenders attend for two or three hours at a time for a mix of rigorous physical activity and instruction. They are administered by the Home Office and usually operated by the police, often on a Saturday afternoon and using, e.g. school premises. There are single sex (male or female) and mixed centres. Those for this age group are termed 'senior attendance centres'. The offence must be imprisonable—but the order can also be used for fine default (up to the age of 25) and breach of a community rehabilitation order. The maximum aggregate hours of attendance are 36 and the minimum 12. Offenders meet their own costs and journey times are not deducted from the hours set out in the order.

*Justice for All* advances the idea of a 'going straight' contract for young offenders, tailored to the individual and using an integrated approach to rehabilitation and reducing offending—to complement the proposed sentence of 'custody plus', and operate across the entire sentence (*Chapter 15*).

# THE SENTENCING ADVISORY PANEL

The Sentencing Advisory Panel is an independent public body charged by the Home Office with encouraging consistency in sentencing throughout the criminal courts. *Justice for All* proposes a Sentencing Guidelines Council to set guidelines for sentencing across the full range of offences. The council will be chaired by the Lord Chief Justice and members will be drawn from the Court of Appeal, High Court, Crown Court and magistrates' courts. It will have a responsibility to publish its guidelines in a way that is easily accessible to the public as well as to the judiciary and legal practitioners.

# CHAPTER 10

# Appeal and Review

It is fundamental in a democratic state that methods exist by which the decisions of courts can be challenged, reviewed and where wrong corrected. Various national channels of appeal are open to people convicted and sentenced by the Crown Court or a magistrates' court against conviction or sentence. Appeals may be based on the facts (sometimes called 'the merits') of a case, the relevant law or both—when the appeal is described as involving questions of mixed fact and law. National courts now apply English law in the light of the European Convention On Human Rights (*Chapters 1* and *4*). Miscarriages of justice can be corrected by the Court of Appeal following a reference to it of a case by the Criminal Cases Review Commission (CCRC). *Justice for All* proposes giving the prosecutor a right of appeal where the judge withdraws a case from the jury.

## APPEALS TO THE COURT OF APPEAL

Anyone convicted and sentenced by the Crown Court can appeal to the Court of Appeal against conviction, sentence or both. The Court of Appeal (Criminal Division) is situated in the Royal Courts of Justice in London ('The Strand'). Courts are constituted by the Lord Chief Justice and Lords Justices of Appeal assisted by High Court judges as required.[1] A further appeal may be made to the House of Lords when it has been certified by the Court of Appeal that a point of law of general public importance is involved and either the Court of Appeal or the House of Lords grants leave to appeal.

### Appeals against conviction
A defendant may appeal against his or her conviction as of right on any question of law (e.g. whether the judge properly directed the jury by correctly outlining the ingredients of the offence). In cases which involve questions of fact (e.g. whether the jury should have convicted on the evidence) the offender may only appeal if he or she obtains a certificate from the trial judge that the case is fit for appeal or, more usually, obtains leave from the Court of Appeal itself. Originally, the governing statute, the Criminal Appeal Act 1968, provided that:

- a conviction should be set aside on the grounds that in all the circumstances of the case it was unsafe or unsatisfactory

---

[1] For an outline of judicial personnel see *Chapter 12*.

- the judgment of the court of trial should be set aside on the grounds of a wrong decision on any question of law; or on the basis that there was a material irregularity in the course of the trial.

Somewhat tortuously, the court could also dismiss an appeal when, although there had been a wrong decision on a point of law or irregularity in the trial, it considered no miscarriage of justice had actually occurred. Following the report of the Royal Commission on Criminal Justice (*Chapter 15*) and subsequent amendments to the 1968 Act contained in the Criminal Appeal Act 1995, the law was simplified so that there is now a single requirement, i.e. that the court shall allow an appeal against conviction if it thinks that the conviction is unsafe.

### Appeal against sentence
Appeals against sentence to the Court of Appeal always require the leave of the Court of Appeal. The Court may quash a sentence imposed by the Crown Court and in its place substitute any sentence which that court could have imposed. It must exercise its powers so that, taking the case as a whole, the applicant is not more severely dealt with on appeal than he or she was dealt with by the Crown Court. The prosecutor may however in effect appeal against an 'over-lenient' sentence in certain situations (below).

### Application for leave to appeal
In order to obtain leave from the Court of Appeal, the appellant must within 28 days of conviction or sentence file an application for leave and notice of the grounds of appeal. The application is considered by a single judge on the basis of a written application for leave and any supporting material sent with the application. If the single judge refuses the application, the appellant may apply to the full court against that decision. In order to discourage appellants who have no chance of success, the single judge or the full court may direct that time spent in custody pending the appeal hearing shall not count towards the sentence. However, this power is not often exercised and may now, in any event, have human rights implications.

### Procedure on appeal
The hearing of the appeal is by a court of three judges. They will have received a note on the case prepared by a barrister employed by the Court of Appeal, which sets out a summary of the facts and arguments. Counsel on behalf of the appellant and respondent address the Court and the decision is by a majority.

### Rulings of the Court of Appeal and *Practice Directions*
Rulings of the Court of Appeal are regularly reported in the law reports and form part of the doctrine of precedent (*Chapters 1* and *4*). Closely allied to appeal rulings but not stemming from an individual case are *Practice Directions*. These

are of a more general nature and usually set out broad advice on a given aspect of law or procedure and are often promulgated by the Lord Chief Justice.

### Appeals from the Crown Court by way of case stated
Where the Crown Court is sitting to hear appeals from magistrates' courts (below), its decisions cannot be challenged in the Court of Appeal. However, the appellant has the right to apply for a case to be stated by the Crown Court for the determination of a point of law by the High Court. Such appeals are heard by a Divisional Court of the Queen's Bench Division: below.

### Role of the Attorney General
The Attorney General may seek a ruling of the Court of Appeal on a point of law which has been material in a case where a person is tried on indictment. The Court of Appeal has power to refer the point to the House of Lords if necessary. The ruling will constitute a binding precedent (*Chapter 4*), but an acquittal in the original case is not affected.

The Attorney General also has power to refer a case to the Court of Appeal if he or she considers that a sentence passed by the Crown Court for an offence triable only on indictment, or for certain offences which are triable either way (e.g. threats to kill, cruelty to or neglect of children, and serious fraud), was unduly lenient. The Court of Appeal may then increase a sentence within the statutory maximum for the offence.

## APPEALS FROM MAGISTRATES' COURTS

There are different avenues of appeal from magistrates' courts according to whether, in broad terms, the subject matter involves a question of fact or concerns sentence (when the appeal is to the Crown Court) or of law or the proper exercise of judicial discretion (when the appeal or application is to the High Court).

### Appeal from magistrates to the Crown Court
Anyone convicted of a criminal offence by magistrates can appeal to the Crown Court against conviction, sentence, or both. A prosecutor cannot appeal against an acquittal, or against what he or she believes to be an over-lenient sentence (although this latter form of appeal *is* available in relation to certain more serious cases dealt with by a judge and jury in the Crown Court: above). The convicted person must give notice of appeal within 21 days of being sentenced. This period can be extended by the Crown Court (called 'leave to appeal out of time'). The notice of appeal must give details of the conviction and sentence and state the grounds of appeal.

- *Appeal against conviction*
  This is heard by a judge sitting with two magistrates. There is no jury. The case is heard afresh. The Crown Court either upholds the conviction or substitutes an acquittal. If it convicts the accused it proceeds to sentence. The sentence must be within the maximum powers of the magistrates' court (*Chapter 9*), but the appellant risks a more severe sentence within that ceiling.

- *Appeal against sentence* An appeal against sentence is heard by a judge sitting alone. The court is addressed by the appellant or his or her legal representative. The Crown Court can confirm the decision or substitute its own sentence, either more or less severe than that originally imposed by the magistrates but limited to magistrates' maximum powers of punishment (*Chapter 9*). Again, the appellant risks a more severe sentence.

### Appeals from magistrates to the High Court

Appeals on points of law go to the Queen's Bench Division of the High Court of Justice (QBD)—where they are heard by a Divisional Court of the QBD. The court is presided over by the Lord Chief Justice, who may well sit in person. Appeals may involve points of law of general importance the outcome of which will have widescale implications, but such appeals also extend to more mundane or narrow technicalities. Usually, three High Court judges will sit to hear such appeals—which are open to both the defendant and the prosecutor. Rulings (or 'judgements') of the Divisional Court constitute legally binding precedents (subject to any human rights considerations in relation to cases decided before the Human Rights Act 1998: *Chapter 4*).

There are three methods of challenging a decision:

- *Case stated* Here the magistrates are required to state a case for the opinion of the High Court, i.e. to set out in writing what facts they found to exist from the evidence in the case and then to say what law or legal principles they applied to those facts. The Divisional Court either upholds the magistrates' decision or makes some alternative order, e.g. quashes the conviction; or orders the magistrates to rehear the case and apply the correct law and procedure. The process starts with an application by *either* party for the magistrates to state a case for the opinion of the High Court— which must be made within 21 days of the decision of the magistrates' court. Magistrates can refuse a 'frivolous' application, or ask the applicant to identify the point of law at issue (a possibility which should recede with increasing obligations to give explanations in court and allow representations at that time).
- *Judicial review* Anyone aggrieved by a decision of magistrates (which can extend beyond the original parties to other people with a legitimate interest in the outcome of the case: what is called *locus standi*)—may ask the High

Court to review the case in order to see whether, e.g. the magistrates' court acted judicially, fairly and followed correct procedures. If not, the remedy is one or more of the 'prerogative orders': *certiorari* to quash the decision; *mandamus* to compel the magistrates to act properly (e.g. by re-hearing the case in the correct manner); or *prohibition* to prevent magistrates acting in error. Judicial review must normally be pursued within six months.

• *Application for a declaration* Applications for declarations are somewhat unusual (due to the existence of the standard remedies outlined so far). They are applications to the Divisional Court by either party for that court to declare the law on a particular point. Declarations are binding on public authorities (such as the magistrates' court, police, Crown Prosecution Service and Criminal Defence Service) who, it can be taken, will act upon the declaratory advice given.

**Rectification of magistrates' decisions**
The underlying principle is that once a decision has been formerly announced by a court then the court cannot go back on that decision and change it, known as the doctrine of *functus officio*. However, magistrates' courts have a statutory power to alter their own sentences or orders or to correct their own mistakes in certain limited circumstances. These provisions were introduced so that a court can ensure that its original sentence decision is complete and appropriate and based on the facts as they were at the time. Section 142 Magistrates' Courts Act 1980 (as amended) thus confers power, among other things, to amend a sentence if there has been a mistake, unlawful penalty, omission or there are other compelling reasons. Use of these powers can often avoid unnecessary appeals.

**Statutory declaration**
Not exactly a right of appeal as such, but analogous in effect (if only, possibly, temporarily) is the right of a defendant to make a solemn declaration that he or she never knew of the proceedings. The effect is that proceedings will be restarted relying upon the original information.

# CRIMINAL CASES REVIEW COMMISSION

Historically speaking, it was a function of the Home Secretary (acting under the Royal Prerogative) to consider complaints of wrongful conviction and to refer these to the Court of Appeal where he considered this appropriate and if all the normal rights of appeal had been exhausted. This was normally done only where there was new evidence or some other consideration of substance that was not before the original trial court. However, following the Royal Commission on Criminal Justice (*Chapter 15*) this arrangements was superseded by the Criminal Cases Review Commission (CCRC) with analogous authority to review cases and to refer these back to the Court of Appeal.

The CCRC is an independent body set up in 1997 under the Criminal Appeal Act 1995. It reports to Parliament through the Home Secretary and has 13 members (as at 2002) appointed by the Queen on the recommendation of the Prime Minister. One of these is designated as chairman. It also has a chief executive plus around 90 staff (including CCRC members). It can consider cases heard in either the magistrates' court or the Crown Court, its principal purpose being to review suspected 'miscarriages of justice' in England, Wales and Northern Ireland (including cases rejected by the Home Office under the former arrangements), and to refer to the appeal courts a conviction, verdict, finding or sentence if it considers there is a real possibility that it would not be upheld. Except on rare occasions the case must have been through the normal appeal procedures first. The CCRC also investigates and reports on any matter referred to it by the Court of Appeal, assists the Home Secretary as required when considering the exercise of Her Majesty's Prerogative of Mercy and prepares an annual report. It has no power to overturn convictions or sentences itself.

Since the CCRC began its work it has received over 4,000 applications of which approaching three-quarters have been completed, the remainder being cases in progress or new applications awaiting attention. The CCRC provides an applicant with a full explanation of its decision to refer or not to refer the matter to the Court of Appeal known as a Statement of Reasons.[2]

## THE EUROPEAN COURT OF HUMAN RIGHTS

As already outlined in *Chapters 1* and *4*, the correct application of human rights law can be tested either within the national appellate system (as described in this chapter) or by means of a free-standing right of appeal to the European Court of Human Rights in Strasbourg. Similarly, if a provision of English law is incompatible with the European Convention, then a declaration of incompatibility (which should normally only be made by or on appeal to the higher courts) will oblige Parliament to reconsider the matter with a view to 'fast-track' amending legislation. However, it remains the right of every citizen involved in proceedings before courts of law in the UK to appeal to the European Court of Human Rights (either at an earlier or later stage).[3]

---

[2] For a useful exposition of the CCRC, its objectives, functions, procedures and methods of working see 'Investigating Miscarriages of Justice' (2002), Brittan D in *The Prisons Handbook 2002*, Leech M and Cheney D, Winchester: Waterside Press.

[3] See, generally, *Human Rights and the Courts: Bringing Justice Home* (1999), Ashcroft P et al, Winchester: Waterside Press.

# CHAPTER 11

# Before Court

As outlined in earlier chapters there is a nationwide network of law enforcement agencies, investigators and prosecutors in England and Wales. Investigation is normally carried out by an officer of one of the ordinary civil police forces in England and Wales or from one of the special forces or other public bodies charged with confronting specific kinds of crime such as evasion of excise duty, immigration offences or breach of health and safety law (see later in the chapter). Special police forces (see later in the chapter) include the Ministry of Defence Police and British Transport Police.

The Crown Prosecution Service (CPS) has both an advisory and prosecution decision-making function. The Serious Fraud Office (SFO), e.g. has investigation and prosecution responsibilities. The police and CPS are gradually, and since the Glidewell report of 1998, being located in joint Criminal Justice Units (CJUs)[1] a process which *Justice for All* notes will continue until all areas in England and Wales function in this way. The CJU is a single administrative unit, co-locating police and CPS staff 'working together' in order to maximise efficiency, eliminate duplication, improve working relationships and provide early legal advice to the police. CJUs function principally in relation to the magistrates' court whereas Trial Units, often involving similar cross-agency co-operation are being put in place in relation to the Crown Court.

## THE POLICE

There are 43 police forces each covering a county or group of counties, except in London where there is one force for the City and the Metropolitan Police Service covers the rest of the capital. The White Paper *Police Reform* (1993) set out the then main aims of the police as being to:

- fight and prevent crime;
- uphold the law;
- bring to justice people who break the law;
- protect, help and reassure the community; and
- provide good value for money.

Each police force is divided geographically into a number of districts or divisions within the force area, known as a Basic Command Unit and normally led by a police superintendent. Divisional police stations have facilities for charging people, cells, a Criminal Investigations Department (CID) and a communications room. The areas in turn are usually broken down into sub-divisions, based on sub-divisional police stations. Police forces also employ civilian staff in administrative and other posts, thereby releasing officers for

---

[1] Often based at a police station.

operational duties. The police also recruit and use 'special constables' (part-time volunteers) acting in support of regular officers.[2]

Forces are supported by the National Crime Squad (NCS),[3] National Criminal Intelligence Service (NCIS) (which collates information relating to crime nationally and circulates this as appropriate) and a range of centralised databases such as those at Bramshill House, Hampshire and in Derbyshire (of paedophiles) together with specialist or tactical squads and support units which can be called on as necessary. Forces also aid one another in a wide variety of ways. In 2002 there were several reports of forces being assisted by America's Federal Bureau of Investigation (FBI), including to track down paedophiles on the internet and to enhance the quality of video images taken by security cameras.

Police forces work in partnership with a range of other agencies, including with the CPS on case preparation as described in *Chapter 7*. They may also work with the Forensic Science Service (FSS) at the investigation stage and FSS experts may later give opinion evidence in court. FSS scientific support to detectives includes work in the laboratory in relation to exhibits and suspicious deaths, DNA testing and police awareness training. There is a national DNA database which by 2002 contained 1.5 million offender profiles. Other key support organizations are the Police Information Technology Organization (PITO), the National Identification Service (NIS) and the Criminal Records Bureau (CRB) which is operated jointly by the Home Office and a private contractor.

The Crime and Disorder Act 1998 placed fresh obligations on the police, local authorities and other agencies to co-operate in the development and implementation of a strategy for tackling crime in their area. This responsibility is discharged through local Crime and Disorder Reduction Partnerships and as part of the Crime Reduction Programme (CRP). The CRP is a £250 million project which began in 1999, is scheduled to last for three years and involves an evidence-led approach to reducing crime. It comprises a range of diverse initiatives which support projects on the ground as operated by local agencies and monitored regionally by government. The Safer Communities Initiative addresses crime and disorder in individual communities by concentrating on repeat offenders and so-called crime 'hot spots'. There are plans to invest £20 million in 2002-2003 in a number of such projects. Certain schemes aimed at the detection of crime and the prosecution of offenders are mentioned in *Chapter 6*.

*Justice for All* promises an increase in police numbers to 130,000 by Spring 2003; increased spending on the police by around £1.5 billion by 2005-2006 by comparison with 2002-2003; more specialist detective skills; a clear target for increasing the proportion of time spent on frontline work; and better harnessing of science and technology to find the evidence to detect offenders.

## Political accountability

The police are politically accountable through a tripartite structure consisting of the chief constable, the police authority and the Home Secretary. The chief

---

[2] In 2001 the Government broached the idea of 'police auxiliaries' with limited powers to detain suspects, leading to 'community support officers': see later in the chapter.

[3] Unlike the FBI, the NCS—established in 1992 to target criminal gangs—is an operational mechanism rather than an independently functioning nationwide agency with separate powers and jurisdiction.

constable ('commissioners' for the Metropolitan and City of London Police) is responsible for every aspect of the conduct of his or her force. He or she has power to appoint, promote and discipline officers below the rank of assistant chief constable—and a duty to enforce the law: to bring offenders to justice.

### Chief constables and police authorities

Each police force operates under the auspices of a police authority. An autonomous Association of Police Authorities (which works in partnership with the Local Government Association) has existed since 1997. Chief constables are appointed by and make reports to their local police authorities. Police authorities fix the maximum strength of the force, subject to approval by the government, and provide buildings and equipment. They can advise a chief constable, e.g. on law enforcement, priorities and the allocation and deployment of police resources. The Police and Magistrates' Courts Act 1994 made police authorities free-standing bodies, reduced their size and introduced independent members (in addition to local councillors and magistrates).

### The Home Secretary and the Home Office

The Home Secretary can make regulations covering: qualifications for appointment, promotion and retirement; discipline; hours of duty, leave, pay and allowances; uniform; and ranks. He also has various powers to influence practice nationally, for example by participating in senior appointments and by issuing circulars on the general direction of policing policy, which forces are expected to comply with. In 2002 he established a Police Bureaucracy Task Force under a retired chief inspector of constabulary charged with identifying ways in which the burden of bureaucracy shouldered by the police can be reduced.

Within the Home Office, the Organized Crime, Drugs and International Group (OCDIG) and the Policing and Crime Reduction Group support the Home Secretary to promote police efficiency and effectiveness. They provide the administrative framework that enables government policy on policing to be formulated and implemented, and it provides central services to the police.

The Home Secretary also influences policy and practice through HM Inspectorate of Constabulary which carries out full, primary inspections covering all aspects of force activity with a view to improving efficiency; performance review[4] inspections concentrating in greater depth on a limited range of issues; and thematic inspections. HM Chief Inspector of Constabulary (an office which is over 100 years old) is also the Home Secretary's senior professional adviser on police matters including senior appointments. Proposals in *Justice For All* would increase the Home Secretary's authority, via a National Policing Plan and default powers where police forces are under-performing (see later in the chapter).

### Police membership organizations

Police officers are not allowed to join a trade union or to go on strike. All ranks, however, have their own staff associations including the Police Federation for rank and file officers and which is the representative body for all officers below superintendent. The federation was established in 1919 to provide the police with

---

[4] Following preliminary work by Portsmouth University, it was announced in September 2002 that the Home Office is to publish performance tables for police forces.

a ready and lawful means of bringing their concerns to the notice of government and others. Officers of the rank of superintendent can belong to a Superintendents Association whilst beyond this there is the Association of Chief Police Officers (ACPO) which exists 'to promote leadership excellence by the chief officers of the police service, to assist in setting the policing agenda by providing professional opinion on key issues identified by the Government, appropriate organizations and individuals and to be the corporate voice of the service'.

### Police work
The police have a duty to maintain law and order, to protect people and property, to prevent crime (in conjunction with local authorities and communities) and, when crime occurs, to try to detect offenders and prepare case papers with a view to prosecution (*Chapter 6*). They also act as prosecutors in relation to certain minor crimes and at the outset in most other cases until they are taken over by the CPS (below). They control road traffic and advise local authorities on traffic matters. They also carry out certain duties, such as immigration enquiries, for the government. By tradition they assist anyone who needs their help and they deal with a range of emergencies, often in conjunction with other agencies and authorities. Much of this work (aspects of which are described below) is carried out by patrol officers, who make up around 60 per cent of force strength. They are deployed on foot or in vehicle patrols and organized on the basis of beats. Ordinary beat officers normally work a shift or relief. Officers are not usually assigned to a particular beat: they go wherever they are needed. More specialised work is undertaken by operational officers, who make up around a third of force strength.

### Maintaining public order
The maintenance of public order ranges from the day-to-day policing of the streets to the control of crowds and demonstrators and responses to terrorist attacks. Patrol officers are supported by special patrol groups or task forces, seconded officers specially trained and equipped and put on standby to respond to any incident or potential disorder. Forces also have Police Support Units (PSUs), which are made up of ordinary officers who carry out normal policing duties but who are given special training in the use of shields and riot techniques. PSUs will aid other police forces in emergencies. The Metropolitan police also have District Support Units, mobile instant response units who patrol the streets in vans. Ever since the first real urban riots in the early 1980s, the police have been given more powers and equipment to deal with disorders, and more resources have been devoted to public order training.

### Public safety, crime prevention, crime reduction and fear of crime
The main responsibility within police forces for crime prevention lies with patrol officers. While they may rarely discover 'invisible' (i.e. off-street) crimes such as burglary, it is argued that their presence on the streets may reduce the number of 'visible' crimes and the fear of crime. In addition to these officers, every force employs crime prevention officers in their own right. These officers carry out security surveys of domestic and commercial premises and advise on appropriate security, and distribute crime prevention publicity.

Forces are also involved—often in partnership with local authorities in pursuance of their own responsibilities—in a range of other public safety, crime prevention and crime reduction initiatives. They help to establish neighbourhood watch schemes, which involve neighbours in keeping a look out for people acting suspiciously and promote household security measures such as property marking. Other watches have been formed based on similar principles. These include boat, business, cab, campus, caravan, child, farm, hospital, pub, school and shop watches.

Many forces work with other agencies in analysing and tackling local crime problems, e.g. on run-down housing estates and school premises. Some have launched initiatives to protect elderly people, or to involve young people in activities and education programmes and there are now enhanced multi-agency projects to tackle domestic violence across the country following publication of the Cabinet Office/Home Office document *Living Without Fear* (1999). Flowing from this, a Domestic Violence Unit now brings together expertise from the Home Office and other government departments including Health, Education and Skills, the Lord Chancellor's Department and the office of the Deputy Prime Minister. Its main role is to support ministers in driving forward key programmes whereby the agencies work together under a 'common commitment' to reduce levels of domestic violence.

Police officers also become members of youth offending teams (YOTs) (*Chapter 5*) and some officers give up part of their spare time to supervise young offenders given attendance centre orders by the courts. These orders aim to deprive young offenders of some of their leisure time and encourage them to make more constructive use of it.

## Special constables

Special constables are part-time police officers who work on a voluntary basis alongside regular, full-time, police officers. Although supported and supervised, they have the same legal powers as their full-time colleagues and sometimes provide a vital resource where large numbers of police officers are required at a given place or event. The emergence of community support officers from 2002 onwards may alter the balance in terms of who will fulfil which role in future.

## Community support officers: A note

The Police Reform Act 2002 confers powers on chief officers to designate civilian support staff as community support officers (CSOs) and to set up accreditation schemes for street wardens, security guards and similar staff employed by other agencies: accredited community safety officers (ACSOs). CSOs and ACSOs, who will be able to exercise limited police powers, will assist the police in tackling anti-social behaviour and minor disorder and will provide increased reassurance and contact with the public.

CSOs and other civilian patrollers will perhaps have the greatest impact on the public as a result of this Act. They are not a replacement for fully trained police officers but, according to the Home Office, will play 'a different but complementary role to the record numbers of police officers currently in post'. CSOs will be fully trained and tackle low-level crime such as burglaries, anti-social behaviour and petty crime as well as acting as the eyes and ears of the community. It is planned that they will be a visible and reassuring presence.

Powers of detention of individuals by CSOs pending the arrival of the police who are empowered to make an arrest are to be piloted in six areas of the country and the data analysed before being rolled out nationally.

# INVESTIGATING CRIME

Minor crime is investigated by uniformed patrol officers including, in some forces, officers designated as beat crimes officers.[4] Broadly speaking, plain-clothes CID officers take over the investigation of more complex and serious crimes often after an initial assessment by uniformed officers. Modern methods have seen increased reliance on surveillance by way of CCTV and the development of advanced identification techniques such electronic face, voice and iris recognition. A scheme known as Scanning Analysis Response Assessment (SARA) has been used for a number of years with regard to what has become known as 'problem-oriented' or 'problem solving' policing, a means of attempting to methodically solve problems.

CID officers are usually based at sub-divisional or divisional police stations or in central specialist sections, such as a stolen vehicles squad, a commercial fraud squad, a 'special branch' (responsible for dealing with threats to public order, terrorism, espionage, sabotage, subversive activities, immigration, personal protection etc.), a robbery squad, a drugs squad (see below), a serious crimes squad and a cheque fraud squad. These squads are supported by a number of services such as the NCIS mentioned earlier in the chapter, scenes of crimes officers, fingerprint and photographic officers, firearms and explosives experts and a criminal records office. CID officers may also be seconded to regional crime squads covering more than one force area.

Together with Customs and Excise, the police have established a National Drugs Intelligence Unit which gathers, collates and circulates information on drug misuse, drug-trafficking and drug-related or crime-related financial transactions through a financial section which receives information from banks and other institutions about funds suspected of having been derived from such sources. This information is checked out and passed to operational officers.

The central drugs squad in London and the drugs wings of the regional crime squads investigate national and international drug trafficking. In addition, every force has a local drugs squad which tackles middle-level dealers in its area, often in co-operation with a regional drugs wing. At a divisional level, local uniformed and plain-clothes officers deal with individual misusers and street pushers in the normal course of their duties. From 2001, there has been greater tolerance of soft drugs and the Government has indicated that it intends to reclassify some prohibited drugs by downgrading their criminal status.

### Police registration of sex offenders
The Sex Offenders Act 1997 imposed a requirement on offenders convicted or cautioned for specific sex offences to notify the police of their name and address and any subsequent changes thereto. The length of the obligation is based on the sentence imposed. Failure to comply is a criminal offence. Later, the Crime and

---

[4]  See *Chapter 6* for detection, investigation and charge as part of the criminal process.

Disorder Act 1998 introduced 'sex offender orders' whereby the chief officer of police may—if a convicted sex offender later acts in such a way as to give cause to believe that serious harm may be caused to the public—apply to a magistrates' court for an order imposing prohibitions on the individual concerned. The order is a pre-emptive measure (not unlike a civil injunction), breach of which is also a criminal offence. Such registration or monitoring is vital to the modern policing function and to the work of Multi-agency Protection Panels (MAPPs) (*Chapter 6*).

## HELPING VICTIMS

The police play a key role in supporting and advising victims of crime through a range of operational and liaison activities and by their involvement in taking witness statements and 'victim personal statements'. This aspect of police work is dealt with in *Chapter 18*.

## PUBLIC RELATIONS

Overall, public confidence in the police is high. However, over the years, surveys have found that attitudes to the police differ strikingly according to age, race, gender and area of residence. Research shows that a substantial proportion of the black population lacks confidence and trust in the police. This applies not only to the young but also to middle-aged and older black people and is the case for both African-Caribbean and Asian people, although there are differences in the way the problem is experienced. The Stephen Lawrence case (*Chapter 16*) has caused police forces to review their methods and priorities in this regard.

The police have two distinct roles in their relationship with the public. They police the public—by stopping, questioning, controlling, arresting, summoning, detaining and applying a variety of sanctions. They also provide services to the public as outlined earlier in the chapter and generally work to enable ordinary life to continue. They must be seen to carry out these roles fairly and now in accordance with human rights principles. Towards this end, the Police and Criminal Evidence Act 1984 (PACE) (*Chapter 6*) regulates police powers on the streets, on premises and at the police station. Lay visitor schemes have been introduced to assess and report on detention conditions in police stations and on the way rules governing the treatment of detained people are applied.

Most forces now have specialist community liaison officers whose remit is to develop contacts with voluntary and statutory agencies, minority ethnic organizations and schools. Under PACE, police authorities are required to consult local people about the policing of their area. Police authorities have set up consultative committees on which authority members, police officers, councillors, statutory agencies and voluntary and community groups are represented.

Policing depends to a large extent on public co-operation (sometimes referred to as 'policing by consent'[5]), and this is more likely to be forthcoming if the police are seen to be responding sufficiently vigorously to their priorities. The

---

[5] For a discussion of policing theory see *Principled Policing: Protecting the Public with Integrity* (1998), Alderson J, Winchester: Waterside Press.

public want more officers on foot patrol and the police to be more responsive to calls for help. The police have responded by deploying more officers on foot and changing shift systems to ensure that police cover more accurately reflects public needs. In addition to patrol officers, forces also deploy home beat officers. These officers are given responsibility for a particular beat and are expected to get to know the people who live and work on it. They maintain contact, e.g. with local schools, collect information about racial incidents and investigate minor offences.

## COMPLAINTS AGAINST THE POLICE

A complaint about the police may be informally resolved between the police and complainant or formally investigated by the police. It can be considered for informal resolution if it would not justify criminal proceedings. If the complainant agrees to informal resolution, a senior officer will investigate and mediate between the complainant and the officer subject to the complaint. If mediation fails, another officer will be appointed to deal with the complaint formally.

The Police Complaints Authority (PCA) is the independent body that oversees complaints against serving police officers in England and Wales.[6] Additionally, voluntary (or 'non-complaint') referrals to the PCA can be made by the police themselves and certain complaints or events must be referred to and be supervised by the PCA, e.g. where death or serious injury occurs in police custody or stems from firearms being used by the police or 'hot pursuit' in police vehicles. Where the complaint is of assault occasioning actual bodily harm, corruption or a serious arrestable offence by a police officer the PCA can decide whether or not to supervise the investigation. Some people sue the police in the civil courts for damages as an alternative to using the PCA procedure.

In order to give greater reassurance that complaints against the police are investigated openly, fairly and impartially, *Justice for All* proposes the formation of an Independent Police Complaints Commission (IPCC) to be established by April 2004 to investigate and oversee serious complaints against the police. The commission, it is urged, will encourage greater openness and transparency in complaints procedures, and will lead to increased confidence 'in the robustness of the complaints system'.

## THE POLICE AND PROSECUTION

A principal function of the police where a crime is detected is to decide whether or not to arrest the suspect, to make inquiries (*Chapter 6*) and whether to launch a prosecution. In terms of the future course of a criminal case, the police gather the evidence necessary to support a prosecution, often in the form of witness statements and exhibits (*Chapter 8*). This will also involve incidental decisions about whether the suspect or accused person should be granted bail or whether

---

[6] There has been a general downward trend in complaints, but the figures show that a disproportionate number of complainants are unemployed, black (11 per cent), or of Asian origin (4.5 per cent) (compared to 1.8 per cent and 3 per cent of the population as a whole, respectively). More information is available at the PCA web-site www.pca.gov.uk

he or she should be brought before a court with a view to an application for a remand in custody (*Chapter 8*). As indicated earlier, the move is towards joint-working with the CPS whilst *Justice for All* proposes a more prominent role for the CPS which would, in effect, determine the charge in all but straightforward cases and those where the police need to prefer a 'holding charge'.

**Prosecution or diversion**
Even where there is clear evidence to support the initiation of a prosecution, the police may decide against that course in favour of a formal caution (or in the case of a juvenile a reprimand or warning) or other form of diversion from the criminal justice process: *Chapters 5 and 7*

*Fixed penalties*
The police and certain other public bodies have statutory powers to operate schemes in relation to minor offences whereby offenders are issued with a fixed penalty, either at the time of the offence or soon afterwards. The 'ticket' may be issued, e.g. by a police officer, traffic warden or employee of a local authority. Currently such penalties range up to £80 according to the offence involved (and there are surcharges in some cases if the initial fixed penalty goes unpaid and thus has to be registered with a court for enforcement as if it were a fine: *Chapter 9*). Fixed penalties avoid the need for prosecution or other court proceedings provided that the penalty is accepted and paid within the period specified in the notice, normally either 21 or 28 days.

As part of a visible (and what some people view as a questionable) offensive on 'anti-social behaviour', the Police Reform Act 2002 introduced new powers for the police to issue 'on the spot' fines for a range of (ostensibly) lesser offences.[8]

*Mitigated penalties*
Prosecutors such as Customs and Excise and the Inland Revenue may accept a 'mitigated penalty', which is analogous to a fixed penalty but usually in a more substantial amount.

# OTHER AGENTS OF LAW ENFORCEMENT

Among other law enforcement agencies with an investigation or prosecution function are:

- a number of what are called 'non-geographic' forces such as the British Transport Police (the largest of these and the one that the general public is most likely to encounter), Ministry of Defence Police, United Kingdom

---

[8]  These so-called 'on the spot' fines for 'anti-social behaviour' (what some sections of the media have termed 'yob offences') do not in fact involve immediate payment, but operate along the lines of other fixed penalties, with time allowed for payment or the option of prosecution in the normal way. The behaviour concerned ranges from being drunk and disorderly to threatening behaviour, wasting police time and making hoax calls (some of which could be quite serious matters: although the police retain the discretion to bring a conventional prosecution). The scheme is being piloted in six areas (one 'area' is the British Transport Police). Also being tested is a further police power, under the Criminal Justice and Police Act 2001, to close disorderly or noisy public houses.

Atomic Energy Constabulary, Port of Dover Police and NCS (already mentioned above)

- the Serious Fraud Office (SFO). The SFO is headed by a Director of Serious Fraud and has authority to take over prosecutions from other agencies where the matter falls within its remit.
- Customs and Excise which is responsible for ports, airports, drug trafficking, rivers and tunnels and such items as the seizure of drug-related cash and non-payment or evasion of Value Added Tax (VAT)
- the Health and Safety Executive which deals not only with everyday prosecutions of employers for day-to-day failures to comply with safety legislation but also with serious cases, e.g. where an accident or even a fatality has occurred or where the defect complained of may require a change of manufacturing practices generally
- TV Licence Records Office (TVLRO) which prosecutes people for having no TV licence and other broadcasting offences
- local authorities who (apart from bringing civil care proceedings in respect of children and having responsibility for vulnerable adults) have a public safety function, special responsibilities in relation to juveniles (*Chapter 5*) and a number of prosecution responsibilities, e.g. enforcement of bye-laws; consumer protection (including misrepresentations etc. relating to products offered for sale); and school attendance.

Among voluntary sector organizations, the following have been given statutory powers to prosecute within their field of operations:

- the National Society for the Prevention of Cruelty to Children (NSPCC)
- the Royal Society for the Protection of Animals (RSPCA).

# POLICE REFORM

Various proposals contained in *Justice For All* (*Chapter 15*) are likely to affect the work and role of the police (as did the White Paper *Policing a New Century: A Blueprint for Reform* (2001)). The Police Reform Act 2002 forms what the Home Office describes as part of its 'ambitious police policy' which will:

... support the police service in tackling crime and anti-social behaviour. It contains measures to ensure that the most effective policing methods are used by all police forces, and so tackles the variations in performance between forces. The Act will make anti-social behaviour orders more flexible and widely available. It will enable trained civilians to execute some police powers, freeing a growing number of police officers from unnecessary duties and providing a presence in local communities. And it will enable the police to work closely with other agencies like neighbourhood and street wardens. (News and Press Release, 25 July 2002)

According to John Denham, Minister of State for Policing and Crime Reduction:

The ... Act will do a great deal to create a modern and efficient police service, not only capable of and properly equipped to fight crime in the twenty-first century, but also able to react flexibly to the needs of a changing society. It is a vitally important piece of legislation both for the police and the public they serve.

Among other measures, the Act provides for the following:

- a National Policing Plan, which will set out the Government's priorities for policing, their delivery and indicators by which performance will be measured
- powers enabling the Home Secretary to issues codes of practice to chief officers and make regulations governing the use of police equipment or requiring forces to adopt particular procedures or practices in order to spread good practice throughout the police service and to help raise the standards of all forces to the level of the best
- the strengthening of the powers of police authorities to remove chief officers in the interests of efficiency and effectiveness
- arrangements whereby, in exceptional circumstances and where a police force is manifestly failing in its duty to protect and serve the public, the Home Secretary will be able to intervene. Existing powers that require a police authority to take remedial action have been strengthened. An adverse report by Her Majesty's Inspectorate of Constabulary could trigger intervention, which would require the police authority and the chief constable to produce an action plan to address failings within 12 weeks. The Home Secretary will have the right to comment on the action plan, and his comments will be considered by the police authority before they implement the plan.
- the formation of an Independent Police Complaints Commission (see earlier in the chapter)
- chief constables will also be able to confer appropriate police powers on civilian investigating, detention and escort officers, thereby freeing up police officers for front line duties and enabling forces to employ specialist investigators to help in the fight against fraud and IT crime
- strengthened and streamlined procedures for obtaining anti-social behaviour orders (ASBOs) through the introduction of interim orders and extending the geographical area to which an order can apply. The British Transport Police and registered social landlords will be able to apply for orders, county courts will be able to impose orders, and an order could be imposed on conviction for any offence where evidence of persistent anti-social behaviour has been presented to the court
- measures to improve the use and effectiveness of sex offender orders by giving police throughout England and Wales greater flexibility as to how they apply for the orders, making them apply across the United Kingdom as a whole and providing for interim sex offender orders in England and Wales to deal more effectively with the most urgent cases
- provision for community support officers (see earlier in the chapter).

# In Court

## JUDGES

Every criminal court above the magistrates' court relies on professional judges[1] drawn from the legal profession, principally from leading practitioners at the Bar—although, increasingly, judges have been appointed from the ranks of solicitors and occasionally academics. All judges are appointed by the sovereign on the recommendation of the Lord Chancellor as head of the judiciary. In the case of the most senior appointments, those to the Court of Appeal and House of Lords, the recommendation is routed via the Prime Minister. The way in which judges are appointed has been criticised as unduly secretive. *Justice for All* (*Chapter 15*) announces that a Judicial Appointments Commission will be established, which it claims will be more open and accountable. Relevant parts of this chapter should thus be understood in the light of possible changes to the present arrangements.

### Law Lords

As outlined in *Chapter 4*, judges of the House of Lords are known as Lords of Appeal in Ordinary or 'Law Lords' and on appointment become life peers. By convention they do not participate in the general business of the House except where there is a direct legal or judicial context such as debates on Criminal Justice Bills or measures affecting the powers, jurisdiction or administrative arrangements for the courts and other agencies on whom the courts depend for the proper and effective administration of justice.[2] The Law Lords number between nine and eleven. They sit as an Appellate Committee of the House in an ante-room (not in the chamber of the House) to hear appeals from the Court of Appeal (Criminal Division) and the Queen's Bench Division of the High Court of Justice (and non-criminal courts). The Lord Chancellor is the head of this committee and of the judiciary as a whole and may sit with other Law Lords to hear cases on occasion.

### Lords Justices of Appeal

Each of the of the 30 or so judges of the Court of Appeal is known as 'Lord Justice'. Lords Justices (often shortened in writing to LJJs) are promoted from among High Court Judges (some of whom who may also depulise as Court of

---

[1] District judges (magistrates' courts) sit in magistrates' courts. Their role and the arrangements for their appointment are described later in the chapter.

[2] For example the debates on the Police and Magistrates' Courts Bill (subsequently Act of 1994) where the then Lord Chancellor was obliged to withdraw certain proposals which touched on judicial independence (*Chapter 1*) following speeches by the Lord Chief Justice and senior Law Lords.

Appeal judges from time-to-time). They sit regularly in the Civil Division of the Court of Appeal and some also in the Criminal Division.

### High Court judges

There are around 100 High Court judges who, as well as sitting in the High Court to hear cases, may also sit in the Crown Court. At Crown Court centres where a High Court judge sits, cases are assigned between different types of judges on the principle that the High Court judge should usually try the more serious or difficult allegations (sometimes called 'first tier' cases). A High Court judge will often serve as the presiding judge for a court centre or circuit. These functions apart, the main significance for the criminal process is that High Court judges sit to hear appeals by way of case stated and application for judicial review and declarations in the Queens Bench Division (and also as stated above in the Court of Appeal (Criminal Division) from time to time).[3]

The Lord Chancellor appoints High Court judges who are selected from among senior barristers, normally Queen's Counsel (QCs) or solicitors, who are also eligible for appointment. Again, this mechanism has been under scrutiny.

### Circuit judges, recorders and assistant recorders

The Lord Chancellor appoints circuit judges, recorders and assistant recorders to sit in the Crown Court. Any reasonably senior barrister or solicitor can apply to be interviewed and assessed.

Circuit judges, who sit in one of the Crown Court circuits (*Chapter 3*), are drawn mainly from the middle ranks of senior barristers. However, solicitors are also eligible for the circuit bench if they have served for a period as a recorder although they number less than a fifth of the 500 or more regular circuit judges. A recorder is a practising barrister or solicitor who sits as a part-time circuit judge. There are some 900 recorders who sit for around 20 days a year in the Crown Court whilst continuing with their normal legal practice or other legal occupation for the rest of the year. In addition, there are approaching 400 assistant recorders. Each centre has a 'resident judge' who acts as a link between that centre, its administration, and other courts, judges and agencies.

### The role of the trial judge

As explained in *Chapter 8* the trial judge supervises the conduct of a jury trial and ensures that rules of law, procedure and evidence are kept. In essence, he or she decides any legal issues that arise during the trial, e.g. concerning the admissibility of evidence; sums up the case to the jury, setting out the main factual points covered and guiding the jury on the law as it applies to the case in question. He or she also passes sentence following a plea of guilty or a verdict of guilty by a jury (below). Proposals in *Justice for All* (*Chapter 15*) would allow certain cases to be tried by a judge alone either because the accused person requested this or the case was one of serious fraud or involved similarly complex issues.

---

[3] For the appellate system see *Chapter 10*.

# THE JURY

The jury is the incarnation of the right of citizen's to be tried by his or her peers (which is presumed to stem from Magna Carta). Jurors are chosen at random from the electoral roll. Qualifications for jury service are contained in the Juries Act 1974. At present a juror must:

- be registered as a Parliamentary or local government elector
- be not less than 18 years old, nor over 65
- have been ordinarily resident in the UK for a period of at least five years since his or her thirteenth birthday.

and must not be ineligible for or disqualified from jury service. The Auld report suggested that the qualification criteria be broadened and this found favour in *Justice for All* which proposes widening the make-up of the jury so as to 'increase the proportion of the population eligible to serve'. Whilst the proposals could remove some current exemptions, disqualifications and categories of ineligible citizens these are currently as follows:

*People entitled to be excused jury service as of right e.g.:*

- members of Parliament
- members of the armed services
- members of the medical or psychiatric professions
- people who have served on a jury within the last two years (in some instances, after a long or arduous trial, a judge may excuse members of the jury for life).

The following people fall within classes of people who are currently ineligible or disqualified:

*Ineligible*
- past and present members of the judiciary (including magistrates: below)
- other people who are or have been, within the last ten years, concerned with the administration of justice (barristers, solicitors, clerks to justices, police officers etc.)
- the clergy
- the mentally ill.

*Disqualified*
- people who have at any time been detained during Her Majesty's Pleasure, or sentenced to imprisonment or youth custody or detention, for a term of five years or more
- people who within the last ten years have been sentenced to a term of imprisonment, youth custody, detention or have been made the subject of certain community sentences within the last five years
- people who are on bail (*Chapter 8*).

Jurors are summoned to attend at the Crown Court by the Central Jury Summoning Bureau (CJSB) (*Chapter 3*). Failure to attend at court is punishable as a contempt of court by a fine. However, any juror may apply to the summoning officer before the date for his or her attendance to be excused from this obligation for sound reasons.

### Jury challenges

Prosecuting counsel can challenge any juror without putting forward a reason by calling on him or her to 'stand by for the Crown', but this right of what is known as 'peremptory challenge' is rarely used in practice.[4] Both prosecution and defence can also challenge for cause, i.e. seek to reject a juror for good reason, e.g. that the juror is disqualified or ineligible, or because for reasons explained to the court—such as financial interest or strongly held views on a given topic—the juror in question might be biased or otherwise likely to prejudge the case.

### Jury oath

Each member of the jury is required to swear on oath (or if he or she so chooses to make an equivalent affirmation) as follows:

> I will faithfully try the several issues joined between our Sovereign lady the Queen and the prisoner at the Bar, and give a true verdict according to the evidence.

## LAY MAGISTRATES AND DISTRICT JUDGES

There are around 29,000 lay magistrates or 'justices of the peace' (JPs)[5] in England and Wales. They undergo special training but are essentially unqualified and not paid other than their expenses and any loss of earnings. They are ordinary members of the community drawn from a cross-section of society and are chosen for their character, integrity and judgment. They sit on the bench as a form of public service. Magistrates are advised at a senior level by justices' clerks and, on an everyday basis, by other qualified court legal advisers.

### Appointment of lay magistrates

Lay magistrates are appointed by the Lord Chancellor on behalf of the Sovereign. He receives recommendations from local Advisory Committees. Most large cities and town have an Advisory Committee, whilst other parts of the country are served by committees with responsibility for a county (and possibly divided for the purposes of interviewing and making initial assessments of candidates into Advisory Sub-committees). A special arrangement exists in Greater Manchester, Merseyside and Lancashire, where appointments are made by the Chancellor of the Duchy of Lancaster.

There has been a drive to broaden the bench, i.e. to make it more representative of the community. This move has led to a greater number of appointments from minority groups and disabled people, including since 1998

---

[4]   It has been argued that this ancient form of challenge should be dispensed with.
[5]   These terms are synonymous. For an overview see *Introduction to the Magistrates' Court* (2001), edn. 4, Gibson B, Winchester: Waterside Press.

blind people (for whom training and other materials have been translated into braille). Another aim is to achieve balance. Committees thus look for applicants from a range of backgrounds and walks of life. They seek nominations by such methods as asking local organizations or businesses to encourage suitable people to come forward, and through notices in the press or in public libraries. There is nothing to prevent an individual putting himself or herself forward by contacting the secretary to the local Advisory Committee, completing an application form and adding the names of people prepared to recommend him or her. Political views are only relevant to prevent benches becoming weighted in any particular direction.

### District judges
There are also around 100 district judges (magistrates' courts): full-time salaried judges, but otherwise of equivalent status to lay magistrates, although empowered to sit alone to hear cases and dispense justice and who, by virtue of their professional status and expertise, are likely to play a leading role in areas where they operate—principally London and larger urban centres, but also across many counties. District judges are appointed by the Lord Chancellor on behalf of the Sovereign. Many also sit as Crown Court recorders (see above).

Despite the role of the district judge successive Lord Chancellors have repeatedly indicated that wholesale replacement of the lay magistracy by professionals is not an objective.

### Commission of the Peace
Magistrates are appointed to a Commission area and are assigned to a Petty Sessions Area or 'PSA' (*Chapter 2*). They must retire from the bench at 70 years of age when they normally transfer to the supplemental list (as opposed to serving on the active list) and after which they can still carry out a somewhat restricted range of purely administrative duties.

### Training
Training is a high priority. Before being appointed, candidates must give an undertaking to comply with the relevant requirements. If someone fails to complete an appropriate stage, he or she is expected to resign unless there is an acceptable explanation. There are schemes of Induction Training and Basic Training for new magistrates and comparable schemes for magistrates appointed to the specialist panels, i.e. youth court panel and family proceedings panel.[6]

The Magistrates New Training Initiative (MNTI) introduced in 1998 is based on magistrates acquiring a range of identified competencies for each area of responsibility as a magistrate (e.g. adult court, youth court, family court, chairmanship in the adult court and specialist panels) and demonstrating these through a process of mentoring and appraisal. Newly appointed magistrates are supported by suitably selected and trained experienced magistrates appointed as mentors to assist them to acquire basic competencies for the adult court—through attendance at training events, experience of sitting in court, support from the

---

[6] The magistrates' court has a wide-ranging family jurisdiction. It is possible in future that appointments may be made by the Lord Chancellor direct to either of these specialist panels (as already occurs in London)—as suggested by *Justice for All* in relation to the youth court panel.

mentor and a programme of visits to their home court, other courts, National Probation Service (NPS) facilities and custodial institutions. A magistrate is appraised when he or she and a mentor agrees that the magistrate is able to demonstrate the required basic competencies, normally around two years after appointment.

Under MNTI, a new magistrate receives a personal log in which progress and development is recorded and can expect to be re-appraised at least every three years. Through a mix of training and experience, all magistrates are expected to acquire a working knowledge of the law sufficient to follow the general run of summary cases, and an understanding of the main rules of evidence and procedure. They must, in particular, grasp the basic law and practice of sentencing—including a knowledge of local facilities for community sentences. There are also special training courses, e.g. in court chairmanship, for members of youth court panels, family panels and so on. Additionally, most courts run regular sessions to keep magistrates up-to-date with developments in relevant law, practice and procedure. The local magistrates' courts committee (MCC) is primarily responsible for training arrangements and there is also a Bench Training Committee and a local Development Committee to oversee aspects of the scheme, such as the appointment of mentors, appraisers, the approval of new court chairmen etc. The transition of the administration of magistrates' courts to the umbrella of the Court Service is likely to affect how training is provided—as it will affect other aspects of the administration of summary justice.

Apart from the input of local training officers, various bodies are involved in providing training and materials: the Judicial Studies Board (JSB) (below); the Magistrates' Association (below); and external organizations such as Cambridge University whose Board of Extra-Mural Studies runs regular courses at Madingley Hall. Training programmes tend to include components from various sources.[7]

### Duties and responsibilities
The main duty of a magistrate is to sit in court on a regular basis. The minimum requirement is 26 sittings a year. Most magistrates sit more than this and senior magistrates may find themselves sitting many more times. Apart from duties in their own PSA, magistrates may be called upon to sit elsewhere within the Commission area on occasion, e.g. where someone closely connected with another bench is charged with an offence. Additionally, magistrates can volunteer to sit in the Crown Court alongside a judge to hear appeals (but no longer to sit on committals for sentence as they once did): *Chapter 10.*

### Bench chairmen and deputy chairmen
Each PSA—or local bench—has a bench chairman whose role it is to oversee the general affairs of the bench, as well as to chair the court when present. The chairman is influential in shaping bench policy (e.g. the local starting points for sentences for particular offences; preferred ways of conducting court proceedings). He or she will also act as a sounding board for the views of

---

[7]  In 1997, the Magistrates' Association, Justices' Clerks Society, Judicial Studies Board and Waterside Press formed a Project Board to develop a workbook for use in court. The *Magistrates Bench Handbook* was first published in 1998, and a revised version in 2000. In 2002 a similar project was begun to create a *Family Bench Handbook.*

members of the bench—who as ordinary members of the community are exposed to every shade of public opinion and concern on matters such as law and order.

A secret ballot for the post of chairman takes place at the bench Annual General Meeting in October—when the successful candidate must obtain more than 50 per cent of the votes cast. The term of office is one year from the following January 1. If re-elected, the same individual may serve up to a maximum of five one-year terms. Local practice can often mean that, e.g. a voluntary three year rule is observed.

A local bench will usually have one or more deputy chairmen (sometimes called vice-chairmen) who are appointed in a similar way, but without any requirement to obtain a minimum percentage of the votes cast. The PSA can, if it wishes, adopt a statutory nominations procedure in relation to the appointment of the chairman and deputies. Otherwise there is a secret ballot. It is now possible for there to be a postal ballot.

**Presiding justices**

For many years PSAs have appointed 'court chairmen', 'day chairmen' or 'presiding justices'. A busy centre may have a dozen or more courts running every day and all needing someone other than the chairman proper or one of its deputy chairmen to preside. Since 1996, only magistrates whose names appear on a list of approved court chairmen appointed by a local bench selection panel are eligible to act as such (except under supervision for training purposes). Similarly, no-one can preside unless they have undertaken a course of instruction under arrangements approved by the Lord Chancellor.

# THE MAGISTRATES' ASSOCIATION

The Magistrates' Association was established in 1920 and incorporated by Royal Charter in 1962. It enjoys the patronage of the Sovereign, publishes a regular journal, *The Magistrate,* an annual report and responds to government proposals (and those of other agencies) affecting magistrates' courts, as well as initiating projects and proposals of its own. The association publishes the *Magistrates' Court Sentencing Guidelines* (latest edition 2000)—now formulated in conjunction with a range of other interested parties—which are promulgated nationwide. Membership is by voluntary subscription but the vast majority of magistrates in England and Wales belong to the association.

The association's headquarters are at 28 Fitzroy Square, London W1P 6DD. There is a full-time secretary and staff, including a training officer. The association operates via local branches based on a county or several counties. Each branch organizes its own events and elects representatives to a national council of around 100 members. There are various standing committees covering sentencing, youth courts, road traffic matters, and legal matters generally.

# JUSTICES' CLERKS

Formerly, justices' clerks were both the chief legal advisers to magistrates and managers of their courts. They are still the main legal advisers and PSAs must, in effect, operate under their auspices—but since the Police and Magistrates' Courts Act 1994 (as subsequently amended) the administrator is the justices' chief executive[8] for the magistrates' courts committee (MCC) area and an individual justices' clerk will only carry out management functions to the extent that these have now been delegated. Central to this relationship are the arrangements whereby the justices' clerk is free from direction in legal and judicial matters. However, he or she can direct his or her own court legal advisers—essentially people who deputise for him or her on a day-to-day basis in order that several courts can function simultaneously. Many justices' clerks are in fact now known as directors of legal services. At the time of the first edition of this handbook (1995) there were 230 justices' clerks, but now only around 150 people fulfil that role[9] assisted by some 3,000 court legal advisers. There are 42 MCC areas.

### Duties in court

These were the subject of a *Practice Direction (Justices: Clerk to Court) 2000* issued by the Lord Chief Justice, Lord Woolf, shortly after the Human Rights Act 1998 came into effect. Quite apart from giving judicial advice or repeating it in open court if it was given in private—and so that the parties can comment or make representations concerning that advice—there is a legal duty to assist unrepresented parties (i.e. people with no legal representative) to put their case but without acting in a partisan way. There is a duty to take a note of any evidence; or at least of all the main points. This will be relied on in the event of a dispute about what was said, or on appeal.

The *Practice Direction* also covers the situation where the adviser is conducting enforcement proceedings (which following the Access to Justice Act 1999 are for the justices' chief executive to bring). The legal adviser must not seek to 'prosecute' (as tended to happen in the past when such matters were the responsibility of the justices' clerk[10]). Whilst the direction acknowledges the practice in some areas whereby another member of staff is allocated the task of prosecuting enforcement cases, it does not comment on this beyond saying that it is not a breach of human rights law.

### In the retiring room

As can be seen from the 2000 *Practice Direction*, the justices' clerk must advise *on request*, but he or she can also act of his or her *own initiative*—and, in effect, must do so if the magistrates are about to go wrong in law. He or she may be invited into the magistrates' private retiring room but should never go there automatically and normally not unless specifically asked to do so. This invitation should only occur where there is a genuine need for legal advice or support. There is a duty to interrupt magistrates' private deliberations if by not doing so this would result in some legal error being made. The modern practice sanctioned by the 2000 *Practice Direction* is for advice to be given or repeated in open court. The parties can then comment if they wish. This is an aspect of ensuring a fair trial[11] (i.e. the adviser

---

[8] For a fuller outline of the role, powers and responsibilities of the justices' chief executive see *Introduction to the Magistrates' Court*, mentioned in footnote 5.

[9] They must be barristers or solicitors of at least five years' standing.

[10] A justices' clerk (or some other staff member) can be authorised to act in that capacity by the justices' chief executive delegating the function.

[11] Which also involves human rights considerations: *Chapter 1*.

must not appear to be involved in the final decision) and safeguarding the principle of open court.[12] There are limitations: magistrates may wish to discuss doubts or reservations—when common sense indicates such exchanges should be in private.

### Judicial duties

The justices' clerk has certain judicial or quasi-judicial powers and duties, e.g. to grant summonses, adjourn cases and to extend bail. These have been extended in recent times: in broad terms the justices' clerk now has many of the powers of a single justice—including to conduct a pre-trial review or criminal directions hearing at the start of a case—but not those which directly affect verdict, sentence or individual liberty.

### Appointment and status

Justices' clerks are appointed by local MCCs who must submit one or more names to the Lord Chancellor for approval—the final choice then being restricted to an approved candidate. Reasons must be given if the Lord Chancellor declines to give approval. Approval is also required for removal against the wishes of the local bench—who must also be consulted by the committee in this and a variety of other situations affecting their justices' clerk, including on appointment. The Justices' Clerks Society is the professional representative body for justices' clerks and certain other legal advisers of similar status.

## THE JUDICIAL STUDIES BOARD: A NOTE

The Judicial Studies Board (JSB) provides training and instruction for all full-time and part-time judges in England and Wales (including district judges) in the skills necessary to be a judge. Additionally, it has an advisory role in the training by local MCCs of lay magistrates. The JSB is based at Millbank Tower, Westminster although many of its training functions take place at other locations.

As part of its general remit, the JSB provides a range of courses, materials and related support or advice for members of the judiciary at all stages of their development. It has been to the fore in encouraging working manuals such as the *Magistrates Bench Handbook* in partnership with the Magistrates' Association and Justices' Clerks' Society.[13] Quite courageously, the JSB was one of the first organizations within the criminal justice process to take a stand on race (and other discrimination) issues, to the extent of setting up its own advisory board and providing extensive training and materials for judges and magistrates from the 1980s onwards.

## LAW OFFICERS

The law officers of the Crown are the Attorney General and the Solicitor General. They are appointed from among the senior lawyer MPs of the party in power and

---

[12] Which involves both statutory and human rights considerations: *Chapter 1.*
[13] (2000). Published by Waterside Press and now in its second edition.

are either peers or members of Parliament. Apart from his or her role in the courts, which may involve appearing as prosecuting counsel in high profile or nationally sensitive cases, the Attorney General has a political role which is to act as the government's principal legal adviser and in this capacity he or she answers members' questions in the House of Commons. Additionally, he or she is accountable to Parliament for the CPS and the SFO, the directors of which agencies report to him (*Chapter 10*). Along with the Lord Chancellor and Home Secretary the Attorney General is one of the three signatories to the White Paper *Justice for All* and as head of one of the three departments of state with responsibilities for aspects of criminal justice is part of the triumvirate which stands at the pinnacle of efforts to improve the workings of criminal justice as whole.

# CROWN PROSECUTORS

As explained in *Chapters 7* (which also outlines the nature of the prosecutor's role) the overall national head of the CPS is the Director of Public Prosecutions (DPP)[14]—who must issue a Code for Crown Prosecutors pursuant to section 10 Prosecution of Offences Act 1985—and the responsible Government law officer the Attorney-General (above). Crown prosecutors are usually solicitors, but may be barristers by training. Other senior personnel include a chief executive, directors of casework and policy, chief Crown prosecutors, assistant chief Crown prosecutors, area business managers and specialist higher court advocates. Crown prosecutors and senior Crown prosecutors operate at local level assisted by designated caseworkers (below).

### Headquarters and the regions
The CPS has headquarters in London and York and operates under the now standard structure of 42 areas coinciding with police force and other agency boundaries across England and Wales. In 1999, following publication of *Review of the CPS* by Sir Iain Glidewell in the previous year the CPS changed from 14 to 42 geographical areas. Each area lines up with existing police force boundaries apart from in London where the area covers the forces of the City of London Police and the Metropolitan Police Service. This structure 'meets the Government's aim of a co-ordinated criminal justice system with national policies delivered locally'.

### External representation and opinions
Largely speaking, the CPS functions through in-house lawyers and managers. However it does sometimes employ solicitors in private practice to act as its agents, and did so extensively in its early days. CPS agents have only limited authority concerning the conduct of a case. Also, it can happen that a case is unusually complex, involves specialist technicalities, or needs to be managed away from the distractions of day-to-day prosecution. It may then be more

---

[14] The director originally had a limited responsibility for approving and supervising the prosecution of very serious offences at a time when prosecutions generally were conducted by the police or their own prosecuting solicitors. The office of DPP and those arrangements were transformed by the creation of the CPS in 1985.

expeditious or cost-effective for the CPS to employ outside lawyers. Likewise it may be appropriate at the outset of a substantial case to take the opinion of counsel (i.e. a practising barrister) and to retain that person's services for all aspects of the future conduct of the case. Every such advocate prosecuting on behalf of the CPS is expected to be familiar with a booklet *CPS Instructions For Prosecuting Advocates* first published in 2000, which covers a range of day-to-day issues such as custody time limits, plea and directions hearings, disclosure of the prosecution case, racially aggravated offences and human rights issues.

### Designated case workers

In 1998 the law was changed to allow CPS staff who are not qualified as lawyers to review cases and present them in magistrates' courts. The powers extend to a limited range of cases involving straightforward guilty pleas, including, e.g. minor thefts, simple possession of certain drugs and non-contentious motoring offences. Under the supervision of experienced Crown prosecutors, designated caseworkers divide their time between police stations (where they review cases) and local magistrates' courts. Before they can undertake this work they must pass an intensive training course validated by an external body and be formally designated as caseworkers by the DPP.

## ADVOCATES

Lawyers are either barristers (sometimes called 'counsel') or solicitors, according to their training. Both have rights of audience in the magistrates' court and barristers and authorised solicitors in the Crown Court. When appearing in court both are also known as 'advocates', i.e. they speak for their client, advocating—putting forward—matters in the best light. It can be viewed as an essential feature of democratic and decent society that everyone is entitled to have their case argued in this way no matter how unpopular the thought might be to some people on occasion. Both professions have their own codes of conduct and ethics but, generally speaking, provided that they do not positively mislead the court there is no duty to disclose matters which are adverse to a client and which have not otherwise emerged in the proceedings (a consequence of the English adversarial system).

The kind of advocate regularly seen in magistrates' courts is the local solicitor specialising in criminal and family work. He or she will usually undertake state funded representation (below). Some solicitors find it cost effective to employ recently qualified barristers for advocacy work. This is a common feature in London and other urban centres where there are barristers' chambers. Senior barristers are known as Queen's Counsel (or 'silks') and must normally appear in court accompanied by a junior barrister (although this allegedly restrictive practice is being questioned in the European Union).

### Duty solicitor schemes

Local duty solicitor schemes may provide legal assistance and advice to people when they are first detained. There are no great formalities, but the schemes do not allow for or guarantee any choice of solicitor, or for continued services by the same solicitor after the defendant is released from police custody or when he or she appears in court. Duty solicitor schemes in magistrates' courts provide a 'first aid' service to defendants in criminal cases who arrive at court without a lawyer. Duty solicitors can advise defendants in custody; make bail applications; represent defendants in custody who are pleading guilty; give advice to and represent non-custody defendants who, in the duty solicitor's opinion, need such help; and help defendants to apply for state funded representation which is now free of charge in magistrates' courts for everyone regardless of their financial circumstances (below).

# CRIMINAL DEFENCE SERVICE

A key aspect of reforms which took place in 2001 to the former arrangements for legal aid was the creation of a Criminal Defence Service (CDS) which provides legal assistance to people suspected or accused of crimes through a mix of contracts with private and salaried defenders. The purpose of the CDS is set out in a circular from the Lord Chancellor's Department as

> . . . to ensure access for individuals involved in criminal investigations to such advice, assistance and representation as the interests of justice require. The CDS will move to funding criminal defence services through a flexible system of contracts with private sector lawyers and salaried defenders, with the aim of achieving quality assured services and value for money. Suspects and defendants will have a choice of representatives.

The CDS operates under the auspices of the Legal Services Commission (below). Only solicitors with a franchise from the LSC or who work full-time for the CDS can apply for a representation order for a defendant. The application, usually in the magistrates' court, can be made to a court or justices' clerk, the matter being referred to the court if he or she is not prepared to grant representation.

# STATE FUNDED LEGAL REPRESENTATION

State funded legal representation used to be provided by way of 'legal aid'[15] under a system which took both the interests of justice and the financial circumstances of the applicant into account. In April 2001, the Legal Aid Board was replaced by a Legal Services Commission (LSC) that assumed responsibility for funding advice and assistance in criminal proceedings. This reform—based on the Access to Justice Act 1999 and the Criminal Defence Service (Advice and Assistance Act) 2001—had a number of key effects:

- legal aid as such was abolished and replaced by representation at public expense under the 1999 Act
- legal aid orders have been replaced by 'representation orders'

---

[15] The term 'legal aid' appears to have continued in everyday parlance.

- a representation order will be granted where it is in the interests of justice to do so[16]
- all publicly funded representation in the magistrates' courts is now free of charge. There is no means test.[17]

Where a case is finalised in the Crown Court, the judge has a power to make an order at the end of the case requiring the defendant to pay some or all of the defence costs, known as a recovery of defence costs order (but *not* if a case starts and finishes in the magistrates' court).[18]

## THE McKENZIE FRIEND

A defendant may be assisted by what is sometimes called a 'McKenzie friend'[19] (even if that term may have been superseded in case law), i.e. someone to take notes, quietly make suggestions and give advice. This needs to be authorised by the court and the device can only be used as a means of assisting the defendant and the court, not of hindering the proceedings, e.g. by filibustering, playing to the gallery or otherwise spinning out the case. Courts can hear from whoever they wish in a given case—a principle enshrined in the House of Lords ruling in *O'Toole v Scott* [1965] AC 939. Conversely, the Courts and Legal Services Act 1990 acknowledges a general right for a court to refuse to hear someone who would normally have rights of audience for reasons which apply to him or her as an individual—but the court must give its reasons.

## WITNESSES AND EXPERTS

A key contribution to the criminal process in court is made by witnesses attending to give evidence about events that they have seen, heard or otherwise experienced and who in many instances will also be victims of crime. The proper treatment of witnesses is high on the agenda within all the criminal justice agencies something which (together with Victim Support and witness schemes) is considered in *Chapter 18*. That chapter also looks at the specialist contribution of expert witnesses.

---

[16] The relevant considerations reflect what used to be known as 'the Widgery criteria' (named after Lord Widgery, Lord Chief Justice, who originally laid them down), e.g. whether: the accused is likely to lose his or her liberty; his or her reputation is at stake; the complexity of the proceedings; whether the accused will be able to understand the proceedings etc.

[17] Even a millionaire would qualify, it seems, once the interests of justice test is satisfied—assuming that he or she does not wish to forego this bonus and instruct and pay for a lawyer privately.

[18] There is thus a disincentive to elect trial by jury.

[19] One of those characters who spring up in the law from time to time and lend their identity to some legal concept, such as 'The Man on the Clapham Omnibus'—who became a by-word for reasonableness—and the unsuspecting Mr. Newton whose name is synonymous, in magistrates' courts, with the notion of a 'trial within a trial' to settle disputed facts following a plea of guilty: the Newton hearing.

# INTERPRETERS

Increasingly, the need for interpreters[20] has been recognised in a wide range of criminal justice situations from the outset of an investigation to assistance in the prison setting, and indeed human rights considerations now often mean that such assistance is essential where the accused person's first language is not English (unless he or she clearly indicates that an interpreter is not required). In court, interpreters take a special oath (or affirm) to 'truly interpret' the evidence from one language to another, or by sign language to someone with impaired hearing. The task is a highly skilled one given the degree of precision required in legal proceedings, and the need to communicate information without adding to it, detracting from it or injecting any value judgment.

Courts, police and other practitioners now have, or have access to, lists of people who are qualified to interpret into and from English and other languages as well as interpreters skilled in dealing with sign language. People serving custodial sentences may or may not be fortunate enough to have ready or immediate access to an interpreter although this is an area where a number of initiatives have been developed by HM Prison Service, including remote interpreting over the telephone.

---

[20] For an overview see *Interpreters and the Legal Process* (1996), Colin J and Morris R, Winchester: Waterside Press.

# CHAPTER 13

# Community Provision

This chapter and *Chapter 14* look at community provision and custodial provision respectively, i.e. the existence of facilities, resources or arrangements to deal with offenders within the community or alternatively—where this is not possible in accordance with sound sentencing practice (*Chapter 9*)—in prisons or other custodial establishments.

The National Probation Service (NPS) and HM Prison Service (HMPS) have become increasingly committed to joint working and cohesive strategies in an effort to enhance crime reduction through both community sentences and custodial ones (most of which are served partly in the community in any event: *Chapter 14*). Indicative of such developments is the appointment of a Prisons and Probation Minister[1] and, since 2002, a joint Correctional Services Board and Correctional Services Accreditation Panel[2]—whose aims include maximising the numbers of offenders dealt with via a range of schemes and programmes in accordance with methods of intervention with offenders which are effective in reducing re-offending—and the extension of the Prison Ombudsman's office to cover both prisons and probation. Identifying the best options for tackling offending behaviour—essentially 'what works' with offenders—is a key feature of the proposals in *Justice For All* (*Chapter 15*). The term 'seamless sentence', which implies that work with an offender whilst in prison will, in many cases, be carried over into the community on his or her release, further emphasises the existence of a co-ordinated approach.

## THE NATIONAL PROBATION SERVICE

The National Probation Service (NPS) was established in April 2001 under the Criminal Justice and Court Services Act 2000. It comprises 42 area Probation Services throughout England and Wales together with the National Probation Directorate based in London.[3] The service is a directorate of the Home Office. These arrangements replaced those whereby area probation services operated under the auspices of local probation committees in conjunction with a Probation Unit at the Home Office, and the central directorate now undertakes the former functions of that unit and a number of new ones of a directly managerial nature.

At the same time, probation committees were replaced by local Probation Boards (below) and to accompany the creation of the NPS there have been many changes in organization, structure, priorities, qualifying training arrangements

---

[1] At one stage called the Minister for Community and Custodial Provision. See *Chapter 14* for the Prisons and Probation Ombudsman. For a while there were rumours that there might be just one 'Corrections Service' and one director.

[2] Formerly the Joint Prison/Probation Services Accreditation Panel.

[3] Located at Horseferry House, Dean Ryle Street, London SW1.

for NPS officers and day-to-day routines[4]—and the names of the main community sentences administered by the service were changed under the 2000 Act (below).[5]

## Aims of the NPS
The published aims of the NPS are as follows:

- protecting the public
- reducing re-offending
- the proper punishment of offenders in the community
- ensuring offenders' awareness of the effects of crime on the victims of crime and the public
- rehabilitation of offenders.

The service operates within the Government's 'Correctional Policy Framework', contributing primarily to Home Office Aims 3 and 4. These are as follows:

**Aim 3:** To ensure the effective delivery of justice, avoiding unnecessary delay, through efficient investigation, detection, prosecution and court procedures. To minimise the threat to and intimidation of witnesses and to engage with and support victims.

**Aim 4:** To deliver effective custodial and community sentences to reduce reoffending and protect the public, through the prison and probation services in partnership with the Youth Justice Board.[6]

The NPS also has a remit to be a public service that protects the public, operates and enforces court orders and prison licences, and rehabilitates offenders to lead law abiding lives. Its 'collective aim' is that it should by 2004 establish itself as a world leader in designing and implementing offender assessment and supervision programmes that effectively reduce re-offending and improve public safety; and by 2006 be recognised as a top performing public service as benchmarked by the European Excellence Model.

## Organization and structure
The 42 NPS area boundaries are aligned with those of the police, CPS and magistrates' courts. Between the centre and the operational areas are seven regional offices whose task is described in the NPS director's launch document, *A New Choreography*, as 'adding value to the (centre) core team by providing effective connectors between the centre and local areas as well as working with boards to achieve improved performance'.

---

[4] Also, family court welfare and other civil work was moved from the service to a new Children and Family Court Advisory and Support Service (CAFCASS).

[5] The original plan was to alter the name of the service to give it a 'punishment' or 'corrections' edge. This was resisted, the word 'probation' retained in the agency's title and the names of orders changed. Mike Nellis, a seasoned observer, has commented that it might have been better the other way round, i.e. to have retained the well understood names of orders and to have changed the name of the service to, say, 'Community Corrections Agency': *Introduction to the Probation Service* (2001), edn. 2, revised reprint, Whitfield D, Winchester: Waterside Press.

[6] Again emphasising the need for joint working.

A main aim is that this revised structure should bring with it benefits in terms of consistency, uniformity and standardisation, e.g. in the application of *National Standards* for aspects of probation work and in terms of the facilities and programmes which the service is responsible for providing in order that community punishments ordered by the courts can be carried out. Central direction should also mean that each NPS area will use comparable risk and dangerousness classifications when probation officers make assessments of offenders—and, e.g. common computer programmes and more coherent probation and bail hostel provision. However, local understanding, especially with the courts for the area, remains a key component.

### Probation Boards and chief probation officers
Each Probation Board is composed of representatives of the local community appointed by the Home Secretary (except for a judge appointed by the Lord Chancellor) and the chief probation officer is a member of the board. The board acts as the local employer as well as setting the local agenda against a background of national strategy. The chief probation officer for the area is appointed by the Home Secretary who also has power to give directions to boards about how to fulfil their statutory responsibilities. There are 'default' powers whereby he or she can sack and replace boards if they fail to perform effectively. At national level there is an Association of Probation Boards.

### A new choreography and new national priorities
Stationery for the NPS is inscribed with the phrase: 'Enforcement, rehabilitation and public protection'—a reflection of government priorities and the notion that the NPS is now a law enforcement agency rather than a welfare agency (its historical roots). Thus according to *A New Choreography*:[7]

> The NPS is a key statutory criminal justice service working in a highly collaborative way with police and prison colleagues as well as local authorities, health, education, housing and a wide range of independent and voluntary sector partners.

*A New Choreography* deals with the 'nine areas where the greatest challenges or changes lie' as follows:

- more accurate and effective assessment and management of risk and dangerousness
- more involvement of victims of serious sexual and other violent crime
- offender programmes that have a track record in reducing reoffending
- intervening early to take young people away from crime
- prompt enforcement of community orders and release licences
- providing courts with good information and pre-trial services
- valuing and achieving diversity in the NPS and the services it provides
- building an excellent organization; and
- building an effective performance management framework.

---

[7] (2000), Wallis E, London: National Probation Service.

That document also mentions the provision of better information to victims of crime about the release arrangements for offenders, further development of 'what works' programmes, and a special emphasis on young offenders to try and use early intervention and divert young people away from crime. In this last context specially selected probation officers now serve as members of the local multi-agency youth offending teams (YOTs) described in *Chapter 5*.

### A context for change

The shifts so far described occurred at a time when government was working towards other major changes in criminal justice services (as subsequently reflected in the Auld report and *Justice For All (Chapter 15)* or enacted, e.g. in the Police Reform Act 2002 (*Chapter 11*)). Indeed, in the 'rebranding' of the NPS, the changed names of community orders (below) and changed order of priorities, the whole nature of criminal justice can be seen to be altering and adapting to a corrections or punishment oriented political agenda, one which also embraces increasing reliance on technology, surveillance (including electronic monitoring) and faster responses to offending. Thus, according to one commentator with extensive experience as a chief probation officer:[8]

> The picture represented by these changes is clear—the NPS is in the process of being re-shaped to support the government in its political need to be "tough on crime". Community-based orders need to carry conviction and credibility; but they also need to demonstrate a level of effectiveness and be given weight. All the changes . . . from provision for youth justice to long-term supervision for dangerous offenders, were designed with this in mind. Many are undoubtedly welcome, positive and overdue— and they brought a sense of optimism and purpose to probation work which was badly needed. Others seem excessively managerial and bureaucratic, and if a re-shaped service is to retain the drive and imagination which have characterised its approach to the messy, difficult, sensitive and sometimes very rewarding business of supervising offenders in the community it is going to test the boundaries, and its capacity to hold on to its values as well as its enthusiasm to ensure that the communities it serves understand and accept the way it works.

The NPS itself points out that it has accelerated the development of effective ways of working with offenders—and also, indicative of the sheer breadth of NPS responsibilities, that:[9]

- Each year the NPS commences the supervision of some 175,000 offenders. The caseload on any given day is in excess of 200,000. Approximately 90 per cent are male and ten per cent are female. Just over a quarter of offenders serving community sentences are aged 16-20 and just less than three quarters are aged 21 and over.
- Approximately 70 per cent of offenders supervised will be on community sentences, and 30 per cent imprisoned with a period of statutory licence supervision in the community as an integral part of the sentence.

---

[8] From the *Preface* of *Introduction to the Probation Service* (2001), edn. 2, revised reprint, Whitfield D, Winchester: Waterside Press.

[9] NPS Web-site: www.homeoffice.gov.uk/cpg/nps/

- All NPS work with offenders combines continuous assessment and management of risk and dangerousness with the provision of expert supervision programmes designed to reduce re-offending. Enforcement of the order or licence conditions is a priority.
- Each year the NPS assist magistrates and judges in their sentencing decisions through the provision of about 235,000 pre-sentence reports (PSRs), and 20,000 bail information reports.
- Each year NPS staff find and supervise some eight million hours of unpaid work by offenders in local communities, to ensure that they meet the requirements of their community punishment orders (CPOs).
- The NPS makes a critical contribution to decisions about the early release of prisoners through the production of reports (approximately 87,000 annually) which combine risk and dangerousness assessments with community supervision plan proposals.
- 100 approved probation hostels will continue to play a major role in the NPS public protection strategy, providing controlled environments for offenders on bail, community sentences and post-custody licences.
- Where the victims of the most serious violent, including sexually violent, crimes are contactable and wish it, the impact of the offence and their concerns form a part of the pre-custody and post-custody release risk assessments written by probation staff (50,000 cases a year and rising).
- Many probation staff are seconded to work in youth offending teams, prisons and a wide range of other public protection and crime prevention or reduction partnership agencies. Their skills, particularly in assessing risk and dangerousness, are highly valued.

The NPS also works in partnership with other agencies and services, e.g. Mult-agency Protection Panels (MAPPs) already mentioned in *Chapter 6* (and see, generally, the comments on working together and partnership in *Chapter 17*).

### The names of community penalties
A reflection of the Government's determination to 're-brand' the NPS, is the legislation that changed the names of the principal community orders, as follows:

- the probation order became the *community rehabilitation order*
- the community service order became the *community punishment order;* and
- the combination order became the *community punishment and rehabilitation order*.

The criteria affecting the use of community penalties by sentencers and the content of all community orders are outlined in *Chapter 9*. Remarking on these changes, David Faulkner[10] has noted:

> . . . the appearance of "punishment" as a statutory aim of the Probation Service, but with no mention of it for the Prison Service, is at best confusing and at worst alarming. So is the replacement of the community service order by the community punishment order—both for its use of the word punishment and for the loss of the sense of restoration and "paying back the community" which the old title implied.

---

[10] See *Crime, State and Citizen: A Field Full of Folk* (2001), Winchester: Waterside Press.

The change also drains "community" of any positive meaning; combined with punishment—unless it implies that the community is somehow to join in the offender's humiliation—it means no more than "not served in prison" . . . Probation officers must find it ironic that these changes were taking place in their own service at a time when recruitment advertising for the Metropolitan Police depicted the police as performing what is essentially a social service.

### Drug testing

The Criminal Justice and Court Services Act 2000 gave police the power to drug test detainees in police custody (*Chapter 6*) and the courts powers to order drug testing of offenders under the supervision of the NPS and in relation to certain 'trigger' offences. Testing is restricted to specified Class A drugs heroin and crack cocaine. The powers are being piloted in nine areas of the country. See also the drug treatment and testing order mentioned in *Chapter 9*.

### Further change on the horizon

*Justice for All* states:

Where an offender is convicted we will . . . ensure tough, more intensive community sentences with multiple conditions like tagging, reparation and drug treatment and testing to deny liberty, rehabilitate the offender and protect the public.

The route via which such changes are to be delivered is to be found in suggestions for more rigorous community penalties, increased use of electronic monitoring and new sentences of intermittent custody ('weekend gaol'), custody minus (a form of 'suspended' sentence conditional on completion of punishment in the community), and custody plus (where a larger proportion of a custodial sentence is spent in the community). It remains to be seen how the NPS will respond to such sentences—further explained in *Chapter 15*—if enacted.

## KEY ROLE OF THE PRE-SENTENCE REPORT

A central aspect of probation work is writing pre-sentence reports (PSRs) for consideration by courts before they decide upon sentence. PSRs are normally requested by courts in all the more serious cases, although they can be dispensed with where the court thinks that one is unnecessary.[11] In their present form they were introduced by the Criminal Justice Act 1991[12] following which the preparation and content of reports also became subject to *National Standards*. In more recent times, a form of PSR known as a 'specific sentence report'—or SSR—has evolved. This is a more focused form of report which, at the request of the court, is directed towards the appropriateness of certain community orders and their suitability for the offender (e.g. lesser CPOs or CROs with no added requirements).

PSRs are confidential documents and the information in them is limited to what is relevant to the sentencing process. However, following the Pre-Sentence

---

[11] There are stricter criteria before a PSR can be dispensed with in relation to a juvenile: *Chapter 5*.

[12] Now consolidated in the Powers of Criminal Courts (Sentencing) Act 2000. Prior to 1991 courts relied on what were known as 'social enquiry reports' (or SERs) a term which serves to indicate how the ethos of probation work has changed, at least in the political sense.

Report (Prescription of Prosecutors) Order 1998, certain prosecutors (including Crown prosecutors) are automatically entitled to receive a copy of the PSR, whilst the decision whether to disclose to other prosecutors depends on an exercise of discretion by the court. *National Standards* envisage that a copy 'will be provided to the court, the defence, the offender and (where required by [law]) the prosecution'.

The content of the PSR is brought to the attention of the offender by the report writer. This may mean reading it out in private for those who have difficulty in reading, or having an interpreter read and translate it to an offender whose first language is not English. A copy of the PSR is given to the offender and to his or her legal representative. It is important post-Human Rights Act 1998 for a court to ensure that the PSR has been made available to the defendant and that he or she understands it and has had a proper opportunity to consider and, where appropriate, comment on it to both the writer and the court, and to make any relevant representations if, e.g. not satisfied that it contains correct data or a valid conclusion.

The PSR will start by setting out basic factual information on the offence and the offender (including previous convictions and drawing on other information from the CPS). There will also be a summary of the sources drawn upon to prepare the report and steps taken to verify information, a note of other potentially useful sources to which it was not possible to have access, and any doubts about the reliability of particular information. Information will then appear under headings such as:

- offence analysis
- offender assessment
- assessment of the risk of harm to the public and the likelihood of re–offending
- a conclusion (including, if appropriate, a sentence proposal) [13]

## PROBATION OFFICERS

Much of the day-to-day work of the NPS is carried out by what are often called 'main grade' probation officers. This work encompasses:

- *fieldwork:* attending court, writing PSRs and SSRs, supervising offenders
- *probation centre work:* running intensive courses for high risk offenders who attend a probation centre
- *group work:* running offending behaviour groups such as programmes for sex offenders, anger management groups, alcohol education courses
- *community punishment:* supervising non-probation officer staff, attending court, publicising the CPO scheme
- *probation hostels:* managing hostels, selecting and supervising residents, attending court

---

[13] Further information about PSRs is contained in *The Sentence of the Court* (2002), edn. 3, revised reprint, Watkins M and Gordon W, Winchester: Waterside Press and *Introduction to the Probation Service* (2001), edn. 2, revised reprint, Whitfield, D, Winchester: Waterside Press.

- *prison-related work:* working alongside prison officers in the exercise of their welfare function and in relation to bail information, sentence planning and early release plans, forging a link with outside supervisors, rehabilitative and other pre-release work
- *youth justice:* being a member of an inter-agency youth justice team (YOT): see *Chapter 5*
- *bail information:* which is governed by *National Standards* and involves interviewing defendants, verifying information about their circumstances and supplying this to the CPS.

Senior grades—implying management, co-ordination or specialist roles in relation to a geographical area or specialist sphere of operations—are senior probation officer, assistant chief probation officer and deputy chief probation officer. The NPS also employs administrative and clerical staff, and specialists in areas such as information technology and research.

## HM INSPECTORATE OF PROBATION

HM Inspectorate of Probation (HMIP) is a compact, autonomous unit responsible directly to the Home Secretary and charged with inspecting the work of the NPS. HMIP also provides ministers and officials with advice on probation matters and promotes the development of effective probation management and practice. Most probation inspectors are drawn from within the ranks of the NPS. Inspectors generally have considerable experience in the probation field, and may have worked through the grades to reach chief officer level. There is statutory provision allowing suitably qualified people from other professions to become probation inspectors. There are two kinds of inspection:

- *area* inspections, when two or three sections of a an NPS area's work (e.g. court reports, community service, sex offenders) are looked at in detail, with sampling exercises and face-to-face discussions between inspectors and probation staff taking place at all levels within the service being inspected. Such inspections are called 'Quality and Effectiveness Inspections' and make recommendations to the area concerned.
- *thematic* inspections, when a particular area of work is examined, e.g. the preparation of PSRs or post-custody supervision (i.e. the supervision of prisoners following their release from prison: see below and *Chapter 14*). A thematic inspection will normally be carried out across several NPS areas and the final report will contain recommendations to the Home Secretary about national issues as well as recommendations to local areas. Reports of thematic inspections can also contain recommendations concerning the performance of other agencies within the justice process and government departments with an interest in criminal justice.

As well as recommendations regarding action which needs to be taken to improve standards, reports by inspectors may also contain 'commendations' whereby government, Probation Boards and other people can become aware of good work. All such reports are open to public scrutiny.

## POST-CUSTODY SUPERVISION

As indicated at the start of this chapter, the trend is towards the 'seamless sentence' whereby work with an offender in prison dovetails with supervision in the community on release. This is a key feature of *Justice For All* (*Chapter 15*).

## SOCIAL SERVICES

Local authority social services departments work with many young or vulnerable people (see also *Medical and Psychiatric Services*, below). Such work is often carried out independently of the criminal process proper by social workers but also as an integral part of it, e.g. by social services department members of YOTs (*Chapter 5*). Such services also have a wider welfare role in relation to children generally, including child protection and safety, as to which they have both emergency powers and longer-term duties, the latter in many instances requiring an order under the family jurisdiction.[14]

## EDUCATION SERVICES

Local education services are involved with the criminal justice process in a number of ways, including:

- preparing school reports on pupils appearing before the criminal courts, or alternatively providing relevant information to a YOT member preparing a PSR, for incorporation into that report
- participating in a YOT
- bringing prosecutions against parents for non-attendance of their children at school;[15] and
- involvement in a range of multi-agency partnerships.

## MEDICAL AND PSYCHIATRIC SERVICES

The National Health Service, social services departments and the voluntary sector provide a range of facilities for mentally disturbed offenders who are diverted towards appropriate care at the pre-court stage (including the pre-prosecution stage); given community rehabilitaion orders or supervision orders with a condition of psychiatric treatment; given hospital orders or remanded to hospital; made subject to guardianship orders or transferred from prison to hospital. In addition medical services (including the Healthcare Service for Prisoners: *Chapter 14*) prepare reports on the medical and mental condition of defendants to assist courts in their sentencing decisions and HMPS and the NPS concerning post-custody and other community supervision.

---

[14] For an explanation of these powers and how they intersect with the youth justice process, see *Child Law: A Guide for Courts and Practitioners* (2001), Powell, R, Winchester: Waterside Press.

[15] For a detailed explanation see *Child Law, supra.*

In many courts 'duty psychiatrist' schemes and other court psychiatric assessment arrangements have been established: these enable courts to receive speedy professional advice which can also facilitate the (sometimes difficult to obtain) admission of offenders to hospital in appropriate cases.

## THE PRIVATE SECTOR

Private sector involvement with prisons is referred to in *Chapter 14*. The private sector is also involved in the provision of criminal justice services in the community, including the electronic monitoring (or tagging)[16] of offenders subject to curfew orders (*Chapter 9*) or home detention curfew (*Chapter 14*) following release from prison on licence. The whole electronic monitoring service, from the supply and installation of equipment to the actual monitoring of those subject to surveillance, is the responsibility of private contractors.

## THE VOLUNTARY SECTOR

The voluntary sector is heavily engaged in work with offenders and a wide range of such organizations plays a part in work with offenders, from national bodies such as the crime reduction charity Nacro and Victim Support (which also operates the Court Witness Service: *Chapter 18*) to small local organizations managing a single hostel or providing a local service (for example a drug rehabilitation project). Key areas of work for the voluntary sector include:

- *accommodation:* providing hostels, shared housing and supported lodgings schemes for ex-offenders
- *employment:* providing adult and youth training, work experience, and help and advice on finding employment
- *education:* providing offenders with education in basic skills, and information, advice and help on participation in education courses
- *bail:* providing accommodation and support for bailed defendants to help avoid unnecessary remands in custody
- *mental health:* providing hostels, group homes, day care and advice services for people with a history of mental illness
- *drug/alcohol misuse:* providing advice services, residential rehabilitation facilities and day care for people with drug and alcohol problems
- *court-based services:* running help desks at courts providing on the spot advice and information to people attending court, as well as 'tea-bars' and refreshment facilities in some instances; and
- *prisoner's families:* providing support, help and advice to the families and friends of people serving prison sentences.

The voluntary sector also plays a substantial and increasing role in relation to HMPS: *Chapter 14*.

---

[16] For an overview see *The Magic Bracelet: Technology and Offender Supervision* (2001), Whitfield D, Winchester: Waterside Press.

# Custodial Provision

Lawful denial of liberty as a form of sanction has existed since the Roman era (and maybe longer), but it is only in modern times, the last 200 years or so, that prisons and similar establishments have been places where people serve custodial terms ordered by the courts as a punishment. Until the eighteenth century prisons were used mainly for people awaiting trial, exile, execution, transportation or to enforce payment of a debt or other civil obligation.

Similarly, in former times, prisons might operate under private ownership or other vested interest, or as an adjunct to power or status whereby a given individual could imprison someone else at will. The first truly communal or public gaols were local 'bridewells' and 'houses of correction' intended among other things to house petty offenders ('miscreants') and vagrants as well as those people awaiting trial etc. as above—and which were largely administered by local magistrates. Reliance on prisons as, on the one hand, municipal symbols of deterrence, shame and retribution and, on the other, more enlightened places where offenders might be, e.g. educated, trained and rehabilitated developed only gradually from a mix of law and order politics and a strong tradition of penal reform.[1]

Nowadays Her Majesty's Prison Service (HMPS) operates primarily under the Prisons Act 1952 and Prison Rules 1999 (with comparable provisions for young offenders) and an accumulation of internal prison service orders (PSOs), instructions (PSIs) and manuals dealing with every aspect of prison life from the making of a telephone call by a prisoner to race relations, work, pay, religious worship, discrimination and disability—all now subject to human rights law (*Chapter 1*). The former relative isolation of HMPS is being replaced by increased involvement with other agencies and the voluntary and the private sectors to deliver a range of regimes. As noted in *Chapter 13* custodial and community provision are increasingly mentioned 'in the same breath'. *Justice for All* proposes new forms of sentence where such an inter relationship is implicit (*Chapter 15*).

## HM PRISON SERVICE

Custodial provision for offenders convicted of offences that are 'so serious that only a custodial sentence can be justified' or to protect the public from serious harm from certain violent or sexual offenders (*Chapter 9*) is the remit of HMPS which must combine security, control and safety in its establishments with a range of prisoner activities including a variety of offending behaviour and pre-release courses—where HMPS works, in particular, in close co-operation with the

---

[1]   For an outline see *Introduction to Prisons and Imprisonment* (1998), Flynn N, Winchester: Waterside Press; *Punishments of Former Days* (1992), Pettifer E, Winchester: Waterside Press. For the debate about the purposes and utility of imprisonment see *Prison On Trial* (2000), Mathiesen T, 2nd English edn., Winchester: Waterside Press.

National Probation Service (NPS) in relation to adults (*Chapter 13*) and Youth Justice Board in relation to juveniles (*Chapter 5*).[2]

HMPS is obliged to hold all adults (and some juveniles: *Chapter 5*) remanded to custody by the courts pending trial (*Chapter 8*), as well as all people convicted and sentenced to a custodial term (or who are in custody after conviction but awaiting sentence). This it does through a nationwide network of prisons, remand centres, young offender institutions (YOIs), secure training centres and auxiliary premises, all collectively known as 'the prison estate'. The aims of HMPS are crystalised in its statement of purpose displayed in all establishments:

> Her Majesty's Prison Service serves the public by keeping in custody those committed by the courts Our duty is to look after them with humanity and help them lead law abiding and useful lives in custody and after release.

### Status, organization and staffing
HMPS became an executive agency in 1993. In theory, Home Office ministers, including the Prisons and Probation Minister, are responsible for policy but the director general of the HMPS is responsible for the delivery of services—but the distinction is not always straightforward in practice. A Prisons Board acts as the agency's senior management team. There are a number of executive directors in charge of specific areas of operation, including, e.g. healthcare, programmes, the high security estate, personnel and finance, together with four non-executive directors from outside of the service. The role of director can represent something of a 'poisoned chalice' in that there is always the risk of a major disturbance or other threat to security and control (both first order priorities), whilst the demands of items such as prisoner activities, education, rehabilitation, treatment programmes (especially concerning misuse of drugs and alcohol) often require a level of flexibility and compromise.[3]

### Governors, officers and other staff
HMPS employs around 44,000 staff and spends about £1 billion a year on salaries and related costs. Some two-thirds of HMPS staff are uniformed prison officers[4] whilst over a thousand are 'governor grades' (i.e. as opposed to prison officers: below). There are also various operational support grades (OSGs). Each prison has a 'governing governor' with governor grades in support.[5] Until 2002, governors were responsible for disciplinary adjudications under a system whereby prisoners can have days added to their sentence for breaches of prison discipline, but this practice fell foul of Article 6 of the European Convention On Human Rights (the right to a fair trial) (*Chapter 1*).[6] At the time of writing the

---

[2] See also the references to the Correctional Services Board and Correctional Services Accreditation Panel in *Chapter 13*.

[3] A previous director was dismissed by the then home secretary, the latter having refused to accept responsibility for operational matters (the escape of high security prisoners).

[4] For an overview see *The Prison Officer* (2001), Liebling A and Price, D, London: Prison Service Journal. See also 'Prison Officers and Prison Governors', Bryans S and Jones R in *The Prisons Handbook* (2002 Edn.), *supra*.

[5] See *The Prison Governor: Theory and Practice* (1998), Bryans S and Wilson D, London: Prison Service Journal.

[6] *Okichukwiw Ezeh and Lawrence Connors* v. *United Kingdom* (judgement of 15 July 2002).

adjudications process is in some disarray although the Home Office has promised an early solution.

Prison officers with basic nursing training (provided largely within HMPS) may be employed as hospital officers in some places, although the staff of Healthcare Services for Prisoners also includes state registered nurses. Qualified nurses are normally employed in women's prisons. Other key staff include:

- medical officers, prison doctors and psychologists who advise the governor on healthcare and mental health matters and prepare reports for courts on prisoners, as well as providing related day-to-day care for prisoners
- education officers who run full-time or part-time education courses and evening classes (often provided under contract by organizations that also run further education courses in the community)
- librarians who staff libraries in all prisons. They are of varying size, standard and accessibility, although the best provide a service equal to that in the community and notwithstanding the constraints of prison life. Library catalogues include items from an official list of books and other documents which must be available in each prison for the use of prisoners.
- chaplains (Anglican, Roman Catholic and Methodist) who provide opportunities for worship, spiritual counselling and pastoral care, supported by visiting ministers of other denominations and faiths. Many prison chapels are now multi-faith.
- probation officers who work alongside prison officers on programmes and courses and undertake rehabilitative and pre-release work, liaise with a prisoner's home probation officer, write reports for the discretionary conditional release (DCR) process mentioned later in this chapter, and advise the prison management team on issues of throughcare and sentence planning; and
- resettlement workers employed by voluntary agencies such as the crime reduction charity Nacro and contracted to work full-time in an increasing number of prisons.
- administrative and clerical staff who handle contracts, accounts, calculate release dates, service internal boards and committees and keep records.

## Prison establishments and regimes

*The Prisons Handbook*[7] lists 136 HMPS establishments including 12 for women (either whole prisons or dedicated wings).[8] Many prisons were built in Victorian or Edwardian times. Others are much less architecturally grand (although they may be more functional) and many have been built since the Second World War. Some 25 prisons have been built since 1980, including those designed, constructed, managed and financed (DCMF) by the private sector and operated under contract. The prison estate also includes converted castles, manor houses and military bases and one prison on land reclaimed from the sea by prisoners.[9] Prisons are styled 'HMP . . .' or in the case of young offender institutions 'HMYOI . . .'.

[7] *The Prisons Handbook* (annually), Leech M and Cheney D, Winchester: Waterside Press.

[8] The precise arrangements are always difficult to pinpoint. They frequently change as prisons are 're-rôled' to accommodate changing (or increasing) prison populations.

[9] HMP North Sea Camp in Lincolnshire.

By 'regime' is meant how and when events occur on a day-to-day basis ranging from the locking or unlocking of cells to activities such as work, education, meals, association with other prisoners, visits, offending behaviour courses, disciplinary adjudications (but see above) and worship. The regime will depend on the particular prison and the kind of prisoners held there. HMPS's stated aims include 'protecting the public', 'positive regimes' and 'purposeful (or meaningful) activity' for prisoners. There is a special regime for life-sentence prisoners (below) and there are therapeutic communities at HMP Grendon (since 1960), HMP Dovegate (which opened in 2001) and on individual wings or in smaller units at other prisons.[10]

# PRISONERS: FROM RECEPTION TO RELEASE

At the time of writing the prison population is around 71,500,[11] a rise of over one-third over the past decade. Partly as a result of prison overcrowding, in 2001 Lord Woolf, Lord Chief Justice, urged courts to consider whether when they send someone to prison a shorter sentence will suffice and later, in *R* v. *Kefford* (5 March 2002),[12] he indicated that prison overcrowding is a relevant consideration when deciding whether or not to send someone to custody, since it affects the ability of HMPS to tackle offending behaviour and reduce reoffending. Courts should heed the principle 'imprisonment only when necessary and for no longer than necessary'. In 2002, the prison Boards of Visitors (see later) reported that overcrowding increases assaults, suicides and compromises security. However, there are signs that the 'tough on crime' agenda of the 1990s may be suffering a backlash in favour of what has been termed a 'smart on crime' agenda.

### Reception into prison

From court, a prisoner will normally be taken to a local prison or remand centre,[13] usually during the evening after the prison transport—prison vans now operated almost exclusively under private contracts with providers such as Group 4, Securicor and Premier Prison Services—arrives to collect prisoners from a court centre at the end of the day's proceedings.

A prisoner will arrive at reception and be required to shower or bathe, and receive a set of prison clothes. Women prisoners,[14] remand prisoners and, in some prisons depending on the regime, men serving sentences are allowed to wear their own clothes. The prisoner will then be offered a meal, be given a number (which remains with the prisoner throughout his or her sentence) and often a

---

[10] For these regimes see *Grendon Tales: Stories from a Therapeutic Community* (2001), Smartt U, Winchester: Waterside Press.

[11] i.e. virtually at capacity and well above HM Prison Service's 'uncrowded' figure of 64,000. Lord Woolf's sentiments are supported, e.g. by both the former HM Chief Inspector of Prisons, Sir David Ramsbotham, and the head of the Youth Justice Board, Lord Warner who have indicated that much custody is futile compared to work with offenders in the community— to which most prisoners must return in due course.

[12] See also *R v Mills*, 14 January 2002, in the context of the women's estate.

[13] For a description of individual establishments and all aspects of prison life and regimes see *The Prisons Handbook*, *supra*.

[14] See, generally, *Invisible Women: What's Wrong with Women's Prisons?* (1998), Devlin A, Winchester: Waterside Press.

brief medical interview before being taken onto one of the prison wings. During this or a later medical interview or examination the medical officer will assess the prisoner's fitness to work and whether there is a suicide risk. The suicide rate in prisons is roughly four times that for the general population despite extensive efforts and procedures to bring this down.[15] Young offenders, who are more likely to lack the inner resources to deal with imprisonment, are particularly vulnerable.

Prisoners may be fingerprinted and, within a day or two, photographed. On leaving reception, they are given a towel, sheets, wash-things, toothbrush and tooth powder, spare clothing, plastic cutlery, a plate, mug and pillowcase. He or she may be allowed to keep other personal items 'in possession' such as a radio, wristwatch, book, pen and paper. Some such items are allowed according to local practice (there is a standard list but of somewhat uncertain effect) and the discretion of the governor, who will be concerned to ensure the safety and security of prisoners generally. Other personal items will be stored in reception or at an extensive central store in Branston, Staffordshire.

Local and other closed prisons are usually divided into a number of wings or halls, each often holding a different category of prisoner (below). Normally, prison wings have several levels or landings containing cells. Outside each cell is a small metal plate for a card containing the prisoner's number (which stays with him or her throughout the sentence), surname, length of sentence, earliest date of release and religious affiliation.

### Categorisation and allocation

Sentenced adult men (i.e. aged 21 and over) will initially be held in an observation, classification and allocation unit of a local prison or remand centre, after which they will be placed in a security category, depending on their offence(s), the perceived risk of their escaping and the danger they would pose to the public should this happen.

Sentenced prisoners will be categorised A (those 'whose escape would be highly dangerous to the public or the police or to the security of the State'), B ('for whom escape must be made very difficult'), C ('cannot be trusted in open conditions' but who 'do not have the will or resources to make a determined escape attempt') or D ('can reasonably be trusted in open conditions'). Unsentenced prisoners are automatically categorised B, unless provisionally placed in Category A. Women and young offenders are categorised simply for open or closed conditions, apart from a few women who are treated as if they were in Category A. Categorisation is reviewed at least every 12 months and prisoners tend to be moved to less secure conditions as they progress through their sentence and as part of a overall sentence plan or pre-release plan.

The exact establishment to which an adult male sentenced prisoner is allocated will depend on his security category, sentence and the places that are available. Many men serving sentences of 18 months or less serve the whole sentence in a local prison. Those serving longer sentences will usually be transferred to a training prison. Category A prisoners will usually be allocated to

---

[15] See, e.g. *Deaths of Offenders: The Hidden Side of Justice* (1997), Liebling A (Ed.), Winchester: Waterside Press. Annual figures appear in *The Prisons Handbook*, *supra*.

a 'dispersal' prison,[16] which is a high security closed training prison. Category A women are sent to a separate unit such as that attached to HMP Durham. Category D prisoners may be transferred to an open prison. A young offender (i.e. someone under 21) will be held in an open or closed YOI.[17]

There are also around one thousand civil prisoners, mainly immigration detainees who are subject to a separate civil regime but within the same establishments as convicted and remand prisoners.

## Rule 45

Vulnerable prisoners in need of protection and prisoners perceived as a threat to the maintenance of good order and discipline (GOAD) may be segregated from other prisoners under Rule 45 of the Prison Rules.[18] The former generally request segregation, whereas GOAD prisoners are often segregated against their wishes. In addition some prisoners needing long-term protection are held in vulnerable prisoner units (VPUs).

## Sentence planning, drug and alcohol testing and sex offenders

Sentence plans are drawn up for prisoners serving 12 months or more and for all young offenders. These plans seek to ensure that the prisoner's time in custody is spent positively and that problems underlying offending behaviour are confronted. During their sentence many prisoners will join activities and work groups, offending behaviour courses and programmes which seek to address and remedy problems such as alcohol or drug abuse, gambling, aggression or sexual offending. There is mandatory drug testing (MDT) or voluntary drug testing (VDT) in many prisons and a number of special schemes to rehabilitate people who misuse drugs and alcohol.[19] Under CARATS (Counselling, Assessment, Referral, Advice and Throughcare Services) a comprehensive strategy was introduced in 1999 under which HMPS aims by March 2004 to:

- undertake 25,000 CARATS assessments annually
- have 5,700 prisoners entering a rehabilitation programme or therapeutic community annually
- have 27,000 prisoners entering detoxification annually; and
- achieve an annual percentage of positive results from the random MDT programme of no more than ten per cent.

Various establishments run sex offender treatment programmes (SOTPs) ('core', 'advanced' and 'booster') and which aim among other things to counter denial and distorted beliefs; increase awareness of the effect on a victim; get prisoners to accept responsibility; and prevent relapse and high risk situations in future.

---

[16] The term 'dispersal' reflects the decision taken after the Mountbatten inquiry into prison security in the 1960s to disperse those prisoners who present the greatest risk to a number of high security prisons rather than concentrate them in a single establishment.

[17] As indicated in earlier chapters, it is intended that institutions for young people aged 18-20 should be reclassified as prisons, and that the separate sentence of detention in a YOI be abolished, although the change may be one of form rather than substance.

[18] Rule 47 in YOIs under comparable provisions.

[19] Including the RAPt scheme: see *Drug Treatment in Prison: An Evaluation of the RAPt Treatment Programme* (2000), Martin C and Player E, Winchester: Waterside Press.

# Education

Prisoner education currently focuses (somewhat contentiously) on the acquisition of basic skills rather than advanced qualifications, although there are opportunities to pursue a range of courses, including correspondence courses (some funded by outside organizations).[20] There is also a wide range of vocational training courses depending on the arrangements and facilities at a particular prison. However, the availability of fringe activities such as the arts which many people argue can lead to personal change has reduced considerably with increasing prison populations and the fact that such activities do not figure directly in HMPS key objectives.[21]

## Pre-release courses and temporary release

Some prisoners attend prisoner development and pre-release courses. The courses, usually run by prison officers, cover many topics including housing, interview skills, work, benefits and rights and a range of outside agencies often take part in such courses. After serving a part of their sentence, prisoners can be considered for temporary release to take part in regime-related activities such as community service projects, employment, training or education, and for resettlement purposes, usually towards the end of their sentences (see further below). This aspect of prison life, increasingly curtailed in the 1990s, would appear to be gradually re-emerging.

## The prison day

A typical day begins between 7.30 and 8 a.m. in a closed prison, when cells are unlocked and officers conduct a roll-check. Prisoners are counted frequently, and there are regular roll-calls throughout each day. All cells now have sanitation, or access to sanitation, so that the practice of 'slopping out' plastic chamber pots into a communal sluice has almost disappeared. Prisoners may collect hot water for washing and shaving, then their breakfast from heated trolleys to consume in their cells (although some may collect a cold breakfast the night before).

Regime activities begin between 8.45 a.m. and 9 a.m. Many prisoners will go to work, training or education classes, though some, mainly those in local prisons, may be inactive for much of the day. Prisoners are employed as cleaners, kitchen and laundry staff; in farming and gardening activities; in clothing, carpentry and engineering workshops; in assembling components for outside industry—and in sewing mailbags. Prisoners in some open and other training prisons work outside prison with elderly people, with physically and mentally handicapped people and on community projects. The opportunities for such constructive work were severely reduced by changes to temporary release arrangements in the mid-1990s. Several prisons have won contracts in competition with private sector organizations to supply goods or services provided by prisoners.[22]

---

[20] See *Prison(er) Education: Stories of Change and Transformation* (2000), Wilson D and Reuss A, Winchester: Waterside Press.

[21] See, e.g. *Inside Art: Crime, Punishment and Creative Energies* (2002), Brown M, Winchester: Waterside Press. Drama is used in some prisons, see, e.g. *The Geese Theatre Handbook: Drama with Offenders and People at Risk* (2002), Baim C, Brookes S and Mountfield A, Winchester: Waterside Press.

[22] One aim is to provide meaningful work, enhance self-esteem and get away from the stereotypical image of prisoners 'sewing mailbags'. Thus *The Bookseller* reported in August 2002 that one

Prisoners who are employed within a prison can earn from around £7 to £15 per week although the amounts are typically towards the lower end of this scale. Earnings can be spent in the prison shop[23] which prisoners can usually visit (or order from) once a week to buy food, tobacco (although many prison wings are now no-smoking zones), toiletries, batteries etc. Prisoners who do not have work or classes to go to are paid a flat rate allowance.

During the morning (and, in many establishments, the afternoon), prisoners in closed establishments exercise outdoors, weather permitting. In many establishments exercise involves walking with other prisoners in a circle in a yard. Prisoners in open prisons do not have exercise periods as such. Juveniles and young adults serving short sentences should have an hour of physical education each weekday. Physical education is popular with many prisoners. It raises self-esteem, provides a sense of achievement, serves as a means of letting off aggression, and prisoners are allowed a shower afterwards.

After lunch, activities are resumed. Some prisoners will receive visits from family and friends. Some prisons allow visits in the morning. Unconvicted prisoners can normally have visits on at least three days a week, totalling a minimum of one and a half hours, and another visit on Saturday or Sunday. Convicted prisoners are normally allowed a minimum of one visit every two weeks. Close relatives on income support or low incomes may get the cost of two visits a month paid for by the Home Office.

The final meal of the day in local prisons, tea, is often eaten quite early, around eight or nine hours after breakfast, though many prisons have now introduced more flexible arrangements. Some prisons allow prisoners to prepare snacks on the wings.

Subject to there being provision, some prisoners will attend classes during the evening while others will be allowed association, often by rota. Association may be withdrawn in the interests of security and control or if there are not enough staff to supervise it. Many prisoners not allowed association will be locked up—often with another prisoner[24] in a cell for one and typically measuring 12 feet by nine by eight. After lock up and lights out, the cell light is turned off from the outside. In this context, it is worth noting that *Justice for All* claims (in somewhat broad terms) that the Government has already increased prison capacity by 18 per cent, improved conditions inside prisons and invested £20 million in boosting prisoners' learning facilities.

## REQUESTS AND COMPLAINTS

Formal interchanges between prisoners and HMPS are conducted via a system of 'requests and complaints' (now substantially revised and being implemented during 2002). The scheme provides a formal mechanism for grievances, albeit

---

contract bid was later dropped. This was to drill holes in overstocked volumes before they were sent for pulping, to guarantee that they could not sold on.

[23] Traditionally known as 'the canteen' but this term seems to be disappearing. Many prison shops are now operated by private sector contractors such as Aramark and involve 'bagging systems', i.e. a kind of internal mail order with the goods arriving on the wing in bags for forwarding to individual prisoners.

[24] The practice of requiring three prisoners to share a cell was brought to an end in the early 1990s.

that in practice prisoners are encouraged to discuss their concerns with prison officers to see whether these can be resolved informally (which the vast majority are).

Under the revised scheme requests have been separated out from complaints and are dealt with by way of a simple applications procedure. Anything which proceeds beyond this stage is treated as a complaint. Complaint forms are freely available to prisoners on prison wings and completed forms are posted in locked boxes to which only a complaints clerk has access. Complaints are then considered and responded to in three potentially cumulative stages within the HMPS establishment:

- a response from the wing officer within three days (i.e. weekdays)
- a response from a governor grade within seven days
- a response from the governing governor within seven days.

A former HMPS headquarters appeal stage has been abolished other than in the case of certain reserved subjects so that now—once the above three stages are complete—a prisoner can apply directly the Prisons and Probation Ombudsman (below), ask to see a member of the Board of Visitors (below), petition the Home Secretary or pursue the complaint outside the prison system through, e.g. the civil courts or his or her member of Parliament.

## PRISONS AND PROBATION OMBUDSMAN

The Prisons and Probation Ombudsman acts, in effect, as a final appeal stage for grievances: he or she is totally independent of the agencies concerned but can make recommendations to HMPS, the NPS or to the Home Secretary. He or she is appointed by the Home Secretary. The ombudsman will investigate complaints which have already been through all other stages in relevant procedures from:

- individual prisoners who have failed to obtain satisfaction from the requests and complaints system (above) (if eligible in other respects); and
- people who are, or have been, under the supervision of the NPS or housed in NPS accommodation or who have had pre-sentence reports (PSRs) prepared on them by the NPS and who have failed to obtain satisfaction from the NPS complaints system (and who are eligible in other respects).

The ombudsman will reply to all people whose complaints have been investigated (the target is to do so within 12 weeks of determining eligibility), sending copies to the relevant service, and making any recommendations at the same time. He or she also informs complainants of the response to any recommendations made. The ombudsman publishes an annual report.

## BOARDS OF VISITORS

Each establishment also has its own Board of Visitors (BOV), a body of lay people in effect selected by the prison governor and appointed by the Home Secretary, which is intended to act as a 'watchdog' and oversee the activities of the prison and the treatment of prisoners. The BOV reports direct to the Home Secretary. BOVs have a long history, going back to the visiting committees under the Prison Act 1877, and were at one time the main disciplinary authorities for the prisons.

# RELEASE

Prisoners are normally released after breakfast.[25] Their property and clothes are returned from store and fresh clothes supplied where necessary. Most sentenced prisoners are entitled to a discharge grant to cover immediate expenses.

The Criminal Justice Act 1991 introduced fresh arrangements for the release of prisoners and for their supervision and liabilities after release.[26] All sentences of imprisonment now comprise a custodial part which is served in prison, and a part which is served in the community. Prisoners serving sentences of less than 12 months are released unconditionally after serving half their sentence; those serving longer sentences are released on licence with a requirement to comply with the conditions specified in the licence and are under the supervision of the National Probation Service (NPS). If the sentence is one of 12 months up to four years, release on licence is at the half-way point of the sentence; if it is one of four years or more, release is automatic at the two-thirds point, but the Parole Board may release the prisoner once half the sentence has been served, if he or she is suitable, or recommend release to the Home Secretary if the sentence is for 15 years or more. In all cases the licence remains in force until the three-quarter point of the sentence is reached. There are special provisions for the extended detention and supervision of sex offenders.

The Home Secretary may release any prisoner on licence at any time if there are special compassionate reasons, but this power is rarely used.

A prisoner aged 21 or over serving a sentence of under four years may also be released early under what is known as home detention curfew (HDC), with a requirement for electronic monitoring. *Justice for All* proposes that this mechanism should be more widely used.

Offenders who fail to comply with the conditions of their licence, or who commit further offences, can be returned to prison; and an offender sentenced to four years or more can be recalled to prison at any time if the Home Secretary considers recall to be 'expedient in the public interest' (principally if the individual concerned is a danger to himself or herself or other people, or at risk of committing further offences).

The 1991 Act abolished the longstanding system under which prisoners could earn remission for good conduct, or lose it for offences against prison discipline. It substituted a provision under which a prisoner could be awarded 'added days', but the arrangements for giving effect to that provision have been found to contravene the European Convention On Human Rights (see above).

### Aims of post-release supervision
There are NPS *National Standards* for post-custody supervision. The aims are:

---

[25] The superstition being that a prisoner who fails to eat this breakfast will return to do so.

[26] The terms 'automatic unconditional release' (AUR), 'automatic conditional release' (ACR) and 'discretionary conditional release' (DCR) are normally used to signify the three main forms of release summarised in the text.

- protection of the public
- prevention of re-offending
- successful reintegration of the offender into the community.

As well as setting out frequency of contact and targets, a post-release supervision plan will identify resources which will:

- confront offending behaviour—challenging the offender to accept responsibility for his or her crime and its consequences
- make offenders aware of the impact of the crimes they have committed on their victims, themselves and the community
- motivate and assist the offender towards a greater sense of personal responsibility, to aid re-integration as a law abiding member of the community
- remedy practical obstacles which impede rehabilitation, e.g. education, training, skills needed for employment, and action to counter drug or alcohol misuse, illiteracy or homelessness.

### Young offenders and juveniles

The conditional release system applies to young people serving sentences of detention in a YOI of 12 months or more. Those serving less than 12 months will be subject to a period of supervision on release of not less than three months. Supervision is carried out by social services or the NPS. The detention and training order for juveniles (D&TO) is constructed so that half of the sentence is served in custody and half in the community, i.e. post-custody supervision is in-built: see *Chapter 5*.

### Conditionally discharged patients from mental hospitals

An offender who is adjudged to be seriously mentally ill and who poses a serious risk to the public can be made the subject of a restriction order for a specified period or indefinitely by the Crown Court under mental health legislation. In due course, the Home Secretary has the power to order that:

- the restriction order should cease to have effect; and
- the patient should be discharged absolutely; or
- the patient should be subject to conditions and the possibility of being recalled.

It is likely that supervision will be by a local psychiatrist and a 'social supervisor' who can be a probation officer or social worker. The discharged patient must live at an agreed address and is likely to be on supervision for at least two years. Concern about the patient can lead to the psychiatrist using his or her civil powers to admit the patient to hospital compulsorily, and ultimately the Home Office can order a recall.

### Voluntary after-care

The possibility of voluntary aftercare arises where a short sentence attracts unconditional release (above). There is then a duty on the NPS to provide assistance if the prisoner requests it. The absence of any form of compulsory supervision for short-sentence prisoners was one of the criticisms which led to the Halliday review (*Chapter 15*). If proposals in *Justice for All* are implemented, all prisoners will be subject to some form of supervision after release.

## THE PAROLE BOARD

The Parole Board is an independent non-executive and non-departmental public body which, in broad terms, makes risk assessment to inform decisions on the release and recall of prisoners. It operates in accordance with statutory directions, issued by the Home Secretary, which cover subjects such as the criteria to be used and the procedures to be followed. The board comprises a chairman and some 80 members a small proportion of whom are full-time. Members include judges, psychiatrists, chief probation officers, criminologists and independent members. The board meets in panels of three or four members to consider cases. Its role in relation to release of prisoners is noted under the section headed *Release* above. The Board publishes an annual report.

## LIFE SENTENCE REGIMES

The different types of life sentence are outlined in *Chapter 9*. Lifers are subjected to a continuous process of review, risk assessment and, depending on progress, periodic downgrading of their security category. Because of the length of time served under many life sentences (around 14 years on average and in some cases much more for mandatory life sentences for murder) it is likely that a chain of HMPS and NPS personnel will be involved in discharging the sentence plan and in the throughcare, education, categorisation, assessment and release processes.

Lifers will typically complete an accumulation of offending behaviour courses and may undertake longer-term educational or other self-development projects. On release, they remain on licence for the rest of their natural lives and are subject to recall if their behaviour suggests that they might once again be a danger to the public. The requirement to report to a supervising probation officer can be removed after a period, but the licence remains in force.

## HM INSPECTORATE OF PRISONS

Each prison is inspected periodically by HM Inspector of Prisons or his or her team of full-time or specialist inspectors, the latter attached to the team for particular inspections or purposes. The inspectorate publishes an annual report and a report of each inspection, and carries out thematic inspections on particular aspects of the prison system. Essentially, the inspectorate looks at the treatment of prisoners, regime quality, the morale of prisoners and staff, the quality of healthcare, the way an establishment is managed and the physical condition of the premises. The chief inspector reports directly to the Home Secretary. HMPS is required to publish a considered reply. Reports have often been critical.[27]

---

[27] Report summaries appear in *The Prisons Handbook, supra*.

# CHAPTER 15

# From the Royal Commission to *Justice for All*

As can be seen from earlier chapters the last 30 years or so have witnessed a number of key events in the development of English criminal justice. These include, e.g. the creation of the Crown Court, youth court and Crown Prosecution Service—and more recently a Youth Justice Board, National Probation Service and Criminal Defence Service. There have been various Criminal Justice Acts, perhaps most notably those of 1991 which introduced a comprehensive (and at that time what many people believed to be a coherent) sentencing framework (*Chapter 9*) and the Crime and Disorder Act 1998 with its reforms of youth justice (*Chapter 5*) and racially aggravated offences (*Chapter 16*). Other key measures include the Police and Criminal Evidence Act 1984 (PACE) (*Chapter 6*) which altered the nature of police investigations, the Bail Act 1976 which among other things required courts to give reasons for their decisions publicly for the first time (*Chapter 8*) and the wide-ranging Human Rights Act 1998 (*Chapter 1*). Other milestones include the Mountbatten and Woolf reports into aspects of the penal system (*Chapters 14* and *15*), the Macpherson report on the police investigation into the murder of the black teenager Stephen Lawrence (*Chapter 16*), reliance on increasingly sophisticated technology in the investigation of crime and the Police Reform Act 2002 (*Chapter 11*). Other events have affected the process incrementally such as advance disclosure of the prosecution case (*Chapter 12*) and changes in relation to the right to silence (below). There has also been a notable shift towards joint working (*Chapter 17*) and in the way victims of crime and witnesses are treated (*Chapter 18*).

This chapter focuses on four events that serve to link the past and future:

- the Royal Commission on Criminal Justice of 1993
- Lord Justice Auld's Review of the Criminal Courts in 2001
- John Halliday's review of sentencing in 2001; and
- the Government's White Paper *Justice For All* in 2002.

## THE ROYAL COMMISSION

A Royal Commission on Criminal Justice was announced in 1991[1] (to be chaired by Viscount Runciman of Droxford). Its terms of reference began:

To examine the effectiveness of the criminal justice system in England and Wales in securing the conviction of those guilty of criminal offences and the acquittal of those

---

[1] On the same day that the Court of Appeal quashed the convictions for murder of the 'Birmingham Six'—men sent to prison for bomb explosions in public houses in 1974 who served over 16 years in prison.

who are innocent, having regard to the efficient use of resources, and in particular to consider whether changes [were] needed in [certain aspects of criminal justice which were then listed]:

The general tenor of the work of the commission (and the preoccupation of those times) can be gleaned from the fact that the commission was required to look into the conduct of police investigations, the role of the prosecutor, the role of experts in criminal proceedings, the arrangements for the defence of accused people, the opportunities available for them to state their position and the extent to which the courts might draw proper inferences from primary facts, the conduct of the accused, and any failure on his or her part to answer questions. The commission was also required to look into the powers of the courts in directing proceedings, the possibility of their having an investigative role before and during a trial, pre-trial reviews (then the exception), and the court's duty when considering evidence, including uncorroborated confession evidence. Specifically, it was to look at the role of the Court of Appeal in considering new evidence on appeal and the then process by which alleged miscarriages of justice were investigated by the Home Office.

### Proposals

In its 1993 report the Royal Commission made 352 recommendations including for an independent Criminal Cases Review Authority (see *Chapter 10*),[2] research and monitoring into areas of potential discrimination (see *Chapter 16*) and that judges should be able in exceptional cases to order the selection of a jury containing up to three people from ethnic minority communities.[3] As to the police, they should be able to take samples from suspects for DNA profiling, and it was recommended that a databank should be set up to contain samples from people convicted of serious criminal offences (the present existence of which is noted in *Chapter 11*). Also, there should be training in basic interviewing skills and police should be able to impose bail conditions (*Chapter 8*).

Famously and controversially, the Government rejected the recommendation that the *status quo* should be maintained in relation to the 'right of silence' (i.e. the rule that no inferences could be drawn from a defendant's silence at various points during the criminal process). Instead, the Criminal Justice and Public Order Act 1994 provided that, when a defendant questioned under caution (*Chapter 6*) has not mentioned a fact that he or she could reasonably have done, such inferences as appear proper can be drawn by the court. Further, it was enacted that if the defendant elects not to give evidence at his or her trial it is open to the magistrates or jury (properly directed by the judge) to draw such inferences as appear proper from that failure to give evidence.

Recommendations that committal proceedings in magistrates' courts should be abolished and that defendants should lose the right to insist on trial by jury for certain offences, whilst not enacted, have to all intents and purposes resurfaced in a new guise in *Justice for All* (see later).

---

[2]  Now the Criminal Cases Review Commission (CCRC).
[3]  Never acted upon but revived in the Auld report, though rejected finally by Government, it would appear, as the idea does not reappear in *Justice for All*.

Various recommendations concerning disclosure of the prosecution case were acted upon, whilst those concerning pre-trial procedures to assist in clarifying and defining the issues in the case before trial became, over the years, a part of day-to-day practice—though not perhaps in quite the mandatory fashion envisaged by the commission (something which *Justice for All* again picks up on with some vigour).

A plea for a more open system of sentence discounts—with earlier pleas of guilty attracting higher discounts—remains to be fully formalised and structured following the present White Paper, as do recommendations that at the defendant's request judges should be able to give an indication of the sentence if the defendant were to plead guilty (though this often occurs in practice already). Many other, less prominent, recommendations have been woven into the fabric of the everyday work of the agencies, such as the commission's recommendations concerning the recording of police interviews and of activities in custody suites.

# THE AULD REPORT

Although concerned primarily with the structure of the courts as opposed to their sentencing or other powers, Lord Justice Auld's *Review of the Criminal Courts* (2001) is a further key to future developments. Another is the Halliday report on sentencing, *Criminal Justice: The Way Ahead* (2001) (see next section). Together, these reports form a basis for *Justice for All* and to an extent can be taken to have been superseded by the wide-ranging—and sometimes quite different and at some points controversial—proposals in the White Paper.

The Auld proposals included those for a Unified Criminal Court which, although they do not appear in *Justice for All* (as opposed to proposals for a single administration under the Court Service or its successor), are to an extent reflected in jurisdictional and other changes proposed by the White Paper in relation to the Crown Court and magistrates' courts. Other recommendations from the Auld report such as in relation to jury trial, procedure and evidence are reflected in the Government proposals, if not in the exact same form as envisaged by Auld.

## Strategies for criminal justice
Among other things, Auld recommended that there should be a National Criminal Justice Board to replace all existing national planning, operational and strategic bodies (*Chapter 1*). The new board should be the means by which the criminal justice departments and agencies provide overall direction. At a local level there should be Local Criminal Justice Boards responsible for giving effect to the national board's directions and objectives for the management of criminal justice in local areas. These boards should be supported by a centrally managed secretariat and consult with the judiciary. A Criminal Case Management Agency accountable to the board would be responsible for the implementation of common systems including standard information technology.

Auld also suggested that a Criminal Justice Council, to be chaired by the Lord Chief Justice or a very senior Lord Justice of Appeal, should be established to replace all existing advisory or consultative bodies, including the Criminal Justice Consultative Council (*Chapter 1*) and its area committees.

In broad terms, these recommendations concerning a Criminal Justice Board and Criminal Justice Council—together with a further suggestion in favour of a Sentencing Council—are reflected in *Justice for All*.

## Juries

On juries, Auld recommended that these should be more widely representative of the national and local communities from which they are drawn. A number of public lists should be used, not just the electoral roll, and although people with criminal convictions or suffering from mental disorder should continue to be disqualified, no-one should be ineligible or excusable as a matter of right (*Chapter 12*). However, Auld rejected the idea that the law should be amended to allow more intrusive research into the workings of juries than is currently possible, but suggested that both trial judges and the Court of Appeal should be entitled to examine alleged improprieties in the jury room: 'The law should be declared, by statute if need be, that juries have no right to acquit defendants in defiance of the law or disregard of the evidence'.[4] The make-up of juries should be adjusted in some cases to allow for minority ethnic representation (an aspect seemingly rejected in view of later proposals in *Justice for All*, below).

Among suggestions for procedural reform, the Auld report proposed that the judge be allowed to put a series of questions to the jury which would serve to determine the structure and validity of their findings. It also proposed a comprehensive review of the law of evidence to identify and establish coherent principles and to make it an efficient and simple agent for securing justice, with a move away from often highly technical rules, in effect, in favour of the court deciding what weight to give to such evidence or information as is available. Auld also recommended that the quality and objectivity of expert evidence and the availability and quality of interpreters (*Chapter 12*) should be improved.

### The Government's initial reaction

Before *Justice for All*, in *The Criminal Courts Review Report: A Government Statement* (2001)[5] the Government described the Auld review as 'a major contribution to its continuing programme of reform of the criminal justice system—modern, in touch with the community, efficient and fair'. It went on to comment that Auld:

> makes some radical and far-reaching recommendations, some of which would involve making changes to longstanding structures and procedures. Such changes will need to be carefully considered, in the light of the fullest possible range of comment . . . whilst we are inviting views . . . in a few cases we can already see difficulties . . .

Thus, whilst taking a generally positive stance, it was clear, at an early stage, that there was to be no wholesale or overall commitment.

---

4. It is sometimes said that it is the democratic right of a jury to make a 'perverse' decision. Indeed, by way of a dubious honour, the term 'Liverpool jury' has been coined for this scenario. Non-interference with the jury is usually argued along the lines of freedom from external pressure (or where does this stop?) and the fact that it is not they who are on trial but the accused.

5. Issued jointly by the Lord Chancellor's Department, Home Office and Attorney General.

# THE HALLIDAY REPORT

As already indicated, in 2001 the Home Office published *Making Punishments Work: Report of a Review of the Sentencing Framework for England and Wales*[6] which looked at sentencing in its present and historical contexts, ranging from underlying principles to the costs and benefits of particular outcomes. The Halliday report recommended, among other things, a new sentencing framework which should do more to support crime reduction and reparation while at the same time meeting the needs of punishment.

Among the supporting recommendations were: modification of the just deserts sentencing principle; abandonment of the 'so serious' test for community sentences; a new generic community punishment order 'whose punitive weight would be proportionate to the current offence and any additional severity for previous convictions'; greater control by courts of what sentences involve; continuing review of certain sentences by judges and magistrates; a formalised system of sentencing guidelines; new criteria for custodial sentences; changes to post-custody supervision; the provision of costs and benefits data to courts; and increased emphasis on giving sound, accessible reasons for decisions.

# JUSTICE FOR ALL

The 2002 White Paper makes far-reaching proposals concerning jurisdiction, trials, juries, sentencing, evidence, procedures and other key matters, including ways in which the criminal process overall should function, making its potential impact greater than any single measure already mentioned in this chapter. Some of its proposals have been noted in earlier sections, above. In other key proposals, *Justice for All*, in building on the Auld and Halliday reports, suggests that the upper limit of magistrates' jurisdiction be increased to 12 months imprisonment per offence and there is a fresh emphasis on lesser sentences being served in the community. There are proposals for 'more rigorous community penalties' and an increased use of electronic monitoring, and new sentences of intermittent custody ('what has been termed 'weekend' or 'night-time' gaol), custody minus (a form of 'suspended' sentence but conditional on completion of punishment in the community), and custody plus (where a larger proportion of a custodial sentence is spent in the community than at present: *Chapter 14*). These changes would be accompanied by new and less compartmentalised sentencing criteria, sentencing guidelines and restorative elements. This represents a significant departure from the 'prison works' mantra of the 1990s and has been described as a 'smart on crime' agenda.

According to the Home Office the White Paper sets out a 'coherent, long-term strategy to modernise the criminal justice system from end to end—from detection to the rehabilitation of offenders—with a clear focus on fighting and reducing crime'. The proposals seek to create what is described as a transparent, joined up system that commands the respect of the public by delivering faster,

---

[6]   Home Office (2001). Also known as 'The Halliday report'.

more effective justice for victims and the wider community while safeguarding the rights of defendants. At the heart of this strategy is the aim of

ensuring a better deal for victims and witnesses, fairer more efficient trials, clearer, consistent and constructive sentencing, more effective punishment and rehabilitation, and measures to join up the system and engage the public.

To achieve this, the Government promises (in the following terms):

- tough action on anti-social behaviour, hard drugs and violent crime
- rebalancing the criminal justice system in favour of the victim; and
- giving the police and prosecution the tools to bring more criminals to justice.

The White Paper emphasises that most crime is committed by a relatively small number of persistent offenders. Despite progress, it says, there are signs of weakness in critical areas: too few criminals brought to justice; too many defendants offending on bail; the process too slow in bringing them to trial; and too many guilty people going unconvicted or without the sentence they and society need.

### Aims of *Justice for All*
After noting developments in police reform[7] the document continues by outlining certain key aims, including:

- reducing offending on bail via new police powers to impose conditions on bail *before* charge and an extension of the prosecution's right to appeal bail decisions
- getting more defendants to court, with 'the closest possible working' between the police and the CPS to make sure that cases do not slip between the cracks through poor case preparation or inadequate charging
- ensuring that cases focus on the relevant issues, and do not have 'any surprises' via prosecution and defence disclosure of cases more fully pre-trial—thereby leading to the 'conviction of more of the guilty'
- ensuring that magistrates, judges and juries are able to hear all relevant evidence that fairly bears on a defendant's guilt or innocence
- ensuring, where someone is convicted, that if they are a danger to the public or a serious or persistent offender they will be put into custody and for other offenders the existence of a range of penalties which are effective in punishing them and tackling reoffending.

The purpose of the White Paper is stated to be 'to send the clearest possible signal to those committing offences that the criminal justice system is united in ensuring their detection, conviction and punishment'. Specific promises include:

- an increase in police numbers to 130,000 by Spring 2003
- an increase in spending on the police by around £1.5 billion by 2005-2006 compared to 2002-2003

---

[7] See the Police Reform Act 2002 (*Chapter 11*).

- encouraging more specialist detective skills
- setting a clear target for increasing the proportion of police time spent on frontline work; and
- better harnessing of science and technology to find the evidence to detect offenders.

To get defendants to court more quickly the Government proposes:

- continuing to co-locate the police and CPS in joint CJUs (*Chapters 10* and *11*)
- allowing the CPS to take more responsibility for determining charges 'so that the right cases go to court on the right charges'
- investing over £600 million in CJS information technology to manage cases more efficiently through the system
- giving sentence indication to encourage early guilty pleas; and
- giving magistrates greater sentencing powers of up to 12 months so that they can hear and sentence more cases appropriate to them. In the process, committal for sentence (*Chapter 9*) would be abolished.

To prevent offending on bail the Government proposes:

- giving police power to impose conditions on a suspect's bail during the period *before* charge
- weighting the court's discretion against granting bail to a defendant who has been charged with an imprisonable offence committed whilst already on bail for another offence
- extending the prosecution's right to appeal against bail to cover all imprisonable offences; and
- piloting in high crime areas a presumption of remand to custody if a suspect tests positive for Class A drugs on arrest but refuses treatment.

Moves to improve case preparation and trials (see above) include:

- improving defence and prosecution disclosure by increasing incentives and sanctions
- allowing the use of reported evidence ('hearsay') where there is a good reason, such as when a witness cannot appear in person
- allowing trial by judge alone where the accused requests this or in serious and complex fraud trials, some other complex and lengthy trials or where the jury is at risk of intimidation
- extending the availability of preparatory hearings (see *Chapter 8*) to ensure that serious or complex cases are properly prepared
- allowing courts to be informed of a defendant's previous convictions 'where appropriate'[8]
- removing the double jeopardy rule (*Chapters 1* and *16*) for serious cases if compelling new evidence comes to light
- giving witnesses greater access to their original statements at trial

---

[8]   This appears to mean where such evidence has probative value and is not otherwise prejudicial. The proposal is among the more controversial ones in the White Paper.

- giving the prosecution the right of appeal against rulings which terminate the prosecution case before the jury decides; and
- increasing the proportion of the population eligible for jury service.

Following conviction, the intention is that when sentencing (see, generally, *Chapter 9*) courts will

- focus custody on dangerous, serious and seriously persistent offenders and those who consistently breach community sentences
- ensure that dangerous violent and sexual offenders can be kept in custody for as long as they present a risk to the public
- ensure tough, more intensive community sentences with multiple conditions like tagging, reparation and drug treatment and testing to deny liberty, rehabilitate the offender and protect the public
- ensure more uniformity in sentencing through a new Sentencing Guidelines Council
- enable courts to offer drug treatment as part of a community sentence for juveniles
- introduce a new sentence of 'custody minus'—community supervision backed by automatic return to custody if the offender fails to comply with the conditions of their sentence
- introduce a new sentence of 'custody plus' to ensure that short sentence prisoners are properly supervised and supported after release; and
- introduce intermittent custody to enable use of weekend or night-time custody for low risk offenders.

## Some early reactions

The proposals themselves contain numerous qualifications, sub-proposals and exceptions and are accompanied by explanations consistent with what can be described as a new regime. The crime reduction charity Nacro has responded by welcoming the White Paper's emphasis on focusing imprisonment on serious cases and improving the rehabilitation of prisoners. It goes on to say:

> The sentencing proposals would create a more rational framework for using prison and community penalties . . . However, there is a risk that some of these measures could backfire if courts misuse them. While the custody plus sentence could shorten the periods offenders spend in prison, courts could alternatively decide to use it for offenders who at present receive community sentences. While custody minus and intermittent custody could replace jail sentences, courts could alternatively use them instead of non-custodial penalties.

It is perhaps worth noting that the history of criminal justice has often been one of unintended effects as judges, magistrates, police, prosecutors, probation officers and others apply their own legitimate discretion (*Chapter 1*) and interpretation to aspects of legislation and other exhortations from government. It may well be that due to the enhanced mechanisms for working together described in *Chapter 17* which have developed in recent years and the present

Government's own insistence that the criminal justice process is now a system[9] there is a greater chance that people within the system will 'sing from the same hymn sheet'. But as Nacro notes—and which is classically demonstrated by the 'prison works', 'tough on crime' and 'talking up sentencing' agenda of the 1990s—much will depend on the overall climate:

> Whether these measures increase or reduce the prison population will depend on the prevailing climate towards the treatment of offenders, to which the courts react. Government ministers could make a key contribution by doing all they can to talk down the prison population. This requires sustained high profile efforts to persuade courts to reduce their current over use of prison.

From a criminal policy standpoint there seems to be a discernible difference of approach as between Halliday and *Justice for All* on the one hand and the framers of the Criminal Justice Act 1991 on the other. At the beginning of the 1990s many people were highly sceptical about the extent to which, if at all, changes in the structure and practice of sentencing could have any real effect on crime levels, but fairness in sentencing had a very high priority. The political emphasis now lies in protecting the public and satisfying victims of crime—within a 'rebalanced' system—and, if the White Paper proposals are implemented, the idea of being fair to offenders at the point of sentence will need to be understood in this fresh context.

---

[9] See *Chapter 1*. This is the clear underlying tenor of both *Justice For All* and a range of other relevant publications issued by government in recent years.

# CHAPTER 16

# Protection from Discrimination

Section 95 Criminal Justice Act 1991 requires the Home Secretary to publish each year:

> . . . such information as he considers expedient for the purposes of . . . facilitating the performance by [people engaged in the administration of criminal justice] of their duty to avoid discriminating against any person on the ground of race, sex or any other improper ground.[1]

The provision applies to everyone engaged in the criminal justice process whether, e.g. as a judge, magistrate, administrator, police officer, Crown prosecutor, probation officer or whosoever. Materials on race and gender have been published at regular intervals ever since.[2] From 2000 the duty to avoid discrimination was reinforced by the European Convention On Human Rights which requires, by virtue of Article 14, that Convention rights are applied without discrimination.[3]

### Part of a wider strategy

Measures to prevent discrimination in criminal justice are part of a wider strategy. This includes, e.g. developments such as the Commission for Racial Equality (CRE) (which works in partnership with individuals and organizations to achieve a fair and just society which values diversity and gives all people an equal chance to work, learn and live free from discrimination, prejudice and racism), Race Equality Schemes, the keeping of employment statistics and targets (including within the criminal justice agencies) and the Home Secretary's Race Relations Forum (which advises him on issues affecting minority communities). Broader social considerations of discrimination have sometimes merged with criminal justice concerns as where minority communities have become involved in urban riots or there have been organized or persistent attacks on minorities.

### Policy and practice

There were many developments after implementation of section 95, including, e.g.

- the Lord Chancellor's Department and Home Office issuing guidance requiring courts and other agencies to develop policies and working practices to ensure equality of treatment
- the Judicial Studies Board (JSB) setting up an influential Ethnic Minorities Advisory Committee

---

[1]   The existence of a duty not to discriminate (presumably at common law) is assumed.

[2]   Starting with *Race and the Criminal Justice System* (1992), *Gender and the Criminal Justice System* (1992), *Digest: Information on the Criminal Justice System in England and Wales* (1993) and *Race and the Criminal Justice System* (1994). Statistics on both race and gender have also been published regularly since, see the example at footnote 9. The evidence giving rise to section 95 is summarised in *Chapter 6* of *Criminal Justice in Transition* (1994), Ashworth *et al*, Winchester: Waterside Press.

[3]   Including of course the right to a fair trial in Article 6 (*Chapter1*).

- the incorporation into the regular training of members of all the agencies of modules on discrimination and minority issues (later incorporating training on fairness and human rights)
- the Law Society and the Bar establishing Race Relations Committees and relevant codes of practice and equality policies
- the National Probation Service (NPS) (as it is now) taking steps to promote equality in all aspects of its work
- the issuing by the Association of Chief Police Officers (ACPO) and CRE of a booklet, *Policing and Racial Equality,* police forces adopting equal opportunities policies and seeking to increase recruitment from minority ethnic groups
- preparatory work by the CPS for use of an 'ethnic code' in its COMPAS computer system due to come into operation in 2003, and a major research study covering 15,000 cases. The CPS also includes racial motivation in its *Code for Crown Prosecutors* as a factor to be considered when applying the public interest criterion (*Chapter 7*)
- HM Prison Service developing a comprehensive race relations policy and *Race Relations Manual* setting out the arrangements for monitoring, access to facilities, work, education and training, allocation of accommodation, religion, diet, discipline, racially derogatory language, complaints of racial discrimination, and contacts with minority ethnic organizations outside prison. Race relations liaison officers (RRLOs) have been appointed in all prisons and racial offences are included in both prisoner and staff disciplinary codes.

### Racial offences and racial aggravation
In the 1990s concern for victims of racist crime led to measures being introduced in the Crime and Disorder Act 1998 creating a number of racially aggravated offences with greater maximum sentences than their non-racially aggravated counterparts i.e.:

- racially aggravated assaults including common assault, actual bodily harm, grievous bodily harm and wounding
- racially aggravated criminal damage, including arson; and
- racially aggravated harassment,[4] including: pursuing a course of conduct likely to cause harassment and pursuing a course of conduct causing fear of violence. In addition, on conviction the court can make a restraining order under harassment legislation to prevent given conduct in the future.

An offence becomes 'racially aggravated' for the purpose of such offences if:

- at the time of committing it, or immediately before or after doing so, the offender demonstrates towards the victim of the offence hostility based on the victim's membership (or presumed membership) of a racial group; or
- it is motivated (wholly or partly) by hostility towards members of a racial group based on their membership of that group.

---

[4] Two of the original suspects in the Stephen Lawrence case (see later in the chapter) were in 2002 convicted of this offence and sent to prison after driving a car at an off-duty black police officer.

Under separate provisions a court must normally increase sentence (*Chapter 9*) for *any* crime if it is shown to be racially motivated. The court must:

- treat that fact as an aggravating factor (i.e. so as to increase the seriousness of the offence); and
- state in open court that the seriousness of the offence was aggravated in this way and the specific enhancement applied.

In 2002, in *Racist Offences: How is the Law Working?: The Implementation of the Legislation on Racially Aggravated Offences in the Crime and Disorder Act 1998,*[5] a publication that contains extensive data on the above matters, authors Elizabeth Burney and Gerry Rose conclude:

> The law is now widely accepted in principle, and a great deal of effort is being expended upon it. For it to work effectively it needs to be used both with greater finesse and more firmly. What matters is not the quantity of prosecutions, but their quality, and it is concluded that victims would agree.

### Ethnic monitoring
The Home Office itself has targets for and monitoring of all aspects of its responsibilities. Research by its Research Development and Statistics Directorate (RDSD) supports the work of a Race Equality Unit and other policy units in the development of race equality policies across the board. The department acknowledges that much of its work on the criminal justice side now flows directly from the Stephen Lawrence inquiry (below). A long-term aim has also been to ensure a comprehensive system of monitoring across all the criminal justice agencies based upon compatible record-keeping and which allows greater understanding of the experiences of ethnic minorities. In 1997, in his Foreword to *Race and Criminal Justice,* Lord Justice Rose, the then chairman of the Criminal Justice Consultative Council (CJCC), noted:

> Since its inception in 1992, the CJCC has identified race in the criminal justice system as a priority issue and has been closely involved in work to encourage action at both local and national levels. Significant progress has been made in many areas, and the level of awareness of race issues within the criminal justice system has risen considerably. However, in the absence of accurate information on the stages of the criminal justice process at which unfair discrimination may be occurring, many agencies have found it difficult to target initiatives effectively.[6]

He went on to urge that the extension of ethnic monitoring throughout the criminal process would help to address this problem and to 'pinpoint areas in which discrepancies may be occurring . . . so that appropriate action may be taken'. He also described this as an uncomfortable process for the agencies concerned adding that:

> The value of ethnic monitoring exercises as a whole will depend, to a large extent, on the willingness of each agency to address the problems identified by monitoring exercises and the need for further work.

---

[5] (2002) Home Office Research Study No. 24.
[6] (1997) London: Home Office.

It is this mix of tasks—pinpointing discrepancies and ensuring effective action—which information under section 95 can assist. Over the years, the Home Office publications have contained extensive statistical data and analysis and dealt with a range of decision-making functions across the criminal process beginning with the stopping and searching by the police of suspects, arrest rates and cautioning and early warning rates (see, generally, *Chapters* 6 and 7). The fact that people from minority ethnic groups often figure disproportionately compared to their white counterparts at these and later stages of the criminal process (such as pre-sentence reports, sentencing, imprisonment and deaths in custody) has been a key feature of information published by both the Home and independent sources. Thus, e.g. studies such as that by Roger Hood and his colleagues at Oxford University into patterns of sentencing in the criminal courts have done much to sustain the view that something is amiss[7] and certainly published accounts of the direct experiences of people from ethnic minorities support the view that much remains to be done.[8]

But gains have been made so that by 2000, Jack Straw, Home Secretary, was able to state that the section 95 report for that year

> documents both the strides which have been taken, and the fact that we still have more to do to eradicate racism and to achieve racial equality in the criminal justice system. The data contained in this publication will again inform the initiatives already underway and provide the impetus to achieve the improvements we all seek.[9]

Such initiatives along with improved information and analysis are now likely, perhaps, to go hand in hand with the installation of compatible computer systems and software across the agencies as envisaged in *Justice For All*. It is also important to note that discrimination can take many forms and that with enhanced systems it ought to be possible to monitor a wider range of abuses, not least those concerning religious discrimination.

### Some recent trends

At the time of going to press the latest Home Office figures were those published in 2000 and focussing principally on the data for 1999/2000. 'Latest estimates' indicate that of the population aged ten and over in England and Wales people of black ethnic origin comprise two per cent, of Asian origin three per cent and 'other' non-white ethnic groups one per cent. Set against this, examples from the main findings[10] include:

- 800,000 stops and searches were recorded by the police in 1999/2000 (a general fall since 1998/1999) of which eight per cent were of black people, four per cent of Asians and one per cent 'other' non-white people

---

[7]  *Race and Sentencing* (1992), Hood R, Oxford: Clarendon Press.

[8]  For a valuable analysis, see *Chapter* 16 of *Crime, State and Citizen: A Field Full of Folk* (2001), Faulkner D, Winchester: Waterside Press.

[9]  *Statistics on Race in the Criminal Justice System: A Home Office Publication Under Section 95 of the Criminal Justice Act 1991* (2000), London: Home Office.

[10]  Many of the statistics involve sub-findings and further qualifications.

- 2003 homicides were recorded by the police from 1997 to 2000 of which ten per cent were of black people, six per cent Asians and three per cent 'other' non-white people and of which 15 homicides were recorded as 'racially motivated'. The police were statistically less likely to identify suspects for homicides involving black victims than for white or those from other ethnic groups (although differences in the method of killing, it is claimed, may play a part).
- there were 1.3 million arrests for notifiable offences of which seven per cent were black people, four per cent Asian and one per cent other non-white. Black people were four times more likely to be arrested than white or other ethnic groups. Black people showed a higher likelihood of being arrested for robbery and both black and Asian people for fraud, forgery and drugs (white people stood a higher likelihood of being arrested for burglary and criminal damage).
- of 180,000 police cautions for notifiable offences six per cent concerned black people, four per cent Asian and one per cent 'other' non-white.
- in June 1999, ethnic minorities accounted for 18 per cent of the men's prison population (12 per cent black, three per cent Asian and three per cent 'other') and 25 per cent of the women's prison population (19 per cent, one per cent and five per cent respectively), including foreign nationals who make up eight per cent (men) and 15 per cent (women) of that population
- black and Asian prisoners tended to be younger than white prisoners and white and Asian prisoners tended to be serving shorter sentences
- estimates from the *British Crime Survey* suggest that although racist incidents fell by 27 per cent from 1995 to 1999, there was a general fall of 22 per cent in all incidents both racial and non-racial over this period
- racist incidents recorded by the police rose by 107 per cent to 47,810 in 1999/2000 (which probably reflects better recording practices)
- during the first full year of recording for racially aggravated offences 21,750 offences (one half of harassment) were recorded of which one third were detected
- nine per cent of complaints made against the police in 1999/2000 were from black people, six per cent from Asian and two per cent from other ethnic minority groups
- ethnic minorities are under-represented in all the criminal justice agencies although there are 'some small improvements' over previous years in most criminal justice agencies.

One finding which appears to go against the trend of disproportionate representation (certainly of black people and to some extent Asians) within the above figures is based upon information collected from five pilot areas and involving magistrates' decisions. This data showed that—excluding defendants committed for trial—white defendants were more likely to be convicted (65 per cent) than black or Asian defendants (both 56 per cent). Neither were there 'substantial differences' in the use of custody at the magistrates' courts concerned although black defendants were more likely to be sentenced to a community sentence and less likely to be given a conditional discharge.

## Institutional racism

For many people racism and criminal justice has come to be linked to the high profile Stephen Lawrence case. Stephen Lawrence, a young black man, was killed by a group of white youths in South London in 1994. The inadequate police investigation into that death led to the Stephen Lawrence Inquiry, chaired by Sir William Macpherson of Cluny, into the circumstances and their investigation by the Metropolitan Police. The Macpherson report was severely critical of the Metropolitan Police, which it characterised as 'institutionally racist', and made a large number of recommendations for reform addressed both to the police and to central government. Almost all of these recommendations were immediately accepted.[11] The report can be said to have transformed the attitude of the police and the criminal justice services to race and racism and also the character of the debate at all levels. However, even as late as 2001, HM Prison Service and the CPS were admitting to being institutionally racist also.

The Home Secretary has a published Action Plan with regard to the Stephen Lawrence inquiry and also publishes annual reports concerning its progress.[12] The acquittal of the suspects in a private prosecution for murder is a factor leading to recommendations contained in the 2002 White Paper *Justice For All* concerning the abolition of the double jeopardy rule mentioned in *Chapters 1* and *15* in relation to serious cases.

## Race, discrimination and sentencing: the future

The Halliday report has been criticised—and *Justice for All* could be—for having practically nothing to say about the racial impact of their respective proposals on sentencing or the precautions needed to prevent them from having a discriminatory effect. Whatever, racial and other forms of discrimination are matters to which the Sentencing Advisory Panel and the new Sentencing Guidelines Council might be expected to pay particular attention.[13] Indeed, what seems to be needed is a general momentum to ensure that the undoubted work which has been done in this area across the agencies—by way of research, information, training, commitment and the creation of non-discriminatory policies and statements—is to be seen into daily practice.

---

[11] The Macpherson report did, however, attract severe criticism from some newspapers and from certain sections of the police service.

[12] For further information see www.homeoffice.gov.uk. There is also a Stephen Lawrence Charity, e-mail: information@stephenlawrence.org.uk

[13] For further discussion see *Crime, State and Citizen: A Field Full of Folk* (2001), Faulkner D, Winchester: Waterside Press and 'Taking Account of Race, Ethnicity and Religion' by the same author in *Reform and Punishment* (2002), Rex S and Tonry M (eds.), Devon: Willan Publishing.

# CHAPTER 17

# Working Together and Partnership

Policy and operational decisions by one agency will almost always affect the capacity, workload, output, and resource requirements of other services. Effective cooperation within the system is thus crucial to efficient management and performance. For many years, exchanges between the different agencies have taken place at both national and local level (and often at regional or area level also)—with a view to creating understandings; agreed aims; working practices and targets (e.g. concerning the length of time it should take to complete a given stage in the criminal justice process); and establishing sound and sustainable operating methods. Protocols and Best Practice have been agreed through liaison, negotiations and even so-called 'contracts', to ensure optimum service delivery. Some mechanisms have been mentioned in earlier chapters, e.g. court user groups, the Strategic Planning Board (*Chapter 1*), joint-working in police/CPS Criminal Justice Units (CJUs) (*Chapter 11*) and the cohesive resettlement strategies of HMPS and the NPS (*Chapters 13 and 14*).

## A Criminal Justice Board

Even so, there is at present no overall and effective brake on the inefficient use of resources, despite the existence under section 95 Criminal Justice Act 1991[1] of a statutory duty on the Home Secretary to keep people involved in the administration of justice informed of the costs involved. As noted in *Chapter 15*, Lord Justice Auld proposed a national Criminal Justice Board (linked to local boards). In terms the recommendation states that the board

> should replace all existing national planning and 'operational' bodies, including the Strategic Planning Group, and the Trial Issues Group. The new board should be the means by which the criminal justice departments and agencies provide overall direction of the criminal justice system It should have an independent chairman and include senior departmental representatives and chief executives of the main criminal justice agencies (including the Youth Justice Board) and a small number of non-executive members. At local level, Local Criminal Justice Boards should be responsible for giving effect to the national board's directions and objectives and for the management of the criminal justice system in their areas.

This recommendation finds favour in *Justice For All* and the idea has considerable potential to standardise arrangements which have developed in a fragmented and unco-ordinated way across the years. Such a board could also lend validity to what currently often remains voluntary—and even sometimes grudging—participation in strategies from which it may have been all too easy for one participant to withdraw.

---

[1] Which also deals with discrimination: see *Chapter 16*.

# ORIGINS OF WORKING TOGETHER: A NOTE

Whilst the term 'working together' has often been applied to initiatives such as those described above, it probably first began as natural response to day-to-day problems locally, a response without which the criminal process would hardly function at all. As outlined in *Chapter 1*, the various criminal justice services are independent of one another, but they cannot act in isolation and the decisions they make have effects that are never confined to their own spheres of operation. The term 'interdependence' has been applied to this situation.

From the 1980s a range of liaison and other groups began to emerge, at both local and national level, to discuss and agree ways forward and to provide the agencies with an understanding of each other's requirements. The expression 'criminal justice system' came into regular use, and ministers spoke of the process needing to be managed as a system. The once highly disparate nature of criminal justice began to diminish from the 1980s onwards culminating, from 1992 onwards, in a national Criminal Justice Consultative Council (and area committees) comprising leaders of the different services (see further below).

One striking example of the potential of partnership in action is the work of the Youth Justice Board and local multi-agency youth offending teams (YOTs) (*Chapter 5*). It was, in fact, in relation to the old juvenile court (i.e. pre-1991 and well before that), and such events as the development of the then local intermediate treatment projects, that many of the first effective inter-agency arrangements began.[2] Their success in improving cooperation between criminal justice services meant that they became a blueprint for other aspects of the criminal process. This success also lent respectability to a method of working which until then was often viewed by some sections of the criminal justice process with a degree of suspicion.[3]

**The Criminal Justice Consultative Council (CJCC)**
The setting up of the national Criminal Justice Consultative Council (CJCC) (and area committees) flowed from a recommendation by Lord Justice Woolf (now Lord Woolf, Lord Chief Justice) in his report on prison disturbances in 1991. The council has in practice concentrated more on questions of process and performance than on the strategic thinking that Lord Woolf may have intended, but it may well now prove to be the forerunner of a Criminal Justice Council proposed by *Justice for All* to act as a major source of advice and information and as a forum to be consulted by government and the agencies.

At present, membership of the CJCC and its committees includes senior representatives of the police, NPS, CPS, Criminal Defence Service, HMPS, judges, magistrates and the legal profession. Both the national council and the

---

[2] The voluntary sector was to the fore in encouraging and often facilitating such developments, as when Nacro co-ordinated a major 1983 initiative to promote intermediate treatment nationwide.

[3] The first author of this book recalls that well into the 1980s some justices' clerks still relied on a yellowing circular issued by a former Lord Chancellor advising magistrates that involvement with other agencies could compromise judicial independence. Fortunately, with hindsight, for some magistrates and justices' clerks a certain frisson attached to testing the parameters of that edict.

area committees are chaired by members of the judiciary,[4] their overall purpose being to promote better understanding, cooperation and co-ordination in the administration of criminal justice.

Membership of the national CJCC also includes Permanent Secretaries from the Home Office, Department of Health and Lord Chancellor's Department, executive agency heads or representatives, a chief constable, a senior solicitor and barrister, the chairman of the Magistrates' Association, a circuit judge, a justices' clerk and a director of social services.

Area committees are chaired by a resident judge. Their membership includes the Crown Court circuit administrator, a chief probation officer, chief constable, chief Crown prosecutor, justices' clerk, chairman of a magistrates' bench, barrister, solicitor, director of social services and either the HMPS area manager or the governor of a local prison. Such committees have the responsibility of promoting better understanding, cooperation and co-ordination in the criminal justice process by, in particular:

- exchanging information and giving advance notice of local developments which may affect other parts of the system
- formulating co-ordinated area priorities, strategies and plans to give effect to national and locally agreed policies
- considering problems and issues raised by services and court user committees and developing solutions
- considering issues and proposals from the national CJCC and raising issues with that council or with government departments where these seem to require a national solution; and
- promoting the spread of good practice.

## Partnership

Multi-agency initiatives under the auspices of different lead services have often existed in relation to such matters as crime prevention and crime reduction, community safety, drug misuse and domestic violence, as well as local arrangements between the police, local authorities and other agencies in order to discharge statutory responsibilities. These have often been described as 'partnerships'.[5] Partnership is also a word now used increasingly in discussions about the improvement of the services delivered by all public sector organizations. Within the criminal justice arena, the relevant agencies have more and more been required to think of themselves as part of a co-ordinated team or network, and to give active consideration to working in collaboration with not

---

[4] Whilst this lent weight, status and credibility it may be that committees have lacked a keen business edge, and too often discussions may have focussed on the niceties of a particular course rather than firm objectives, solid outcomes and results. *Justice for All* envisages that the new national Criminal Justice Board would be chaired by the Permanent Secretary at the Home Office (as the Criminal Justice Consultative Council was when first established).

[5] Albeit courts might still be swift to reject the idea that they can become partners, as such, with anyone due to the need to preserve judicial independence. There are many examples of the judiciary and its representative bodies working in partnership amongst themselves, however, e.g. to produce guidelines and training materials, but judges and magistrates tend to meet with other participants as 'outsiders'. There have been comments to the effect that in inter-agency discussions judicial independence has sometimes been played as a 'trump card' to halt developments or take control of events. See also footnote 3.

only other services but also the non-statutory, voluntary and private sectors to create a cohesive framework for responding to crime.

Looking back, the Criminal Justice Act 1991, together with a change to the Probation Rules made in 1994, gave the then probation committees (now boards) authority to make grants to voluntary and private sector organizations for partnership work. In *Partnership in Dealing with Offenders in the Community* (1992) the Home Office set out requirements when working with outside agencies, i.e.:

- an expectation that the probation service should expect to spend a minimum of around five per cent of its total revenue budget on partnership work with the independent sector
- the establishment of a National Partnership Forum to develop guidance, monitor developments and make recommendations on the 'core' funding of voluntary organizations at national level
- the submission of local partnership plans for approval nationally
- the establishing of local strategy groups including representatives of the independent sector to be responsible for the development of agreed plans for dealing with offenders in the community, including plans for local funding of independent sector organizations.

The National Partnership Forum already mentioned was established and guidance on the development of partnership plans drawn up in consultation with the forum. HMPS has also been to the fore in working with both the private sector and the voluntary sector and in 2002 launched a major initiative aimed at working with the voluntary sector.[6]

Developments which have demanded sound working partnership are the arrangements for sentence planning and resettlement for prisoners already mentioned above which involve close collaboration between HMPS and the NPS. A jointly agreed national resettlement framework is underpinned locally by such mechanisms as 'contracts', and business and development plans agreed between chief probation officers and prison governors. Effective partnerships not only between HMPS and the NPS but also involving housing, employment, education, training and health agencies will be essential if the intention to reduce re-offending, stated in *Justice for All*, is to be realised.

## SOME MODERN DEVELOPMENTS

When elected in 1997, the Labour Government placed a new emphasis on strategic planning, management and 'joined up' thinking at national level. A more coherent framework and systematic approach would seem to be emerging (*Chapter 1*). Increasingly there is close contact between government departments at ministerial level and by officials of the Home Office, Lord Chancellor's Department, CPS and others. Various strands can be identified in *Justice for All* which indicate that what began maybe 30 years ago as a marginal activity—upon which some agencies or their members may have occasionally frowned—has become both mainstream and central to Government strategy, to wit:

---

[6] See *Working With the Voluntary Sector (2002)*, Bryans S and Walker R, Winchester: Waterside Press.

- the establishing of a Cabinet Committee chaired by the Home Secretary, including the Lord Chancellor and Attorney General to ensure a coherent approach to criminal justice reform
- the appointment of a Minister for Justice Systems Information Technology who will chair a ministerial sub-committee with oversight of the delivery of IT across the criminal process and its effective implementation
- the establishing of a new Criminal Justice IT organization
- the Government's claim that the system is 'united' in ensuring the detection, conviction and punishment of offenders (*Chapter 1*)
- the extension of police/CPS Criminal Justice Units until they cover all 42 areas together with a promise of 'closer working' between the two agencies
- a partnership approach in relation to various types of crime, including drug and drug-related crime and domestic violence
- the proposal for a Sentencing Guidelines Council (*Chapter 9*)
- the promise of better joint working between HMPS and the NPS
- a tranche of other proposals addressed to 'joining up the criminal justice system' in order to make it more efficient and to ensure accountability
- the proposal for a Criminal Justice Board and local boards (above)
- the proposal for a Criminal Justice Council (above)
- the creation of a secure e-mail system for criminal justice professionals by 2003[7]; and
- the move to ensure that all criminal justice organizations will be able to exchange case files electronically by 2005.

Other often linked developments can be seen at virtually all points in the criminal process. Thus, e.g. as noted in *Chapter 6* the Government has established a Case Preparation and Progression Project which brings together all the participants in the pre-trial process to provide a smoother, more efficient passage of cases through the courts 'from charging to sentence'. That chapter also mentions Multi-Agency Protection Panels (MAPPS), the Persistent Offender Task Force and the Street Crime Initiative whilst *Chapter 7* notes the development of drug action teams. Bail information schemes are mentioned in *Chapter 8* and Crime Reduction Programmes, the Safer Communities Initiative, neighbourhood watch (and other watches) and the national Domestic Violence Unit are mentioned in *Chapter 11*. The joint Correctional Services Board and Correctional Services Accreditation Panel are mentioned in *Chapter 12* one future purpose of which would be to monitor schemes, programmes and methods of intervention with offenders in the context of proposals in *Justice for All* for new forms of sentence (*Chapter 15*) which would appear to rely on a greater interaction of custodial and community provision altogether. As also noted in *Chapter 12* (and earlier in this chapter) HMPS and the NPS have become increasingly committed to joint working and cohesive strategies in an effort to enhance crime reduction.

Analogous developments can be seen in areas less central to the daily workings of criminal justice such as the Community Justice National Training Organization, the Police Skills and Standards Organization and the proposal to bring these together in a United Kingdom Justice Sector Skills Council.

---

[7] Initially it seems this will be for those working within the criminal process but there are already plans to open up the facility to others with a legitimate interest such as lawyers in private practice.

# VICTIM SUPPORT

Local victim support schemes began to appear during the 1970s and their national organization Victim Support was formed in 1979.[4] Trained volunteers and staff are now based in some 400 local areas of England and Wales where schemes are in operation to offer help to over 1.5 million victims of crimes a year from burglary to murder. This free and confidential service includes emotional support, practical help (e.g. with home security, insurance claims, criminal injuries compensation (below) and information). Victim Support also runs the Court Witness Service via which trained volunteers offer emotional support and practical information to victims, witnesses and their families before, during and after a court hearing. Since 2000, the service operates in relation to each Crown Court centre[5] and magistrates' court. Each court has a co-ordinator with a team of specially selected volunteers, trained to give practical and emotional support to victims of crime and other vulnerable witnesses attending court.

In 1995, Victim Support published 'The Rights of Victims of Crime: A Call for Action' together with a policy paper 'The Rights of Victims of Crime'. It began:

> In modern times, the state has rightly taken over from victims the duty of prosecuting offenders and dealing with them if convicted. Victim Support believes that victims should therefore have a right to certain standards of treatment—not merely out of concern for their welfare, but because it is in the interests of society as a whole.

It argued that victims should have the right to:

- be free of the burden of decisions relating to the offender
- receive information and explanations about the progress of the case
- have the opportunity to provide their own information about the case for use in the criminal justice process
- be protected in any way necessary
- receive compensation; and
- receive respect, recognition and support.

# LEGAL REMEDIES

There are a variety of ways in which victims can be compensated or have their property reinstated. A victim can sue in the civil courts (usually for 'tort', a generic legal name for a civil wrong). Awards are also made by the Criminal Injuries Compensation Authority in cases of violent crime (below).

The criminal courts have powers to make compensation, restitution, confiscation and (in relation to juvenile offenders) reparation orders. From 2002

---

[4]  The organization was originally known as the National Association of Victim Support Schemes.
[5]  Each Crown Court centre also has an official witness liaison officer to act as a focal point for the criminal justice agencies and witnesses and XHIBIT which enables the Witness Service to keep witnesses informed of the progress of cases by e-mail and text messages. There are also public information screens.

there is an Assets Recovery Agency (below) some of the proceeds of which will filter through to victims. A victim cannot recover twice over, but proof of a criminal conviction goes a considerable way towards reinforcing a civil claim (assuming the criminal court declined to award compensation).

# COMPENSATION AND REPARATION

Reparation—doing something to repair the harm caused by an offence—is a general object of sentencing (*Chapter 9*) and an aspect which is likely to develop during the coming years. At present, a reparation order as such is only possible in the youth court (see, generally, *Chapter 5*). This is an order requiring the offender to make reparation (as detailed in the order) to the victim of his or her crime or to the community at large. In relation to adults who have caused damage or loss, *de facto* reparation—including, e.g., where appropriate, a letter of apology (or even in some carefully managed instances a meeting with a victim) or repairs to property—can be an integral component of either a community sentence devised by the NPS or an offending behaviour or pre-release programme arranged by HMPS or the NPS.

**Compensation must always be considered**
In terms of pure financial recompense courts are encouraged to award compensation whenever possible. Financial compensation can be ordered as a sentence in its own right[6] or ancillary to any other kind of sentence (subject to what is said about fines below). This is outlined in *Chapter 9* but some points are worth elaborating on.

*When compensation must be considered*
Where an offence causes loss, damage or personal injury, the court is obliged by law to consider whether the offender should pay compensation to the victim or for his or her benefit. Personal injury includes both physical or mental injury. An award can thus be made not only, e.g. for a cut or fracture, but for terror, distress or inconvenience caused by the offence. In the Crown Court the value of a compensation order is unrestricted (and in an appropriate case may be backed by an order for confiscation and sale of the offender's assets). In the magistrates' court there is a ceiling of £5,000 per offence, but within that figure the court can take into account any loss, damage or injury caused by offences which the offender has asked the court to take into consideration (TICs) (*Chapter 9*).

*Priority*
Where a court considers that both a fine and compensation are appropriate but the offender' financial resources are not adequate to cover both, it must give priority (the statutory requirement is 'preference') to a compensation order.

*Application*
Generally speaking, an application is made by prosecuting counsel or the Crown prosecutor. But this is not essential and the victim does not need to apply to the

---

[6] Thereby according with the historic origins of prosecution (see the start of chapter).

court, or request anyone to do so on his or her behalf. The court has power to make an award of its own motion provided that sufficient information is forthcoming to enable it to fix the amount of the award (as to which the 2001 *Practice Direction* mentioned above should mean that such information will be available or at least that the victim will have had the opportunity to provide it).

When a court is considering making a compensation order, it must satisfy itself that actual loss, damage or injury results from the offence (or TICs above). It will then look, e.g. at the cost of replacement, repair or medical reports. Courts use guidelines containing suggested levels of award (or starting points), in relation to frequently occurring types of personal injury. Where items which have been stolen, damaged or destroyed are of sentimental value the court may be prepared to take a common-sense approach, make straightforward comparisons etc. The court can also consider consequential loss, e.g. loss of earnings due to time off work following a violent attack. It will also look at intangible matters such as pain and suffering and any loss of facility.

Often, in practice, the prosecutor and offender will agree the amount of compensation which is appropriate and then ask for this to be ordered by the court (which always has the final say).

*Financial circumstances of the offender*
The court is obliged to have regard the financial circumstances of the offender so far as they appear or are known to the court. The Court of Appeal has interpreted this to mean that a compensation order should be such as to enable the offender to complete payment within a reasonable time. This will normally, in practice, be within 12 months but can be extended to up to three years where the circumstances justify this such as where a substantial order is made by the Crown Court. Sometimes, e.g. where fraud has been involved, the offender may be given the option of paying the amount in question or—subject to his or her assets being confiscated and sold to raise the amount (below)—remaining in custody under an order to serve a further period at the end of his or her sentence if the amount remains unpaid.

Governments have so far resisted the creation of a compensation fund to cover situations where the offender is unable to pay the amount of compensation which would otherwise be justified, or arrangements under which the court would pay the amount ordered from its own funds and recover payment from the offender in due course.

**Reasons**
Under national law the court must give reasons if it does not make an order for compensation where it could have done so. The reasons must be announced in open court and be recorded. This requirement is now reinforced by human rights considerations whereby courts must give proper explanations (*Chapter 1*).

# THE ASSETS RECOVERY AGENCY

The Proceeds of Crime Act 2002 enacts what the Home Office describes as 'a comprehensive package of measures to disrupt criminal enterprises and deprive criminals of their financial lifeblood'. The Act establishes an Assets Recovery

Agency (ARA) to investigate and recover wealth accumulated through criminal activity. It consolidates and strengthens existing criminal confiscation powers, introduces a power of civil recovery, extends investigation powers and enhances existing money laundering legislation. The main functions of the ARA are to carry out investigations leading to criminal confiscation and civil recovery proceedings; to initiate and pursue confiscation proceedings against convicted defendants in respect of their proceeds of crime; to recover proceeds of crime by civil recovery proceedings in appropriate cases; and to tax criminal proceeds.

# RESTITUTION

Where goods have been stolen and someone is convicted of an offence relating to the theft, the court may order the restoration of the goods to the person entitled to them (or of other goods bought by the offender with the proceeds). A restitution order can also be made against a defendant following a conviction for dishonest handling of stolen goods, obtaining property by deception or blackmail. Goods include all kinds of property except land. An order can be made in respect of offences taken into consideration (TICs: *Chapter 9*). Restitution orders can be made by a court of its own volition or on application by the prosecutor. The order takes one of the following forms, i.e. an order that:

- anyone having possession or control of goods restore them to the person entitled to them
- any other goods directly or indirectly representing the original goods be delivered to the person entitled to the original goods; or
- any money found on the convicted person not exceeding the value of the goods be paid to the person entitled to those goods.

In appropriate circumstances a court may make orders for both restitution and also compensation, e.g. if property is recovered but it turns out to have been damaged.

# CRIMINAL INJURIES COMPENSATION

The Criminal Injuries Compensation Scheme, originally established in 1964, provides financial compensation to victims of crimes of violence and to those injured in attempting to apprehend offenders or prevent crime. The minimum award is £1,000 (September 2002). Injuries meriting lower awards cannot be compensated for by the scheme. Applications are made to the Criminal Injuries Compensation Authority (CICA). Compensation for an injury as a result of a crime of violence is intended as an expression of public sympathy and support for innocent victims, and may be refused if the victim has a previous conviction or has not cooperated with the police. It is not, however, necessary for an offender to have been convicted before an award can be made. There are review procedures and in the event of dissatisfaction with the review (by a higher grade staff member), the possibility of an appeal to the Criminal Injuries Compensation

Appeals Panel which has as its members lawyers, doctors and other people with relevant experience.

### Development of the scheme
The original version of the scheme assessed awards on the basis of common law damages—i.e. the amount which would be awarded in the civil courts if the victim had sued his or her attacker. Awards were assessed by members of the Criminal Injuries Compensation Board, which comprised lawyers chosen for their expertise in the field of personal injury legislation. That scheme sought to reflect the losses actually sustained by the individual victim. Nowadays, payments are based on a 'tariff' whereby injuries are classified into bands (from £1,000 to £250,000). Injuries of similar severity are grouped together in a band and cases within each band attract the same lump sum payment. However, as a result of widespread criticism of the tariff scheme, in 1995 a number of additional features were incorporated, including:

- in addition to the tariff payment, people who are incapacitated for 28 weeks or more are entitled to a separate payment for loss of earnings or potential earnings (subject to a cap of one and a half times the national average industrial wage)
- in cases of incapacity for 28 weeks or more there can be a payment for special care costs
- in fatal cases a fixed payment is made to each qualifying beneficiary in addition to payment to cover reasonable funeral expenses. There is also payment in appropriate cases for dependency or loss of support (capped at one and a half times the national average industrial wage).
- special provision is made to enable victims receiving awards of more than £50,000 to purchase annuities to ensure an index-linked, tax free income.

Victims who are claiming social security benefits may however have the amount of any award deducted from this entitlement.

## WITNESSES AND WITNESS CARE

Witness usually attend court voluntarily to give evidence but can be made subject to a witness order (sometimes called a subpoena) or in extreme instances a witness warrant. Witnesses due to appear in the Crown Court are served with a witness order. This may be a full order or a conditional witness order, the latter usually implying that the particular witness' evidence is unlikely to be disputed. Witnesses are later notified of the date if and when they are required to appear at the Crown Court. *Justice for All* proposes giving witnesses greater access to their previous and original statements at a trial and better support for vulnerable or intimidated witnesses.[7] However, the proposal to abolish the double jeopardy rule (*Chapter 1*), albeit designed to bring justice for victims, might not prove to be 'witness friendly' since it inevitably means that some victims and other witnesses would find themselves giving their evidence at a second trial with all the scope

---

[7] It is also proposed to loosen the rule against hearsay or 'reported' evidence.

for fresh cross-examination directed towards showing inconsistencies between the two accounts and consequent suggestions that the witness is unreliable. However, more generally, new procedures would ensure that 'the guilty will have nothing to gain by delaying their plea, saving victims and witnesses from an unnecessary ordeal'.

As already indicated, the Court Witness Service (sponsored by Victim Support) now functions nationwide. It produces leaflets about going to court and giving evidence and also arranges familiarisation visits. *Justice For All* lays new emphasis on proper treatment of witnesses, whether they are victims or attending court to give evidence in some other capacity.

## EXPERT WITNESSES

Expert witnesses may be called by either the prosecution or the defence to give their opinion on a matter within their own field of expertise. Examples are forensic witnesses (including from the Forensic Science Service: *Chapter 6*) who give evidence of tests carried out, e.g. to establish a link between the accused person and the scene of a crime, medical witnesses to give evidence of injury, pain and suffering and engineers to establish the existence or otherwise of a defect in a motor vehicle or in some other piece of machinery. Contrary to the general rule, expert witnesses are not constrained to giving factual evidence but can give evidence of their opinions. Opinion evidence is subject to cross-examination in the usual way when an expert may be called upon to give the reason and explanations for coming to a particular conclusion. Sometimes expert witnesses appear for both parties when there may be a conflict of expert evidence which the court will need to resolve.

It is for the court to decide whether someone is an expert and thus able to give opinion evidence, whether to accept the evidence given, and, if necessary, to choose between two or more conflicting opinions (assuming that any one of them is capable of being accepted).

The cost of calling an expert witness can be considerable. It is borne by the party calling the witness in the first instance but, assuming that the involvement of the expert was reasonable, it is recoverable under the normal rules concerning costs in criminal proceedings (*Chapter 9*). In the case of a successful defence this will be either from public funds or from the prosecutor depending on the order of the court.

Expert evidence is one situation in which, in the spirit of the White Paper *Justice For All,* there would appear to be scope for settling many issues in advance through disclosure between prosecution and defence.

## RESTORATIVE JUSTICE: A NOTE

Issues concerning victims of crime are now linked in many people's minds to notions of restorative justice, i.e. repairing the harm done by the offender to the victim and restoring a degree of harmony as between victim, offender and community.

Restorative justice stems from family or community 'sentencing circles' in various parts of the world (but particularly New Zealand, Australia and the Middle East) whose aims have included acknowledgement of wrong or harm by the offender (sometimes also involving what is called 'shaming', i.e public condemnation before members of an offender's community), remorse and reparation, reintegration and rehabilitation within a community or group.

Whereas the English criminal process is adversarial and most traditional English forms of sentence can be viewed as primarily punitive (whatever their other purposes) and *exclusionary* (particularly custody), restorative approaches tend to be viewed as *inclusionary*. They are, however, in line with much work being done in England and Wales in relation to community sentences, HMPS and NPS courses and in particular work by youth offending teams (YOTs) (*Chapter 5*) (to which it is proposed victim liaison officers be added 'as funds become available'). Making connections between offending and its effects and encouraging offenders to put right the harm they have done, in some cases by repairing damage, achieving something for themselves and the community, and even (as already mentioned earlier in this chapter) in carefully managed situations writing to or even meeting with and apologising to a victim, is an integral part of the developments in this field.[8]

True restorative justice remains something of an ideal, but aspects of social inclusion are invaluable if offenders are not to become marginalised (particularly where this could happen at an early stage in their lives) and exposed to greater risk of further offending. It is longer-term investment through efforts to ensure that offenders change their behaviour and become responsible members of their communities that modern-day pronouncements by Government seem designed to encourage.

There is a national Restorative Justice Consortium of organizations with an interest in work across this expanding this field.

### Restorative justice and *Justice for All*

A restorative theme is now to be found in many official pronouncements, including in *Justice For All* where 'rebalancing' the system is envisaged as a two-way process in which victims are better served by both a reduction in crime and better treatment where crime nonetheless occurs. But beyond these kinds of assertion, restorative justice is also something that the present Government seems to be prepared to acknowledge and subscribe to—even if its sentencing proposals still disclose a relatively punitive edge. Thus, e.g. the following definition appears in the glossary to the White Paper:

---

[8] For a wide-ranging survey of restorative justice including its history, philosophy and present uses, see *Restoring Respect for Justice* (1998), Wright M, Winchester: Waterside Press. Analogous initiatives by the Relationships Foundation emphasise the key importance of relationships in repairing and avoiding harm: see *Relational Justice: Repairing the Breach* (1994), Burnside J and Baker N, Winchester: Waterside Press.

Restorative justice schemes bring together all parties (offender, victim, friends, family, community representatives and others with a stake in a specific offence) to resolve how to deal with the aftermath of the offence and any implications for the future. It can help offenders to understand that their offending behaviour is not just against the law, but also has a damaging effect on their victims, themselves and on their communities. It also gives more of a voice to victims and communities by bringing them into the process and involving them in the solution.

As can be seen from this chapter, victims are being given a voice through various initiatives, but 'conferencing' schemes such as those described in the first part of this quotation do not yet exist in England and Wales other than in pockets and experimental areas and principally in relation to juvenile offenders. Further, such schemes as do exist are ultimately linked to (or operate in the shadow of) the formal processes described in the remainder of this book. Nonetheless, the strength of the restorative movement, both nationally and internationally, is such that further developments in this field are to be expected.

# Index